UNFAIR TRADE PRACTICES
AND
INTELLECTUAL PROPERTY

UNFAIR TRADE PRACTICES
AND
INTELLECTUAL PROPERTY

ROGER E. SCHECHTER
Associate Professor of Law, National Law Center
George Washington University

BLACK LETTER SERIES

WEST PUBLISHING CO.
ST. PAUL, MINN.
1986

COPYRIGHT © 1986 By WEST PUBLISHING CO.
50 West Kellogg Boulevard
P.O. Box 64526
St. Paul, Minnesota 55164–0526

Printed in the United States of America

Library of Congress Cataloging-in-Publication Data

Schechter, Roger E., 1953–
     Unfair trade practices and intellectual property.

     (Black letter series)
     1. Competition, Unfair—United States—Outlines,
syllabi, etc. 2. Intellectual property—United States—
Outlines, syllabi, etc. I. Title. II. Series.

KF3195.Z9S34   1986   343.73'072   86–9152
                             347.30372

ISBN 0–314–98619–7

Schechter–Unfair Trade Practices BLS

PUBLISHER'S PREFACE

This "Black Letter" is designed to help a law student recognize and understand the basic principles of law covered in a law school course. It can be used both as a study aid when preparing for classes and issues and as a review of the subject matter when studying for an examination.

Each "Black Letter" is written by experienced law school teachers who are recognized national authorities in the subject covered.

The law is succinctly stated by the author of this "Black Letter." In addition, the exceptions to the rules are stated in the text. The rules and exceptions have purposely been condensed to facilitate quick review and easy recollection. For an in-depth study of a point of law, citations to major student texts are given. In addition, a **Text Correlation Chart** provides a convenient means of relating material contained in the Black Letter to appropriate sections of the casebook the student is using in his or her law school course.

If the subject covered by this text is a code or code-related course, the code section or rule is set forth and discussed wherever applicable.

FORMAT

The format of this "Black Letter" is specially designed for review. (1) **Text.** First, it is recommended that the entire text be studied, and, if deemed necessary, supplemented, by the student texts cited. (2) **Capsule Summary.** The Capsule Summary is an abbreviated review of the subject matter which can be used both before and after studying the main body of the text. The headings in the Capsule Summary follow the main text of the "Black Letter." (3) **Table of Contents.** The Table of Contents is in outline form to help you organize the details of the subject and the Summary of Contents gives you a final overview of the materials. (4) **Practice Examination.** The Practice Examination in Appendix B gives you the opportunity of testing yourself with the type of question asked on an exam, and comparing your answer with a model answer.

v

In addition, a number of other features are included to help you understand the subject matter and prepare for examinations:

Short Questions and Answers: This feature is designed to help you spot and recognize issues in the examination. We feel that issue recognition is a major ingredient in successfully writing an examination.

Perspective: In this feature, the authors discuss their approach to the topic, the approach used in preparing the materials, and any tips on studying for and writing examinations.

Analysis: This feature, at the beginning of each section, is designed to give a quick summary of a particular section to help you recall the subject matter and to help you determine which areas need the most extensive review.

Examples: This feature is designed to illustrate, through fact situations, the law just stated. This, we believe, should help you analytically approach a question on the examination.

Glossary: This feature is designed to refamiliarize you with the meaning of a particular legal term. We believe that the recognition of words of art used in an examination helps you to better analyze the question. In addition, when writing an examination you should know the precise definition of a word of art you intend to use.

We believe that the materials in this "Black Letter" will facilitate your study of a law school course and assure success in writing examinations not only for the course but for the bar examination. We wish you success.

The Publisher

SUMMARY OF CONTENTS

APPENDICES

*

TABLE OF CONTENTS

APPENDICES

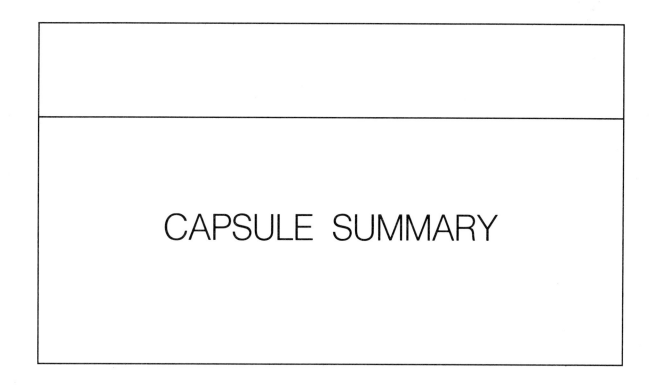

CAPSULE SUMMARY

I. THE PRIVILEGE TO COMPETE

A. THE DILEMMA OF COMPETITION
Competition results in significant benefits to consumers, but at the price of harm to established merchants.

1. Harms
Under competition some firms will necessarily lose patronage to others. This often results in the bankruptcy or economic ruin of weaker firms.

2. Benefits
Competition keeps price low and product quality high while encouraging innovation and product diversity. These virtues inure to the benefit of all consumers.

3. The Legal Compromise
Competition is the approved form of economic activity in the U.S. There is a privilege to enter markets and compete. However, the law imposes limits on how firms may compete. Antitrust rules make sure that competition is not suppressed by undue collusion among firms and that monopoly does not arise. Unfair trade practices law deals with over-zealous behavior that inflicts harm without yielding the benefits of competition.

B.   THE SIGNIFICANCE OF MOTIVATION

A firm's reasons for competing are legally irrelevant, unless the sole reason it goes into business is spitefully to destroy another firm. If spite is the sole motive, the privilege to compete is lost, and the behavior becomes actionable.

1.   Theoretical Basis of Suit

Although there is no specific tort dealing with injury inflicted through spiteful competition, the behavior can be attacked through a general intentional tort cause of action known as "prima facie tort."

2.   Practical Difficulties of Suit

Proving the defendant's spiteful motive is difficult. A plaintiff would probably have to show that the defendant was operating at a loss and intended to leave the business after achieving its purpose in order to succeed.

C.   THE STABILITY OF CONTRACT

1.   Inducing Breach of Contract

The privilege to compete does not include the right to encourage others to breach contracts. Thus, the intentional and improper inducement of a breach of contract is tortious, even if the behavior involved consists solely of persuasion. An inducement is proper in only limited circumstances, such as where the defendant is protecting its own superior contract or property rights or a larger social interest.

2.   Negligent Interference With Contract

There is no cause of action for negligent acts that make performance of a contract more difficult, or impossible.

3.   Interference With Prospective Contractual Relations

If no contract exists between two firms, a third party may offer one of them a better bargain and thus legitimately prevent the consummation of a deal. However, if the third party uses deceitful or coercive means, the behavior ceases to be privileged and will result in liability.

II. TRADEMARKS

A.   THE RATIONALE FOR PROTECTING TRADEMARKS

Trademarks are symbols merchants use to identify their goods. Although there is broad agreement on the utility of some form of trademark protection, there is a debate over how expansive that protection should be.

1.   Justifications for Broad Protection

Those who advocate expansive trademark protection argue that trademarks protect goodwill and thereby encourage firms to be creative; that they provide important information to consumers; and that strict limitations on the use of another firms' marks tend to uphold high standards of commercial morality.

2. Disadvantages of Excessive Trademark Protection

Advocates of more limited trademark rights contend that trademarks can serve as barriers to entry in some industries, making it difficult for new firms to drive prices down; that excessive protection encourages wasteful expenditures on non-informative advertising; and that such protection leads to the monopolization of words and phrases needed by all competitors to describe their goods.

B. THE DUAL SYSTEM OF TRADEMARK PROTECTION

A merchant may obtain trademark rights under state common law, the federal statute known as the Lanham Act, or both. The two bodies of trademark law are independent but interrelated.

1. Common Features of Both Schemes

Both federal and state law require that a firm actually affix the desired mark to its products and use the mark by selling the goods, before any rights can arise. Both schemes also forbid firms from using certain types of words or symbols as marks. Furthermore, both schemes define trademark infringement as any use of another firm's marks which gives rise to a likelihood of confusion.

2. Major Differences Between the Two Schemes

No governmental filing is necessary to obtain common law trademark rights. Under the Lanham Act, however, no rights attach until application for registration is filed and acted upon. Moreover, before federal registration will issue the proposed mark will be scrutinized to determine if it is appropriate. No such "pre-screening" of marks takes place under the common law. Once a federal registration issues, it provides at least presumptive rights nation-wide. Common law rights, on the other hand are limited to the area in which the mark is actually being used.

3. Terminological Differences in the Two Schemes

The exact same terms of art are used to represent different concepts under the Lanham Act and at common law. A focus on the procedural posture of trademark cases is thus unusually important.

C. OBTAINING TRADEMARK RIGHTS: AFFIXATION, USE AND REGISTRATION
1. The Requirement of Affixation

The first step in obtaining the exclusive right to use a word or a symbol is to physically affix it to the goods or their containers. This is to make sure that the public will associate the mark with the product.

2. The Requirement of Use

Rights in a mark do not attach until a merchant makes use of the mark by selling goods with the mark affixed in genuine commercial transactions. For federal registration, these transactions must affect interstate commerce. Sham transactions, intra-corporate transfers, or the sale of goods different from those ultimately intended to carry the mark in question are examples of inadequate uses which confer no rights. A small number of genuine sales will suffice, however. Some courts find even "token" use sufficient to confer rights where there is evidence of an intent to continue the use. If there is a dispute over the ownership of the mark, the first firm to have made bona fide commercial use—known as the "senior user"—will be granted ownership rights in the mark.

3. The Mechanics of Federal Registration

Four types of marks may be registered under the the Lanham Act— trademarks; service marks (symbols identifying services); collective marks (symbols used by associations, clubs, unions, etc.); and certification marks (symbols used to indicate that another firm's goods meet specified standards). A firm desiring federal registration must file an application at the Patent and Trademark Office. An examiner will determine if the mark is suitable for registration. Other parties may intervene and file an "opposition," if they believe registration is inappropriate and that they will be injured thereby. After registration, others may file a petition to have the registration cancelled, although the grounds which may be asserted in such a petition are considerably narrowed after the registration has been in effect for five years. Registration provides numerous advantages, including the right to use the "r in a circle" symbol, nationwide constructive notice of the registrant's claim of ownership and, after five years, the opportunity to have the registration declared "incontestable."

D. DISTINCTIVENESS

The initial question in all trademark disputes is the validity of the mark. Since a mark must identify and distinguish goods, the question of "distinctiveness" is at the heart of the validity inquiry.

1. Inherently Distinctive Marks

Certain types of words are considered distinctive under both the common law and Lanham Act without the need for any evidentiary showing. Fanciful marks are those consisting of made-up or coined words. Arbitrary marks are those consisting of words that have no relationship to the product in question. Suggestive marks are those that provide only an imaginative hint as to the product's attributes. All three of these types of marks are considered inherently distinctive.

2. Marks Which May Become Distinctive

Marks that are not inherently distinctive are protected at common law—and are eligible for federal registration—only if they have acquired "secondary meaning." Secondary meaning is present if consumers have come to think of the term in question as a brand name. The following types of marks require secondary meaning: (1) Descriptive marks, which are those providing a relatively straight-forward description of a product or its properties; (2) Deceptively misdescriptive marks, which seem to provide product information but are actually inaccurate; (3) Geographic terms, unless they are wholly unrelated to the goods in question, and thus arbitrary; (4) Marks consisting of personal surnames; and finally (5) slogans will often require a showing of secondary meaning before being protected as trademarks.

3. Words Incapable of Distinctiveness
The common or generic name for a type of product can never obtain distinctiveness, and thus will never be protected as a trademark at common law, nor will it ever be eligible for federal registration.

4. Loss of Distinctiveness
Over time, a word may cease to function as a trademark and become the generic name for a category of goods. In determining if this has happened, courts focus on how consumers understand the term in question. Although one court attempted to formulate a different test, based on consumers' motivations in using the disputed word, that opinion has been overruled by legislative action amending the Lanham Act.

E. UNUSUAL TRADEMARK TYPES
1. Product or Container Shapes
The shape of a product or its container may be protected as a trademark (and federally registered) if two tests are met. First, the shape must be distinctive, which usually requires proof of secondary meaning. Second, the shape must be "non-functional"—i.e., not improve the performance of the product or container in any way. The non-functionality requirement insures that useful product improvements will be available to all firms unless protected by a patent. A pair of famous 1964 Supreme Court cases suggested that state law could not protect even distinctive and non-functional product shapes as trademarks because of conflicts with the patent policy. Those cases, however, have been sharply limited by subsequent lower court decisions.

2. Colors
No firm may claim exclusive rights to a particular color. Color schemes, however, can be protected as trademarks on the same basis as product shapes—namely a showing of both distinctiveness (i.e. secondary meaning) and non-functionality.

3. Buildings
There is case law holding that the design of a building can function as a trademark if there is both distinctiveness and non-functionality.

F. IMPERMISSIBLE MARKS
1. Deceptive Marks
A mark is considered deceptive if it falsely describes a central and material attribute of the underlying product, and if consumers would likely rely on the representation implicit in the mark when they decide to purchase the goods. Such marks are ineligible for protection at common law and cannot be registered. Absurdly inaccurate marks that no consumer would take literally are not considered deceptive, but rather arbitrary, and hence they are valid trademarks.

2. Immoral or Scandalous Marks
Sexually suggestive or sacrilegious marks are specifically declared unregistrable by the Lanham Act.

3. Other Impermissible Marks
The Lanham Act forbids registration of a mark which resembles a mark or trade name previously used by another, one which falsely suggests a connection with any person or institution, or one comprising a state or national flag or coat of arms.

G. USING ANOTHER MERCHANT'S TRADEMARK
1. The Concept of Trademark Infringement
Any use of another party's mark which gives rise to a likelihood of confusion as to source or sponsorship of the goods constitutes trademark infringement. The clearest case of infringement is the use of an identical mark on directly competing goods sold in the same geographic market. Courts sometimes refer to such obvious infringement as "passing off" or "palming off." However, trademark infringement can occur even if the marks, the products or the markets are not identical. Trademark infringement can harm the owner of the mark by diverting sales from it to the infringer, by limiting the owner's subsequent ability to expand into new product or geographic markets, and by damaging the mark owner's reputation and goodwill if the infringing goods are shoddy or unsatisfactory. If the mark used by the defendant is not identical to plaintiff's mark, the requisite likelihood of confusion can be proved through consumer surveys, or the court can be asked to infer it if there is a high degree of similarity between the sound, appearance, or meaning of the competing marks. The plaintiff in an infringement action need not prove that the defendant's acts were intentional.

2. Non-Competing Goods
A trademark owner can establish infringement even if the defendant sells a different type of goods than it does, provided the mark owner can establish likelihood of confusion. That requires proof that the goods sold by plaintiff and defendant are "related" so that consumers might believe they come from the same source or are sponsored by the same firm. Some courts have held that if the mark is used by the defendant in a decorative fashion rather than

as a symbol of identity, the use is "aesthetically functional" and hence, non-infringing. Other courts refuse to recognize aesthetic functionality and the increasing use of trademark licensing makes the defense more difficult to invoke even where it is accepted. Some states have enacted "dilution" statutes, which protect trademark owners against use of their marks on non-competing goods even where there is no likelihood of confusion.

3. Geographically Remote Users

Under the common law two firms may use the same mark on the same type of goods if they operate in geographic markets distant from each other, provided that the junior user adopted the mark in "good faith," that is, without knowledge of the other's use. Under the Lanham Act, registration is constructive notice of the registrant's claim of ownership. Thus, even if the senior user of a mark only does business in a limited area, once it registers any other firm that subsequently adopts the same mark does not do so in good faith. If the junior user began good faith use of the mark before the senior user registered, however, the junior user may continue to use the mark in its own geographic market, but the federal registrant will be afforded superior rights in the balance of the country. If the junior user was the first to register, the senior user may continue using the mark in its market, but the registrant will obtain superior rights in the balance of the country.

4. Permissible Collateral Uses

It is permissible to use another firm's trademarks when a firm buys trademarked goods and rebottles or repacks them, when it reconditions them and sells them used, and when it provides replacement parts or repair services for them. Reference to a competitor's trademarks in comparative advertising does not constitute infringement.

5. Other Forbidden Practices

It is impermissible to duplicate the packaging of a rival firm in ways that deceive the public. It is also actionable to use pictures of a competitor's goods in catalogues or advertisements and then to supply your own brand when consumers place orders, or more generally to supply a product different than the one the consumer has requested. While these behaviors do not involve trademarks, they are in the nature of passing off and are actionable under both the common law and the Lanham Act.

H. TRADEMARK ABANDONMENT
1. Non-Use

Cessation of trademark use coupled with intent to give up the mark constitutes abandonment. When a mark is abandoned, the former owner loses all rights in it. Under the Lanham Act, non-use for two years is prima facie evidence of abandonment.

2. Failure To Supervise Licensees

A firm that has licensed others to operate under its trademarks must supervise the licensees. If no quality control is exercised, the mark may be deemed abandoned.

I. REMEDIES

1. Injunctive Relief

A party guilty of trademark infringement may be absolutely enjoined from continuing to use the mark, or a qualified injunction can be entered, requiring the use of specified disclaimers.

2. Monetary Relief

The owner of a trademark may recover either damages or profits from a firm found guilty of trademark infringement. If the infringement was intentional, the monetary award is trebled.

3. Destruction of Infringing Articles

The court may order the destruction of labels, packages, advertisements and the like that are in the defendant's possession and bear the infringing mark.

4. Criminal Penalties

If a person is found guilty of "trafficking in counterfeit goods," he or she may be imprisoned for up to 5 years and fined up to $250,000.

III. COPYRIGHT

A. COPYRIGHTABLE SUBJECT MATTER

Copyright subsists in any "original work of authorship fixed in any tangible medium of expression."

1. The Constitutional Basis

The Constitution empowers Congress to protect the "writings" of "authors." These terms have been interpreted broadly to permit copyright protection for a wide variety of intellectual creations.

2. Non-Utilitarian Original Expression Protected

A work is eligible for copyright protection only if it is original, if it is an expression rather than a mere idea, and if it is non-utilitarian. The originality requirement is satisfied if the work required some degree of effort on the part of the author—no judgment as to artistic merit is involved. The expression requirement means that ideas, discoveries or processes cannot be protected by copyright. Only the manner in which an idea is expressed will be protected. If a physical object looks the way it does because of strictly utilitarian consideration, it cannot be protected by copyright.

3.   Fixation Required

A work of authorship must be fixed in a tangible medium of expression before it will be protected by the copyright laws. Thus transitory live performances or any other fleeting artistic creations are not eligible for copyright.

4.   Conventional Subject Matter

The bulk of copyrighted works consist of traditional literary, visual and performing arts such as books, plays, movies, paintings and sculptures. The statute itemizes seven types of works that are specifically protected. A recorded rendition of a copyrighted musical composition—known in the statute as a "sound recording"—is an independent copyrightable work, separate from the underlying musical composition.

5.   Troublesome Subject Matter

Computer programs, compilations of information, commercial prints, labels, translations and architectural plans have all been held eligible for copyright protection, despite earlier doubts. Trademarks, titles, typefaces and the appearance of buildings are not protected however.

B.   PUBLICATION
1.   Historical Significance of Publication

Before 1976, a work was not protected under federal law until it was published. Prior to that time, the work was protected by "common law copyright." Publication was defined as the unlimited distribution of tangible copies of the work to the public, so that performing or exhibiting the work did not constitute a publication that extinguished common law rights.

2.   Current Significance of Publication

The 1976 copyright statute abolished common law copyright and provided that federal protection attaches from the instant the work is fixed in a tangible medium. Publication is still important, however, because the author of a work must insure that a copyright notice appears on the work once it is published or else protection may be lost.

C.   COPYRIGHT FORMALITIES
1.   Notice

Notice must appear on all copies of a published work. However, the omission of notice from only a few copies will be excused. Similarly, if the omission was inadvertent and the copyright owner registers the work and makes reasonable efforts to add the notice, the original omission will be excused.

2.   Registration

Copyright registration is optional, but is a pre-requisite for a suit for copyright infringement. A copyright owner may register after learning of infringement and then file suit, but in that case, certain remedies will be unavailable.

3. Deposit

Once a work is published, the author must deposit two copies with the Library of Congress. Deposit must be accomplished within three months after publication.

D. THE RIGHTS OF A COPYRIGHT OWNER
1. The Statutory Exclusive Rights

The statute confers five rights on copyright owners. Only they may make copies of the work, adapt it into derivative forms, publicly distribute it, publicly perform it, or publicly display it. The owner of the copyright in a sound recording, however, does not have an exclusive right of performance. There are a number of qualifications of these rights permitting limited uses by specified parties such as charities, libraries or educational institutions.

2. Transfers and Licensing

Copyrights may be transferred just like other personal property. A copyright owner may also license others to make use of the work upon payment of a specified royalty. To protect owners against improvident transfers and licenses, such transactions are subject to a statutory right of termination which may be exercised during a five year period beginning at the end of thirty-five years from the date of the execution of the grant.

3. Duration of Rights

Copyright protection runs for the life of the author plus fifty years.

E. INFRINGEMENT
1. Substantial Similarity

Most infringement cases involve unauthorized copying. Copying is often difficult to prove directly but evidence of substantial similarity between the two works at issue is strong circumstantial evidence of copying. Substantial similarity is present if the entire structure of the work has been duplicated in some detail, or if specific phrases have been appropriated verbatim. Copying is also suggested when the two works contain common errors.

2. Access

In addition to proving substantial similarity, an infringement plaintiff also must show that the defendant had access to the protected work in order to make out a claim of copying. Access will be presumed, however, if the degree of similarity is overwhelming.

3. Intent

There is no intent requirement for copyright infringement.

F. FAIR USE
Certain uses of copyrighted material are permitted under the fair use doctrine where the uses are socially useful and will not deprive the copyright owner of significant economic reward.

1. Relevant Factors
Fair use is determined based on four factors—the purpose and character of the defendant's use, the nature of the copyrighted work, the amount and substantiality of the portion used, and the effect the defendant's use will have on the market for the copyrighted work. The last factor is usually considered the most important.

2. Parody as Fair Use
Under the fair use doctrine, a satirist may copy enough of a protected work to conjure up the original without being guilty of infringement.

G. REMEDIES

1. Injunctive Relief
A copyright infringer may be enjoined from continuing the infringing activities.

2. Monetary Relief
A copyright owner may recover his own damages and the defendant's profits if infringement has been proved. Alternatively, if the work in question was registered, the plaintiff may seek "statutory damages" in an amount between $250 and $10,000, as the court deems just.

3. Impoundment
The court may order all unauthorized copies seized and destroyed if infringement has been found.

4. Criminal Sanctions
If an infringing party acted for commercial advantage or financial gain, that party may be subjected to criminal penalties including imprisonment.

IV. MISAPPROPRIATION

A. PROTECTION FOR BUSINESS SCHEMES
Parties who propose clever ideas to others may be entitled to payment if their ideas are used, provided certain requirements are met.

1. Elements of a Protectible Business Scheme
An idea will only be protected if it is concrete, novel and useful. Thus vague or obvious suggestions will not give rise to any claim for payment.

2. Theories for Imposing Obligation to Pay for Ideas

A plaintiff seeking payment for the use of an idea must proceed under a recognized legal theory. The most frequently invoked theories are breach of express or implied contract, unjust enrichment, violation of a confidential relationship and theft of property.

3. Corporate Practice With Unsolicited Ideas

Corporations segregate unsolicited ideas to avoid inadvertently incurring liability if they subsequently adopt a practice resembling a submitted suggestion.

B. PROTECTION FOR INTANGIBLE STOCK IN TRADE

Firms in the business of selling entertainment or information often discover that others have pirated their stock in trade and are selling it in competition with them. These firms may invoke the misappropriation doctrine.

1. Historical Foundations: The *I.N.S.* Case

The misappropriation doctrine dates from the Supreme Court's 1918 decision in the *I.N.S.* case, involving the pirating of hot news stories by one wire service from another.

2. Elements of the Tort

A plaintiff makes out a case of misappropriation if (1) it has created a valuable intangible, (2) the defendant has appropriated that intangible without permission and for profit and (3) the defendant's taking has harmed the plaintiff economically.

3. Comparison of Misappropriation and Passing Off

In a passing off case, the defendant sells its own products under the good name of the plaintiff. Misappropriation is the reverse of passing off, since the misappropriator takes an intangible asset of the plaintiff's and sells it under its own name.

4. Applications of the Doctrine

The misappropriation doctrine has been invoked in many contexts. For instance, it has been used to provide relief against unauthorized reproduction of musical and dramatic performances, unauthorized broadcast of sporting events, and unauthorized use of stock indices by firms selling futures contracts.

C. PROTECTION FOR CELEBRITY'S FAME

1. Right of Publicity: A "Conclusion" or a Separate Tort?

The "right of publicity" refers to the ability of a celebrity to prevent others from making unauthorized use of his or her name or likeness. There is a theoretical dispute as to whether it exists independently of the remedies for trademark infringement, misappropriation and state law privacy infringement, but in most jurisdictions proof of the use of the celebrity's name, likeness, persona or identity without permission is a sufficient grounds for recovery.

2. The "Hybrid" Nature of Publicity Claims

Fact patterns involving the unauthorized use of a celebrity's name or likeness often involve aspects of trademark infringement, misappropriation and invasion of privacy at the same time. That is why plaintiffs in such cases often assert a variety of theories.

3. Who May Assert a Publicity Claim

While most publicity plaintiffs are entertainers and athletes, any famous individual can assert a right of publicity claim.

4. First Amendment Limits on Celebrity's Rights

The ability of a celebrity to invoke the right of publicity is limited by the First Amendment.

5. Descendability

There is judicial disagreement as to whether the right of publicity survives the death of the celebrity. Some courts hold that rights terminate on death, others hold that the rights survive if they were exploited during the celebrity's life, and still others hold that the rights are descendable regardless of exploitation.

D. PRE-EMPTION PROBLEMS

1. Section 301 of the Copyright Statute

State law may not provide any rights equivalent to those specified in the copyright act to any material within the subject matter of copyright. If either the rights provided or the materials protected are not within the scope of copyright, the state law is permissible. State misappropriation remedies are not pre-empted by this provision.

2. Pre-Emption Before the 1976 Statute

Prior to 1972 some courts held that states could not protect any intangibles that were not covered in the copyright act. The Supreme Court repudiated that view in its 1972 *Goldstein* opinion, and the holding of that case was subsequently codified in section 301.

V. PATENTS

A. TYPES OF PATENTS

There are three types of patents—utility patents, plant patents, and design patents. This outline considers only utility patents, which involve "inventions."

B. PATENTABLE SUBJECT MATTER

1. Machines

Any device consisting of parts which function together to produce a result is a machine. Machines are patentable if they meet the statutory tests.

2. Compositions of Matter

A mixture of naturally occurring substances with properties different from its ingredients is a composition of matter. These too are patentable if they meet the relevant tests.

3. Articles of Manufacture

Any man-made object that is not a machine or composition of matter is an article of manufacture, and also may be patented if the relevant tests are met.

4. Processes

A process is a series of steps designed to achieve a particular result. Processes are also potentially patentable subject matter.

5. Unpatentable Material

The courts have held patent protection unavailable for products of nature (such as chemicals or minerals), laws of nature, mathematical formulas, computer programs, methods of conducting a business, new uses for known products and printed material of any sort. A patent on a machine does not grant exclusive rights to the result that the machine accomplishes.

C. THE REQUIREMENT OF NOVELTY

Novelty is the first of the three requirements for a patent. Only novel machines, compositions of matter, articles of manufacture and processes will be protected.

1. Note on Terminology

Some writers refer to the concepts covered in both this section, and in the following section (concerning "statutory bar") as problems of "novelty." This outline uses novelty more narrowly, as encompassing only those problems of unpatentability that flow from events before the applicant's date of invention.

2. Domestic Events Defeating Novelty

If the device or process at issue was (1) patented, (2) described in a printed publication, (3) known by others or (4) used by others before it was invented by an applicant, the device is not novel and no patent will issue.

3. Foreign Events Defeating Novelty

If the device or process at issue was (1) patented, or (2) described in a printed publication, in a foreign country before it was invented by an applicant, the device is not novel and no patent will issue.

4. Single Source With an Enabling Disclosure

If novelty is to be defeated on the basis of documentary material, that cited reference must, by itself, reveal how to make the device or utilize the process in question.

5. Use of Knowledge Accessible to the Public

If novelty is to be defeated because the device or process was previously known or used, the prior knowledge or use must have been available to the public and not a secret use.

6. Accidental Results Are Not Anticipations

Novelty will not be defeated on the grounds that a device or process was previously used, if those engaged in the prior use developed it by accident and were unaware of how to duplicate it.

7. Priority and Diligence

Prior invention by another defeats novelty. Only the first party to invent is entitled to patent protection. However, if the second inventor is the first to reduce the invention to practice and the senior inventor has not acted with continuous diligence to perfect and patent the invention, the patent will be granted to the second inventor.

D. STATUTORY BAR

1. Events Giving Rise to Statutory Bar

If more than one year before a person applies for a patent, the invention has been (1) patented here or abroad, (2) described in a printed publication here or abroad, or (3) in public use here or abroad, the person loses the right to secure a patent, even if he or she was the first to invent. For a printed publication to give rise to this statutory bar, it must completely reveal how to make the invention. Public use is defined broadly in this context to include any non-secret use even if it was not widespread.

2. Differences Between Statutory Bar and Lack of Novelty

Novelty problems occur when specified events happened prior to a patent applicant's date of invention. Statutory bar problems occur when the event happened more than one year prior to the date of the patent application.

E. THE REQUIREMENT OF NON–OBVIOUSNESS

1. Difference Between Non-Obviousness and Novelty

An invention is not novel if it has previously been made or described exactly. Even if the invention has never been made, however, persons skilled in the craft might be able to deduce how to make it quite readily should the need arise. In that case, the invention is "obvious" and not patentable.

2. History of Non-Obviousness Requirement

Non-obviousness was added as a statutory requirement in 1952. Prior to that time, courts demanded that a patent applicant show that the material in question was "inventive." The non-obviousness inquiry involves three steps—(1) identification of the prior art; (2) ascertainment of differences between the prior art and the invention; and (3) resolution of the level of ordinary skill in the pertinent art.

3. The Concept of the "Prior Art"

Prior art consists of documentary and other references that reflect the state of technology in a given field. The relevant prior art includes all material dealing with the same technological problem as the one addressed by the invention.

4. Factual Tests for Determining "Obviousness"

A number of simplified tests are used to determine if a new device was obvious at the time of its invention. Thus, if it resulted from a simple alteration of a pre-existing device or formula, it will be held obvious. On the other hand, if it satisfies a long felt need in an industry, is an immediate commercial success, or meets with widespread professional approval, it will be considered non-obvious.

F. THE REQUIREMENT OF UTILITY

An invention must be useful to qualify for a patent. An item which can only be used for an illegal or immoral purpose will be held lacking in "utility" and is not patentable.

G. PATENT APPLICATION PROCEDURE

1. Drafting the Patent

A patent must contain a "specification," describing the invention, and one or more "claims," indicating the specific attributes of the invention which the applicant alleges are new and inventive. The scope of protection afforded by the patent is defined by the wording of the claims.

2. Patent Examination

A patent application is reviewed by a patent examiner who determines if all statutory requirements are met. Applicants are under a duty of candor, requiring them to disclose all relevant information bearing on their invention. The patent application and all information provided during the examination process is kept confidential until a patent issues.

3. Reissue

If a patentee discovers that the patent is defective in some respect, such as in the wording of the claims, and if the defect was not due to the patentee's own deception, the patentee may apply to have the patent corrected and reissued.

H. PATENT INFRINGEMENT

1. Scope of the Patent

Patents last for 17 years. Under the "doctrine of equivalents," a patent can be infringed even by a device that is not identical to the one described in the patent, if the infringing device does the same tasks in the same manner and achieves the same results as the patented invention. Under the doctrine of "file wrapper estoppel," however, the patentee may not claim infringement under the doctrine of equivalents for anything that corresponds to a claim surrendered during the examination process.

2. Direct Infringement

Infringement consists of making, using or selling a device within the claims of a previously issued patent. There is no intent requirement. Once a patentee sells a product, however, the purchaser is free to use or resell that particular physical item without committing infringement. Repair of patented objects does not constitute infringement.

3. Contributory Infringement

The sale of a substance that has no uses, except as a component of a patented device, to a buyer who lacks a license to practice the invention constitutes contributory infringement, if it is done knowingly.

4. Remedies

A patentee who proves infringement is entitled to both injunctive relief and damages, which may be trebled in the discretion of the court.

VI. TRADE SECRETS

A. MATERIAL CONSTITUTING TRADE SECRETS

1. Uniform Act Definition

The Uniform Trade Secret Act defines a trade secret as any information that is kept confidential and derives economic value from not been generally known by others.

2. Minimal Novelty and Utility Required

Information protected as a trade secret must possess some minimal degree of utility and novelty, although it need not be so inventive as to qualify for a patent.

3. Requisite Degree of Secrecy

The owner of an alleged trade secret must take those steps to preserve secrecy that are reasonable under the circumstances. Absolute secrecy is not required.

4.   Matters Held to Be Trade Secrets

Formulas, manufacturing processes and valuable information about customers, sources of supply and future business plans, have all been held to be trade secrets.

B.   APPROPRIATION BY PARTIES WITH LEGITIMATE ACCESS

Trade secrets are often "stolen" by those who first learn of them legitimately and with the consent of the owner.

1.   Explicit Duty to Maintain Secrecy

To avoid trade secret theft by parties who learn the secret as part of their jobs or for other legitimate reasons, the owner of the secret can contractually impose an explicit duty of confidentiality on them. A trade secret owner can also impose a reasonable covenant not to compete on employees, barring them from opening their own businesses or working for competitors when they leave their present jobs.

2.   Implied Duty to Maintain Secrecy

Courts may imply a duty of confidentiality where one has not been imposed explicitly, if the relationship between the parties warrants. If a party in such a relationship uses the secret to his own advantage or reveals it to another, the trade secret owner will be able to secure judicial relief.

C.   TRADE SECRET THEFT BY STRANGERS

1.   Behavior Constituting Improper Means

It is tortious to learn another's trade secrets by "improper" means. Means are improper if they are successful in uncovering the secret despite reasonable efforts by the owner to keep the matter confidential.

2.   Reverse Engineering Is Not Improper Means

It is permissible to learn a trade secret by taking apart or analyzing another firm's goods that embody the secret. This is known as "reverse engineering."

3.   Innocent Use of Stolen Secrets

A party making use of trade secrets belonging to another, without knowledge that the secrets have been misappropriated, is not liable to the owner until it is informed that the material constitutes trade secrets.

D.   TRADE SECRET DISCLOSURE BY GOVERNMENT

1.   Freedom of Information Act

There is an exception to the Freedom of Information Act that permits the government to refuse to reveal any material that embodies trade secret information.

2.   Reverse FOIA Suits
If a government agency proposes to release trade secret material, the owner of the secret may file suit under the Administrative Procedure Act to enjoin the disclosure, provided it has some statutory basis for its claim of confidentiality.

E.   REMEDIES FOR TRADE SECRET THEFT
1.   Damages
Damages will be awarded for theft of trade secrets.

2.   Injunctions
If the trade secret is still confidential at the time of trial, the court will enjoin the defendant from using it. If the secret has lapsed into the public domain by the time of trial, the courts differ on the remedy. Some deny an injunction, some enjoin the defendant perpetually, and some enjoin the defendant for a limited period.

3.   Criminal Remedies
There is no federal criminal law against trade secret theft, but about 20 states have statutes of this type.

F.   PRE-EMPTION PROBLEMS
1.   Conflict With the Policy of Free Copyability
The patent laws have been held to embody a policy that unpatented material is in the public domain and that anyone can copy it. State trade secret law does not interfere with this policy because it protects only material that is confidential, and by definition does not apply to material that is in the public domain.

2.   Conflict With the Policy of Promoting Disclosure
The patent laws encourage people to disclose their inventions by granting them 17 years of exclusive protection. Trade secret law encourages them to keep their inventions secret. Although the two bodies of law thus seem to conflict, the Supreme Court has held that trade secret law is not pre-empted by the patent laws.

G.   TRADE SECRETS AND OTHER UNFAIR TRADE CONCEPTS
Trade secret law is closely connected with other unfair trade topics, such as patent law, protection for business schemes and, where customer lists are involved, inducement of breach of contract.

VII. COMPETITOR REMEDIES FOR FALSE ADVERTISING AND DISPARAGEMENT

A. COMMON LAW REMEDIES FOR FALSE ADVERTISING

1. No Remedy in Usual Case

If an honest firm competes with a false advertiser, the honest firm usually cannot prove that it would have gotten additional patronage but for the falsehood. Consequently, common law courts do not recognize a competitor cause of action for false advertising.

2. Sole Source May Recover

Where a firm is the only one vending goods with certain attributes (i.e., the "sole source" of those goods), it will necessarily lose patronage when another falsely claims that its goods also have those attributes. Thus, a firm in this situation has a common law cause of action for false advertising.

3. Modern Cases

Newer common law cases permit recovery for false advertising where the defendant's ad was targeted specifically at the plaintiff, even if the plaintiff was not the "sole source."

B. STATE STATUTORY REMEDIES FOR FALSE ADVERTISING

1. Statutory Provisions Are Widespread

Every state has some form of unfair competition statute, many of which provide private remedies to competitors injured by false advertising.

2. No Sole Source Limitation

The state statutory remedies dispense with the sole source limitation that applies at common law.

3. Types of Falsehoods Prohibited

Some state statutes itemize the types of false advertising that are actionable, while others contain only a general prohibition against "unfair" or "deceptive" practices.

4. Limited Utility of State Statutory Remedies

Many state statutes provide only for injunctive relief. Since litigation can be protracted, the offending ad may run for months unless the plaintiff can get a preliminary injunction.

C. FEDERAL LANHAM ACT REMEDIES FOR FALSE ADVERTISING

1. Historical Background

Section 43(a) of the Lanham Act prohibits any false description or representation of goods. Although this section was originally construed narrowly, to reach only "passing off" and other behavior resembling trademark infringement, modern cases regard the statute as providing a federal remedy against false advertising.

2. Standing: Who May Invoke Section 43

A plaintiff seeking injunctive relief under § 43(a) must show a likelihood of economic injury due to the defendant's conduct in order to be entitled to relief. If the plaintiff seeks damages, it must demonstrate an actual loss of sales.

3. What Constitutes a False Description or Representation

Any falsehood with a tendency to mislead or deceive is actionable under section 43(a), provided it is material. The plaintiff need not prove that the defendant acted intentionally.

D. COMMON LAW REMEDIES FOR DISPARAGEMENT
1. Disparagement Defined

Disparagement is a falsehood that tends to denigrate the goods or service being sold by another party.

2. Elements of Disparagement

A disparagement plaintiff must show that (1) the defendant made offending statements about its products; (2) the statements are false; and (3) the statements caused "special damages" (i.e. a loss of sales directly traceable to the disparaging statements).

3. First Amendment Limits of Disparagement Actions

If the merits of a product become the subject of a public debate, a disparagement plaintiff must prove that the defendant acted with "actual malice" in order to establish a right to relief.

E. STATE STATUTORY REMEDIES FOR DISPARAGEMENT

Many state unfair practice statutes also contain explicit causes of action for disparagement.

F. FEDERAL LANHAM ACT REMEDIES FOR DISPARAGEMENT
1. No Remedy for Explicit Disparagement

Because Lanham Act § 43(a) only condemns false statements made by a party about his own goods, disparaging statements made about another firm's goods are not actionable under that provision.

2. Certain Reputational Harms Are Actionable Under § 43(a)

In two situations resembling disparagement, federal courts have allowed § 43(a) actions. The first involves parties who alter or mutilate works of art and then display them with the implied representation that they are the work of the original artist. The second involves parties who use trademarks and trade symbols of other firms in obscene parodies, where there is an implication that the trademark owner endorses or sponsors the parody. In each case the defendant is making a false description of its own goods, which brings the conduct within the statute.

VIII. FEDERAL TRADE COMMISSION REGULATION OF UNFAIR AND DECEPTIVE PRACTICES

A. OVERVIEW OF FTC PROCEDURE

The Commission consists of five Presidential appointees, and a large professional staff. It identifies possible instances of "unfair" or "deceptive" advertising through public complaints and through its own considerable investigatory powers. Prior to commencing formal proceedings, the Commission will usually try to settle the problem by inviting the concerned firm to enter into a "consent" order. If that is not possible, the case will be adjudicated before an Administrative Law Judge at the Agency, with an initial appeal to the Commissioners and then appellate review by the U.S. Courts of Appeals. The Commission is also empowered to promulgate legislative rules.

B. THE MEANING OF UNFAIRNESS
1. Historical Development

Prior to 1938 the Federal Trade Commission Act forbade only "unfair methods of competition." In 1938 Congress added language barring "unfair or deceptive acts or practices" as well. For many years the Commission did not distinguish between "unfairness" and "deception," but in the mid-sixties the Commission developed a separate unfairness doctrine that emphasized the morality of the challenged practice, whether it offended public policy, and whether it injured consumers. This approach was endorsed in dicta in a 1972 Supreme Court opinion.

2. Current Doctrine

The Commission modified its unfairness doctrine in a 1980 policy statement. Under the new approach behavior is unfair if it causes substantial, unmitigated and unavoidable injury to consumers.

3. Illustrative Unfair Practices

Behavior that is coercive, that withholds material information from consumers, or subjects them to harsh remedies for the collection of consumer debt are examples of unfair acts or practices.

C. THE MEANING OF DECEPTION
1. Traditional Definition

Any representation that has a tendency to deceive a significant number of consumers is "deceptive" under the traditional definition. The consumers in question need not be "reasonable" and are assumed to be gullible. There need not be any showing of intent on the part of the advertiser and the Commission need not show that consumers suffered any actual injury other than having been deceived.

2. A New Standard of Deceptiveness?
A 1984 Commission opinion reformulated the definition of deception, holding that it consists of behavior that is "likely to mislead consumers acting reasonably under the circumstances." Whether this new language changed the substantive standard, and if so, the legal status of that change, are currently matters of debate.

3. Factors Influencing Commission Case Selection
The Commission is more likely to challenge deception involving expensive products that are purchased infrequently, or deception that poses a risk of physical injury or foregone treatment to consumers. It is also likely to consider the publicity and deterrence value of a case before deciding to act. It will avoid bringing cases where any remedial order is likely to reduce the amount of information available to consumers.

4. Applications of the Deception Standard
In addition to being used against outright misrepresentations, the deception standard has been used to challenge omissions of material facts, inaccurate claims that a product was unique, mischaracterizations of the type of business the seller was in, falsehoods by endorsers, and the use of misleading television props and mock-ups.

5. Deceptive Pricing and Sales Practices
The Commission has used its deception authority to challenge claims that products are "on sale" or "free" where that is not accurate, and also to attack misleading advertisements of guarantee or warranty terms. Abuses in door-to-door and mail order selling have been eliminated through F.T.C action, as have unfair sales practices such as "bait and switch."

6. Disparagement
False claims about competing firms or their goods constitute deceptive acts or practices under the F.T.C. Act. For First Amendment reasons, however, false statements by individuals not engaged in a given line of business that attack particular kinds of goods or services have been held not actionable under the statute.

D. ADVERTISING SUBSTANTIATION
It is a violation of the F.T.C. Act to promulgate an advertisement unless the advertiser possesses, in advance, a reasonable basis to support every claim that is made.

1. Development of the Doctrine
The requirement of ad substantiation was announced in a 1972 Commission opinion. That case concluded that it was "unfair" within the meaning of the statute for a firm to make claims about its merchandise unless it had documentation to substantiate those claims.

2.   What Constitutes Substantiation

The kind and amount of documentation satisfying the "reasonable basis" standard is determined on a case-by-case basis. Only material in the advertiser's possession *before* the advertisement was disseminated is considered in determining if substantiation was adequate.

3.   Effect of Substantiation Doctrine on Burden of Proof

Although it was argued that the substantiation requirement impermissibly altered the burden of proof in F.T.C. proceedings, that contention has been rejected by the courts.

E.   REMEDIES FOR VIOLATIONS OF SECTION 5

1.   Cease and Desist Order

A firm found guilty of an unfair or deceptive act will be ordered to refrain from the challenged conduct in the future under an F.T.C. "cease and desist" order.

2.   Orders Requiring Affirmative Statements

If the deception in question can only be eliminated by requiring an affirmative disclosure of additional information whenever certain claims are made, the Commission may include a requirement to that effect in the cease and desist order.

3.   Corrective Advertising

When a deceptive advertising claim has continued for such a long period that it will "linger" in the minds of consumers even after the advertisements are discontinued, the Commission may require the advertiser to run a corrective statement in future ads, to eliminate the erroneous impression that was generated by the earlier ads.

4.   Restitution

The Commission may not include a provision in a cease and desist order requiring a firm to refund money to consumers. It may, however, file suit in U.S. District Court seeking a judicial order requiring restitution.

5.   Remedies for Violations of Cease and Desist Orders

A firm that violates the provisions of a cease and desist order entered against it is liable for significant civil penalties. The Commission may also seek penalties against firms that were not parties to the original administrative proceeding if it can show that they knew their conduct was unfair or deceptive.

F.   F.T.C.   RULEMAKING

1.   The Commission's Authority to Promulgate Rules

The F.T.C. was given explicit authority to issue rules declaring specific behavior "unfair" or "deceptive" in 1975.

2.   Scope and Effect of Commission Rules

The Commission has issued rules on a broad variety of subjects. Violation of these rules subjects the violator to civil penalties.

3.   Judicial Limits on Rulemaking

Commission rules are subject to judicial review. The courts have been aggressive in requiring the Commission to document the unfair or deceptive practices it has identified, before upholding a new rule.

4.   Legislative Limits on Rulemaking

Because many rulemaking initiatives are politically controversial, Congress has intervened periodically to limit or suspend particular rulemaking proposals. It also adopted a legislative veto proposal giving itself the right to set aside Commission rules, but that proposal was held defective by the Supreme Court. It is likely that a new provision of this type will be enacted shortly.

5.   The Future of Rulemaking

In the short term, the Commission is unlikely to undertake any new rulemaking activities, opting instead for less controversial case-by-case enforcement.

IX. CONSUMER REMEDIES FOR FALSE ADVERTISING AND OTHER EXPLOITATIVE PRACTICES

A.   TRADITIONAL REMEDIES
1.   Common Law Remedies

Consumers victimized by false advertising may bring common law actions for deceit, contractual recission, or restitution. If physically injured they may also assert a strict product liability claim. Each of these causes of action has shortcomings, however.

2.   Uniform Commercial Code

Consumers may also invoke the warranty and unconscionability provisions of the U.C.C. if they have been deceived by advertisements or other falsehoods prior to purchasing tangible goods.

B.   UNAVAILABILITY OF FEDERAL REMEDIES

1.   No Lanham Act Remedy for Consumers

Consumers lack standing under section 43(a) of the Lanham Act, and thus cannot use that provision as a false advertising remedy.

2.   No F.T.C. Act § 5 Remedy for Consumers

The courts have declined to imply a private right of action under the Federal Trade Commission Act, so that statute is also unavailable as a consumer remedy.

C.   BABY F.T.C. STATUTES

Every state has a statute based on the F.T.C. Act. Most of those provide private actions to consumers who have been deceived by false advertising.

1.   Proof of Scienter and Reliance Not Required

Most state statutes do not require the plaintiff to prove that the defendant knew the challenged representations were false or that he or she actually relied on the representation at issue.

2.   Incentives to File Suit Provided

Baby F.T.C. statutes often provide for simplified class actions, attorney's fees, and multiplied damages to encourage consumers to file suit.

3.   Damages Need Not Be Quantifiable

At least one state has held that any deception is actionable under a Baby F.T.C. statute even if the consumer cannot show economic injury from the transaction.

4.   Relief Against Non-Merchant Sellers

Baby F.T.C. statutes have been successfully invoked against private parties not in the business of selling goods or services, who made misrepresentations in the course of selling used goods.

D.   MAGNUSON–MOSS WARRANTY ACT

The federal Magnuson-Moss Warranty Act specifies how warranty information must be disclosed and provides a federal cause of action for breach of warranty.

1.   Not All Written Material Is a Warranty

Not every piece of paper accompanying a product is considered a warranty. Thus, misrepresentations about products contained in brochures or instruction manuals cannot provide the basis for a Magnuson-Moss suit.

2.   No Remedy for Personal Injuries

The Magnuson-Moss Act does not provide a remedy for personal injuries resulting from a product's failure to perform as warranted.

3.   Jurisdictional Hurdles

To file suit in federal court a Magnuson-Moss plaintiff must satisfy fairly strict "amount in controversy" requirements. These restrictions do not apply in state court, however.

X. PRICE AND SERVICE DISCRIMINATION UNDER THE ROBINSON–PATMAN ACT

Price discrimination is unlawful if (a) the jurisdictional requirements of the Robinson-Patman Act are satisfied and (b) the discrimination is likely to have an adverse effect on competition.

A. JURISDICTIONAL ELEMENTS

1. Interstate Commerce

One of the two sales, which when compared reveal a price difference, must cross a state line.

2. A "Discrimination in Price"

There must be proof that some customers paid a different actual invoice price (net of rebates) than other customers to trigger further scrutiny under the act.

3. Purchases

Only completed purchases are analyzed to determine if there has been a discrimination in price. Offers to sell at specified prices, or refusals to sell at any price, are irrelevant under the act. Purchases by the federal government and non-profit entities are disregarded.

4. Commodities

The statute only covers price discrimination in the sale of commodities. Thus, discriminatory pricing of services or intangibles is not regulated by the act.

5. Like Grade and Quality

The goods sold at the higher price and the goods sold at the lower price must be of like grade and quality for the act to apply. Physically identical goods are of like grade and quality, as are goods that differ slightly but have the same degree of consumer acceptance and marketability.

6. Use, Consumption or Resale in the United States

The act only applies to sales made for the purpose of use, consumption or resale in this country. Sales for export are ignored.

B. HARM TO PRIMARY LINE COMPETITION

1. Overview of Competitive Harm Requirement

Harm can take place at the same level of competition as the seller ("primary line") or on the level of the buyers ("secondary line"). In either type of case, the risk of harm must be substantial, and the harm must be to the competitive process generally, not merely to a particular competitor, in order to violate the act.

2. Theory of Primary Line Cases

When a seller is able to subsidize unusually low prices in one market with higher prices charged to customers located elsewhere, it may be able to harm its primary line competitors who cannot match the low prices. Behavior of this sort is known as predatory pricing.

3. The *Utah Pie* Case

In a 1967 case the Supreme Court suggested that predatory pricing is present whenever there is evidence that price levels in a given market declined and that established local firms lost profit. This case was sharply criticized, and courts and commentators sought a more satisfactory definition of predatory pricing.

4. Identifying Predatory Pricing

Most definitions of predatory pricing specify that the lower price involved must be "below cost." There are several cost figures that might be used however, such as "average total cost," "average variable cost" or "marginal cost." In an important 1975 article Profs. Areeda and Turner argued that prices below average variable cost should be conclusively presumed unlawful. In the ensuing decade, most of the federal Courts of Appeals have adopted an approach to predatory pricing based on or similar to the Areeda-Turner test.

C. HARM TO SECONDARY LINE COMPETITION

1. General Standards

Harm to competition on the buyer level will be presumed where two buyers from the same seller are in direct competition and the amount of the price differential is sufficient to affect their resale prices or to impair the profit margin of the firm paying the higher price.

2. Causation

The harm to firms at the buyer level must be caused by the seller's discrimination and not by other factors, such as consumer preference for certain types of goods.

3. Specific Discounting Practices

Quantity discounts are permissible under the act if they are functionally available to all customers, or if they can be cost justified. The legality of "functional" discounts, in which a firm that does its own wholesaling gets a lower price than ordinary retailers who do not, is a subject of continuing debate.

4. Competitive Injury on Remote Levels of Distribution

Injury on levels several steps removed from the discriminator is sufficient to satisfy the competitive injury element of the statute.

D. AFFIRMATIVE DEFENSES

1. Cost Justification

A seller may charge a lower price to customers whom it is cheaper to serve, provided it can document the cost saving. Developing such documentation is often quite difficult, however.

2. Meeting Competition

A seller may lower its prices to those customers who are being offered an equally low price by one of the seller's own competitors, provided it acts in good faith and seeks only to match, not undersell, the competitor.

3. Changed Market Conditions

It is a defense to a charge of price discrimination that either market conditions or the marketability of the goods has changed between the time of the higher and lower priced sales.

E. BROKERAGE PAYMENTS

Purported "brokerage" payments by a seller to a buyer are forbidden under a specific provision of the act, except for services rendered.

1. When Are "Services Rendered?"

The services rendered exception has been virtually read out of the statute. Any payment directly to the buyer or to a broker controlled by or affiliated with the buyer will violate this provision of the act.

2. Proof of Injury to Competition Not Required

The brokerage provision of the Robinson-Patman Act does not require any showing of harm to competition.

3. Seller's Broker

Sellers may use brokers and compensate them as they see fit, but a seller's broker may not split its commissions with customers without violating the brokerage provision of the act.

F. ADVERTISING ALLOWANCES

1. General Provision

A firm may not provide a customer with promotional services or advertising allowances unless the payments or services are made available on proportionally equal terms to all customers. Provision of such services or payments on other than proportional terms violates the act regardless of whether it causes harm to competition.

2. Services and Facilities Covered

Any items or payments designed to help customers promote the sale of merchandise are included in this provision. Examples include in-store display materials, cash allowances for newspaper advertisements, or cents-off coupons.

3. The Concepts of Proportionality and Availability

A seller can "proportionalize" by basing the amount of services provided on the sales volume of each customer. The seller must take affirmative steps to inform all customers of the program in order for the availability requirement to be satisfied.

4. Dual Distributing Sellers

If a seller sells to both wholesalers and retailers, and provides promotional services to the retailers, it must make those services available to the customers of the wholesalers as well, to avoid violation of the act.

G. BUYER LIABILITY

A buyer who knowingly induces a seller to give him a discriminatory low price is guilty of a violation of the Robinson-Patman Act.

1. The Lower Price Must Be Illegal

Buyer liability only attaches if the seller's price discrimination meets all the jurisdictional tests, has the requisite adverse effect on competition, and is not covered by any affirmative defense.

2. Buyer Need Not Disclose Competing Offers

A buyer does not violate this provision if it accepts the lowest of several bids without informing the seller that it has undercut a rival's prices, because in such a case the seller has a good faith meeting competition defense. Since there is no illegal price discrimination there can be no buyer liability.

H. REMEDIES

Parties injured by violations of the act may sue for treble damages. In addition, the Justice Department and the Federal Trade Commission may enforce the act in civil proceedings. There is also a provision making certain types of price discrimination criminal, but it is almost never enforced.

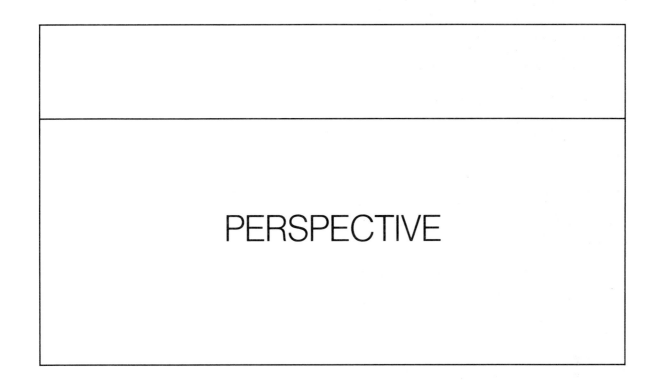

PERSPECTIVE

WHAT IS UNFAIR TRADE?

Most Unfair Trade courses cover a wide variety of topics, including state and federal trademark law, trade secrets, misappropriation, copyright, false advertising, and sometimes either patent or price discrimination. Indeed, the course names vary almost as widely as the subject matter, with the course being variously known as Unfair Competition, Business Torts, Marketing Practices and Intellectual Property. The legal materials used in the typical course also run the gamut. In the same course you encounter detailed and complex statutes (e.g. the patent statute), cryptic and poorly drafted statutes (e.g. the Robinson-Patman Act), cases that interpret statutes, cases that fashion doctrines out of common law, regulations, treaties and perhaps, depending on your text, non-legal materials as well.

Not surprisingly, many students have trouble finding the common theme that runs through this diverse body of subject matter. There are, however, several unifying notions that tie the various components of the course together into a coherent whole.

One approach to synthesizing the material into a coherent whole is *economic*. The free enterprise economy that prevails in the United States is predicated on the notion that competition provides benefits to consumers in the form of low prices and superior goods. Those benefits are realized, to a large degree, because firms in a competitive economy constantly strive to be more creative than their rivals. This creativity can consist of devising a superior way to make the product, coming up with a novel and memorable way to market it, or perhaps cleverly conceiving just what type of new product consumers want.

On this view, behavior that destroys incentives and discourages creativity on the part of others is of serious concern. It is likely to lessen or eliminate the benefits of competition. Unfair Trade Practices can be viewed as the body of law that preserves incentives for creativity. Patent and copyright fit this model most easily since they are explicitly designed to encourage and reward artistic and inventive creativity. Trade secret and misappropriation law are state law doctrines analogous to patent and copyright, that also reward creative activity by protecting it from encroachment. Trademark and false advertising law encourage firms to invest in the development of good will by insuring them that others may not use their trade symbols or lie to the public. Prohibitions against price discrimination encourage small firms to enter markets by insuring that they cannot be destroyed or discriminated against by larger, more powerful rivals or suppliers.

In this economic view of unfair trade law, those behaviors that undermine incentives are labeled unfair. It suggests that for many issues in an unfair trade course, it is useful to ask yourself the question "If left unchecked, will this behavior destroy the incentives that exist for other firms to be creative?"

Alternatively, unfair trade concepts can be seen as implementing *ethical* rather than economic precepts. In this view, the problems taken up in the course are all about preserving a suitable degree of morality and fair dealing in the midst of the otherwise rough and tumble marketplace. Thus, most courses consider topics raising problems of misrepresentation (trademark infringement, false advertising), unauthorized use of another's creative work (patent, copyright, trade secret, misappropriation) or overly aggressive use of economic power to manipulate the market (price discrimination). If you use this perspective to organize the material, you should constantly inquire "Is this behavior consistent with contemporary standards of commercial ethics? Do we want a marketplace in which this type of behavior takes place?"

A third view of unfair trade law is as a body of rules designed to protect commercial *relationships and trade values*. This is the position of McManis, *The Law of Unfair Trade Practices In A Nutshell*, (West 1982). This view posits that firms have certain present or prospective relationships with customers, suppliers, employees, stockholders or perhaps even the government, that are deserving of protection from interference. Thus luring away employees who are under contract, and misleading customers through the use of deceptive advertisements or counterfeit trademarks, are impermissible because they intrude on such relationships. Similarly, this approach recognizes that firms possess numerous intangible assets, such as patents, copyrights, and trade secrets, the theft of which should be impermissible. This view of the subject sets up the recurring inquiries "Does the defendant's conduct interfere with a value or relationship that should be protected from intrusion?" and "Is this relationship or intangible sufficiently unique and specific to deserve protection?"

It should be noted further that one need not adopt any of these general views of the material exclusively. One can think of unfair trade as a subject that deals simultaneously with the preservation of incentives to creativity, commercial morality, and important trade relations and values. My own view is that all three themes are important and each can be helpful in seeing how some doctrines fit with others.

THE FEDERAL/STATE RELATIONSHIP IN UNFAIR TRADE

Some of the topics in the typical unfair trade course are exclusively federal—such as patent or copyright law. Others are exclusively common law creations existing by force of state law—such as trade secrets or misappropriation. Still others have both state and federal aspects—such as false advertising and trademark law. This in itself is uncommon for a law school course.

More important than the diverse sources of authority for different unfair trade topics, however, is the way in which the bodies of law interact. In many areas, state and federal law are consistent and supplementary. Where that is true, no particular analytic problems arise. In unfair trade courses, however, the student frequently encounters situations where the state and federal doctrines appear to work at cross-purposes. For instance state law may forbid copying certain aspects of a product in order to avoid confusing consumers, while federal law may imply that copying should be permitted to encourage competition. As a general rule, state law must give way to federal law when there is a conflict, because of the supremacy clause of the federal constitution. This is known as the pre-emption doctrine. However, courts have been unusually creative in trying to construe both state and federal unfair competition doctrines in such a way as to avoid or side-step these conflicts.

Whenever you confront a problem in the area of unfair competition, you should develop the reflex of thinking through the federal-state interaction. Ask yourself what purposes the state law seems to be striving to achieve, what body of federal law is most relevant to the same subject matter, and whether there are any inconsistent policies imbedded in that federal law. In those areas where there are overlapping—rather than conflicting—federal and state concepts make sure you canvass all the alternative rights and remedies that are provided by both systems before you consider the problem resolved.

THOUGHTS ABOUT OUTLINES

Rare is the law teacher who does not denigrate commercial outlines in the classroom. To the second and third year students in a course on unfair trade practices, the reasons for that hostility are well known. The chief mission of all of your teachers is to teach you *technique,* not *doctrine.* One of the many techniques that marks a good lawyer is the ability to derive doctrine from the raw materials of the law. Resort to a book that summarizes the doctrine insures that you will never master that technique. It can also lull you into a sense that your task is done, so that you never develop the further and more important techniques of a sophisticated lawyer—the ability to critique a doctrine sensibly; the ability to predict how a court will resolve a wholly novel factual problem; the ability to create an argument about which of two conflicting doctrines ought to control in a particular case, and so on.

On the other hand, most teachers hope that you will come away from their courses with some understanding of the vocabulary of the subject and an understanding of the chief doctrinal concepts, even if they do not spend a great deal of class time communicating that information. It is in that regard that this outline can be helpful. It tries to assemble in one place a summary of the key doctrines that mark the field and to present them in an organization that will permit you to see the connections between the various sub-topics and principles that you have studied.

I have tried to construct this outline with that notion in mind. It is designed to render clear and coherent that which may have been murky or disorganized when you first encountered it in the casebook. It is liberally spiced with case citations. This is not to impress you with my research skills. Instead, it is to suggest that after you have read a section of the outline, you might profit from re-reading the cited case, especially if the subject in question was a difficult one for you when it was taken up in class.

The outline also tries to alert you to areas where there is no clear judicial consensus. That is quite common in many areas of unfair trade practices law, and many instructors prefer to teach about and test on these open and controversial areas. Consequently, you ought to pause in your review and think about which of the competing positions you find most persuasive, and why.

Even where the outline states a rule absolutely, you should take it with a grain of salt. First, you (or your instructor) may feel that a case or a statute should be read more conservatively or expansively than I have suggested. Such disagreements are common place and healthy, assuming both parties to the debate can articulate reasons for their conclusions. Even law professors argue about what the law is all the time! Moreover, even if there is complete consensus on a given rule, you must bear in mind that all rules have breaking points. If you apply a doctrine to a state of facts and get an absurd result, re-think your analysis. Be sure that the result is consistent with the economic, ethical, and relational themes that are at the heart of the subject matter. In unfair trade as in all other legal endeavors, remember that common sense is often your most important tool.

OUTSIDE READING IN UNFAIR TRADE

There is an enormous variety of written material available for students who want to go beyond their casebooks and this outline to explore particular unfair trade problems. Two extremely useful student texts are McManis, *The Law of Unfair Trade Practices In A Nutshell,* (West 1982) and Miller and Davis, *Intellectual Property In a Nutshell* (West 1983). The Miller and Davis volume is limited to patent, trademark and copyright issues.

There are also very fine multi-volume works in all of the sub-topics comprehended within the typical unfair trade practices course. In the area of trademark law the two volume treatise McCarthy, *Trademarks and Unfair Competition* is extremely comprehensive and highly influential. Milgrim, *Trade Secrets* is a thorough three volume canvass of every important aspect of trade secret law. Chisum's six volume treatise on *Patents* is an outstanding treatment of all facets of patent law and includes thoughtful analysis of all leading Supreme Court cases. The same comments can be applied to the justifiably authoritative treatise by Professor Nimmer on *Copyright.* In the Federal Trade Commission area, Kanwit, *Federal Trade Commission,* is a useful two volume work that covers both substantive and procedural aspects of the Commission's work. Finally, the intricacies of the price discrimination law are discussed lucidly in the single volume book, Kintner, *Robinson-Patman Primer.*

UNFAIR TRADE EXAMINATIONS

Students in an upper level elective course like unfair trade have undoubtedly heard enough about law school exams to make any discussion here superfluous, and have probably developed their own strategies for dealing with them. Therefore, I will not repeat the conventional advice in all its glory (e.g. review your instructor's old exams, read the question carefully, organize your answer before you begin to write, make sure you answer the precise question posed rather than discourse generally about the law, etc., etc.). Instead, I will make a few observations about some facts that are uniquely relevant to unfair trade exams and then close with one piece of general advice.

First, because the subjects within an unfair trade course interact in so many different ways, you must be cautious in responding to questions on an exam that you consider all alternative causes of action. Thus, in a situation involving false advertising, there are private remedies under both state and federal laws for competing firms, there are state statutory remedies for consumers and there are public remedies under the Federal Trade Commission Act.

Second, as noted previously, unfair trade law bristles with questions of federal/state interaction. Be sure you consider the possibilities of pre-emption of state law on every question before you conclude your response.

Third, for most of the subject taken up in the typical course, there is a standard three step analysis that should be followed to make sure you touch on all relevant points. First, you must determine if the plaintiff has a protectable interest. In other words, start by asking if the alleged trademark is protectable, or if the material is proper subject matter for copyright, or trade secret, etc., as the case may be. Second, you must determine if the defendant's acts interfere with the plaintiff's rights based on some general standard—"likelihood of confusion" in trademark law, for example. Finally, you must address the question of the remedy. This three step technique is effective in making sure you hit the principal issues lurking in most problems.

Now for the general advice. Relax. Exams are somewhat important, to be sure. They are not, however, nearly as important as you think they are when you are taking them. I have always been struck, as I sit reading blue books, how some of the finest answers have been written by students who chose to take my course on a pass/fail basis. I am convinced that their answers are good because they were relaxed while reading, thinking and writing during the exam. You should remember that more than anything else, your answer is an attempt to communicate your version of a solution to your teacher. If you calm down and tell the teacher how you would use the data and techniques at your command to solve the problem he or she has posed, you are certain to do well.

I

THE PRIVILEGE TO COMPETE

Analysis

A. *The Dilemma of Competition*
B. *The Significance of Motivation*
C. *The Stability of Contract*

A. THE DILEMMA OF COMPETITION

Usually, those who engage in intentional conduct likely to harm another are liable for resulting injuries. Competition predictably results in economic harm to others. Competition, however, is also recognized to have extraordinary benefits for our economy and our citizens. Consequently, much unfair competition law is an attempt to balance the economic harm new firms will inflict on established merchants, against the benefits to the public from enhanced rivalry. Understanding this tension puts many unfair trade problems in a clearer context.

1. HARMS

Competition can be thought of as a rivalry for patronage. New firms enter markets and seek to lure away customers from the existing firms. Obviously, if the new firms are successful, the existing firms are injured, because they lose sales and their profits are reduced. Moreover the new entrant inflicts this injury intentionally. The net result can be economic hardship or ruin for established firms.

2. BENEFITS

On the other hand, economic theory suggests that the productivity of an economy—and consequently the benefits to consumers—are maximized in a competitive market structure. With free entry into business, high prices cannot be maintained, because high prices attract new competitors. These new firms will offer the lowest possible prices consistent with their cost of production in an attempt to garner patronage. The older firms will necessarily respond with price cuts of their own. Moreover, product innovation will be commonplace as each firm seeks to "invent a better mousetrap." The result for consumers is a marketplace filled with relatively inexpensive, high quality goods, with enough variety to cater to most tastes. Forbidding entry would permit monopolies to arise, resulting in increased prices and reduced consumer choice.

3. THE LEGAL COMPROMISE

Competition is the approved form of economic activity for most industries in the U.S. Thus, there is a privilege to enter markets and compete. It has been settled for over 500 years that the harm an established firm suffers when a newcomer enters its industry is not actionable. *Schoolmaster's Case*, Y.B. Hilary 11 Hen. 4, f. 47 pl. 10 (1410). However, legal limits on *how* firms may compete are imposed in order to insure both that the predicted benefits will be realized and that the potential harms are kept within tolerable bounds. The law seeks to insure that we have neither "too little" nor "too much" competition.

a. Antitrust Law

The benefits of competition cannot be realized if firms conspire with each other to eliminate rivalry, or if they are allowed to grow so large and dominant that new firms cannot (or are afraid to) enter and compete against them. The antitrust laws are designed to prevent such situations from arising.

Through prohibitions on price-fixing, monopolization, certain mergers, and various distribution practices, they endeavor to insure that healthy rivalry is maintained. Antitrust is theoretically distinct from Unfair Trade Practices law, although both aim to fine tune the balance between the harms and benefits of competition. This outline does not deal with antitrust concepts, and no familiarity with them is required to understand the principle of Unfair Trade Practices law.

b. Unfair Trade Practices

While excessive passivity and collusion deprive consumers of the benefits of competition, excessive ruthlessness in the competitive struggle also works against consumer interests and is undesirable in itself. If a merchant seeks to attract customers by tricking them with false advertisements or the use of someone else's trademarks, or if it seeks to secure a profit by robbing the creative effort of another firm instead of engaging in creative activity itself, its activities do not benefit consumers. Moreover, these activities clearly injure rival firms and fall below the standards of commercial ethics which most persons view as appropriate. Thus, in this case, where the harms of competition are produced without the benefits, we can safely label the competition "unfair." The field of Unfair Trade Practices law is concerned with these methods of engaging in competition, which are other than "on the merits."

B. THE SIGNIFICANCE OF MOTIVATION

Normally, the reasons motivating a firm for entering a line of business are legally irrelevant. Unfair Trade Practices law concerns itself chiefly with *how* competition is conducted, not *why*. However, in extreme cases, an improper motive may cause a firm to lose its privilege to compete. *If a firm does not have a profit motive and enters into a business willing to suffer economic losses, merely to inflict harm on another firm already in that industry, the conduct ceases to be privileged.*

Example: Plaintiff owned the only barber shop in a small town. The defendant, a banker by profession, constructed a new barber shop and sought to rent it at a nominal rent. When no one chose to rent the premises the defendant hired two barbers to operate the shop on salary. The plaintiff alleged that the sole purpose of these activities was to destroy his business. Noting that "when a man starts an opposition place of business, not for the sake of profit to himself, but regardless of loss to himself and for the sole purpose of driving his competitor out of business, and with the intention of himself retiring upon the accomplishment of his malevolent purpose, he is guilty of . . . an actionable tort," the Supreme Court of Minnesota held that the complaint stated a valid cause of action. *Tuttle v. Buck,* 107 Minn. 145, 119 N.W. 946 (1909).

1. THEORETICAL BASIS OF SUIT

Historically, intentional infliction of harm was actionable only if the plaintiff could allege a specified (or "nominate") tort, such as "battery" or "false imprisonment." There was no specified tort category available to a merchant who felt that another firm had entered into competition with the improper—solely malevolent—motivation described above. To remedy that obstacle, some jurisdictions have recognized the concept of "prima facie tort," under which the intentional infliction of injury is made actionable unless the defendant's conduct was privileged. Since there is a general privilege to compete, an injured competitor will only succeed in a prima facie tort action if it can show that the privilege is inapplicable because the defendant acted with a wholly malevolent motive.

2. PRACTICAL DIFFICULTIES OF SUIT

Proving the requisite improper motivation in a prima facie tort suit brought against a competitor is very difficult. Direct evidence of motive will almost never be available, so the plaintiff must rely on circumstantial evidence. Yet, all competition injures rival firms, and all competitors intend, in a general way, to "get all the business" and drive their competitors into bankruptcy. As a result courts require a showing of particularly outrageous behavior before inferring the presence of the illegal motive. Evidence that defendant's business was operated at a loss, or that the defendant intended to retire from the field once plaintiff was destroyed would probably be required by most courts. As a practical matter few cases are brought on this theory and success is rare.

C. THE STABILITY OF CONTRACT

Although competition prompted by the profit motive and carried out through lower prices and better product quality is normally encouraged, there is one situation where it is impermissible. When a firm has entered into a contract, it is not acceptable commercial behavior to try to induce one of the parties to breach the contract. *The privilege to compete ends where contract begins.*

1. INDUCING BREACH OF CONTRACT
a. Elements of the Tort

There are five elements to the tort of inducing a breach of contract. *The plaintiff must show that (1) a valid contract existed between itself and some promisor; (2) the defendant was aware of the contract; (3) the acts of the defendant were the principal cause of the promisor's decision not to perform; (4) the defendant acted intentionally; and (5) the defendant's inducement of the breach was "improper."* The acts of the defendant need not result in an actual breach. It is sufficient if they made the plaintiff's performance more burdensome or in some other way lessened the value of his bargain.

b.   Rationale

Inducing breaches of contract is considered tortious for the same reason that contracts are enforced—to guarantee stability to commercial relationships that have ripened to the stage of a formal bargain.

c.   Factors Making an Inducement "Improper"

Inducing a breach of contract, even through means of ordinary persuasion or the offer of a superior bargain, and even if motivated solely by a desire to make a profit, is improper. If the defendant induced the breach to protect a superior contract or property right of his own, however, his actions may be deemed proper and non-tortious. Among the other factors bearing on whether a particular inducement will be considered "improper" are the nature of the defendant's conduct, the defendant's motive, the interests the defendant seeks to advance, the relationship between the plaintiff and the defendant, and the social interest in protecting the defendant's freedom of action under the circumstances presented in the case. Restatement (Second) of Torts, § 767 (1979).

d.   Contracts Terminable at Will

When a contract is terminable at will one party has a right to withdraw from the bargain at any time, without penalty. While some courts consider inducing breach of a contract terminable at will to be tortious, when the plaintiff and defendant are competitors most courts require the plaintiff to prove that the defendant either used improper (e.g. deceitful, tortious or criminal) means or harbored an improper motive before holding this type of behavior actionable.

2.   NEGLIGENT INTERFERENCE WITH CONTRACT

The vast majority of courts have held that *there is no cause of action against a party who negligently interferes with a contractual relationship.*

> ***Example:***   If a motorist negligently injures a key employee of a small but prosperous business, the proprietor of that business has no cause of action against the motorist, even if there was an employment contract between the employee and the business which now cannot be performed.

3.   INTERFERENCE WITH PROSPECTIVE CONTRACTUAL RELATIONS

Where no formal contract exists, the social interest in the stability of relationships is considerably reduced. Thus the privilege to compete permits one firm to offer a better bargain to a customer or supplier and thwart the efforts of another to enter into a contract without any risk of tort liability. However, if the persuasion is carried out by misleading or coercive means, the behavior loses its privileged character and becomes actionable.

Example: Plaintiff invented and patented a machine to put stripes on men's socks while he was employed by the defendant. Plaintiff alleged that the defendant deceived him into naming another employee as co-patentee, and then used that fact as a pretext upon which to threaten outside parties with patent infringement litigation if they did business with the plaintiff. The Supreme Court of North Carolina held that this was actionable. *Coleman v. Whisnant,* 225 N.C. 494, 35 S.E.2d 647 (1945).

REVIEW QUESTIONS

1. **T or F** The sole merchant in a small village may prevent another party from opening a competing enterprise if it can demonstrate that it will be economically harmed.

2. **T or F** So long as no deceptive means are used, it is lawful to attempt to persuade a firm not to honor a written contract.

3. **T or F** If the doctrine of prima facie tort is invoked by one competitor complaining of the acts of another, the plaintiff must prove the defendant acted with a wholly malicious intent.

4. **T or F** The standards for proving an inducement to breach a contract and an intentional interference with a prospective contract are the same.

5. **T or F** Antitrust law and Unfair Trade Practces law are concerned with opposite problems in the conduct of competition.

6. Alpha Corporation manufactures garden hoses for Beta, Inc., pursuant to the latter's specifications under the terms of a written contract which is to expire in two years. Alpha sells these hoses to Beta for $5 each. Beta then resells these hoses for $10 to retailers. The contract has a clause forbidding Alpha from selling this particular type of hose to any other party. One retailer, Omega, approached Alpha and offered to buy hoses for $7.50 each. Alpha declined because of the contract. Omega then offered to pay $8.00 and Alpha agreed. If Beta files suit against Omega

    a.   It will lose because Omega has a privilege to compete.

    b.   It should proceed on a prima facie tort theory.

    c.   It will prevail because Omega has committed the tort of inducing a breach of contract.

    d.   It can succeed on a theory of interference with prospective contract because Omega used improper means to compete with Beta.

II

TRADEMARKS

Analysis

A. THE RATIONALE FOR PROTECTING TRADEMARKS

Trademarks are devices by which a merchant identifies its goods or services and distinguishes them from those of others. Trademark infringement is considered an unfair trade practice because guaranteeing *exclusive* trademark rights to the originator of a mark is assumed to yield several benefits. However, some have argued that this system of exclusivity also imposes significant costs. Thus, while there is broad consensus in favor of some trademark protection, there is also a debate in both the academic and judicial literature over whether that protection should be broad or narrow. An understanding of the chief arguments on both sides of this debate is helpful in interpreting trademark statutes, cases, and principles.

1. JUSTIFICATIONS FOR BROAD PROTECTION
a. Incentives for Creativity

By insuring that no other merchant can mimic a trademark, the law creates *incentives* for merchants to invest in goodwill. Each firm is assured that if it improves its products and makes them commercially attractive, consumers will be able to reward it with continued patronage by seeking out its unique trademarks. Because of that assurance, trademarks encourage firms to strive to improve their products.

b. Fairness to the Consuming Public

A system of exclusive trademark protection permits consumers to be certain that they are obtaining the same product from the same manufacturer, each time they return to the marketplace. Consequently, they need not gamble on quality every time they buy an item and are saved the expense of conducting research every time they make a purchase.

c. Commercial Morality

Merchants who wait for another to market a successful product and then sell an inferior imitation under the same trademark as the original are engaged in obviously exploitative practices. Broad trademark protection discourages this unscrupulous behavior and prevents unjust enrichment. In a sense, the creator of the mark, by investing effort in promoting the mark, has a property right that is vindicated by the prohibition against trademark infringement.

2. DISADVANTAGES OF EXCESSIVE TRADEMARK PROTECTION
a. Barriers to Entry

Where trademark protection is strong, merchants may try to cultivate brand loyalty on the part of consumers by investing heavily in advertising and promotion that emphasizes their trademarks. If this advertising is successful, consumers will be unlikely to shift away from a well known brand to try a new firm's product unless the new firm also advertises heavily. Some have thus argued that broad legal protection for trademarks makes it harder and more expensive for new firms to enter certain industries and consequently reduces incentives for established firms to keep product quality up and prices down. In economic terminology, this argument says that liberal trademark protection leads to increased "barriers to entry."

b. Encouragement of Wasteful Expenditures

As noted above, exclusive trademark rights makes it sensible for merchants to promote the mark heavily in order to develop and retain brand loyalty. The principal way to do this is through advertising. Some have argued that much advertising of consumer products provides little information and is merely an effort to imprint the trademark on the minds of consumers. In the view of these critics, liberal trademark protection encourages excessive expenditures on advertising, thus diverting funds that could be better used for other purposes.

c. Increased Problems of Commercial Communication

Some have expressed the fear that overly broad trademark protection makes it difficult for merchants to communicate with the public by depriving them of the right to use certain words that they may need to describe their products. The result is less information for the public and an unwarranted advantage for the first merchant to make use of an important term describing its product.

B. THE DUAL SYSTEM OF TRADEMARK PROTECTION

Trademarks may be protected under either state common law, the federal statute known as the Lanham Act, or both. Although the state and federal rules concerning trademark validity and the definition of infringement are similar, they are not identical. The two sources of protection are independent and concurrent. Analysis of a firm's trademark rights requires separate consideration of both state and federal law. The principal similarities and differences between these two bodies of trademark law are discussed below. Further distinctions between them are highlighted in the discussion of specific trademark topics elsewhere in this chapter. A number of states have state trademark registration statutes that supplement the common law. These statutes tend to be of minimal practical significance, however, and are disregarded in the following discussion.

1. COMMON FEATURES OF BOTH SCHEMES
a. Obtaining Trademark Rights
Before any trademark rights can attach, both the federal and state trademark systems require that a merchant actually affix the mark in question to its goods or their containers and then use the mark by actually selling these goods. *There is no way to reserve a trademark prior to actually using it under either the common law or the federal statute.*

b. Choosing a Proper Mark
Under both common law and the Lanham Act, a variety of terms, words and symbols are unacceptable for use as trademarks. The precise categories of

problematic or forbidden terms differ between state and federal law, but *analysis of whether an alleged trademark is a valid type of symbol under the relevant law is always the first step in determining trademark rights.*

c.   Permissible and Impermissible Uses of Another's Mark

Under both federal and state law *it is impermissible to use another merchant's trademarks on your goods if your use is likely to confuse the public.* Case law exists in both systems, specifying the conditions under which courts will find "likelihood of confusion." However, both systems of trademark law specify instances when it is legitimate to use another merchant's trademarks.

2.   MAJOR DIFFERENCES BETWEEN THE TWO SCHEMES

a.   Obtaining Trademark Rights

Under common law principles, once a merchant adopts and begins using a given device as a trademark, it does not have to take any further steps to protect the mark. Rights accrue to the first—or "senior"—user automatically. *Under the federal statutory scheme, it is necessary to file an application for trademark registration,* and for the mark to be found acceptable in an administrative process before federal rights will attach.

b.   Choosing a Proper Mark

Under the Lanham Act, applications for trademark registration are reviewed to determine if the proposed mark is permissible. If the mark falls into one of the categories that the statute declares to be impermissible, registration may be denied administratively, assuming personnel in the Trademark Office recognize the problem or have it called to their attention. *There is, however, no such "pre-screening" of marks under the common law.* Consequently, the invalidity of a mark under the common law usually becomes apparent only after litigation. Moreover, the types of terms that are impermissible under federal law differ slightly from those that are forbidden at common law, as will be further developed below.

> *Example:*   A vendor of soft drinks under the brand name CANADA decides to adopt a Canadian national flag as one of its trademarks. At common law this is a permissible trademark and will be protected as soon as it has first been used. Under federal statute, however, it is impermissible to adopt a mark consisting of the flag or coat of arms of any foreign nation. Consequently, if this merchant applies for federal registration, it will be denied, and no federal rights will ever attach.

c.   Geographic Extent of Protection

Because *the federal statutory scheme of trademark protection is designed to afford nationwide rights,* the first party to federally register a trademark will usually be able to forbid all other firms from using that mark on the same type of merchandise regardless of where they are located. The specifics of this principle and some limitations are noted below. *At common law, trademark rights are limited to the area in which a merchant is actually conducting business and a zone of reasonable expansion surrounding this area.* Thus, it is theoretically possible for two firms who are geographically distant from each other to be selling the same product under the same trademark without violating each other's common law rights.

3. TERMINOLOGICAL DIFFERENCES IN THE TWO SCHEMES

A number of identical terms and phrases have different meanings in the common law of trademarks and under the federal statute. Thus, the student of unfair competition law must be attentive to the context in which various terms are used. The following discussion emphasizes the differences of meaning at common law and under the federal statute as each new term is introduced, and the Glossary in Appendix C contains a complete summary of these terms of art.

C. OBTAINING TRADEMARK RIGHTS: AFFIXATION, USE AND REGISTRATION

1. THE REQUIREMENT OF AFFIXATION

To obtain rights in a trademark, the mark must be actually affixed to the goods or their containers. In the case of services, the mark must be displayed in the sale or advertising of those services.

a. Justification for Affixation Requirement

Trademarks are devices that identify goods as being the output of a particular manufacturer. If a group of words or a symbol is to serve this purpose, consumers must associate the mark with the products. The way to insure that such an association will develop is to require that the mark actually be attached to the goods or their containers.

b. Lanham Act More Flexible Than Common Law

While the affixation requirement is interpreted literally when common law rights are at issue, the federal statute states that its requirements are satisfied if the mark is "placed in any manner on the goods or their containers *or the displays associated therewith . . .*" 15 U.S.C.A. § 1127 (1984). Thus it is possible to imagine a situation where a merchant could apply for federal registration even though it lacked common law trademark rights, because the mark in question appears only on store shelves or on in-store displays, but not on the goods or their containers.

2. THE REQUIREMENT OF USE
a. Type of Use Required

For the purposes of determining if trademark rights have accrued, a merchant must make genuine commercial sales of the goods with the trademark attached. If federal trademark rights are at issue, the mark must be used in connection with sales in interstate commerce. The interstate commerce requirement, however, is interpreted liberally so that intra-state sales of goods imported from abroad have been held sufficiently connected to interstate commerce to permit registration. *In re Silenus Wines, Inc.,* 557 F.2d 806 (C.C.P.A.1977). Sham sales—those which are not bona fide commercial transactions—will not be sufficient to give rise to trademark rights. However, the fact that the principal motivation for a given sale was to establish a basis for trademark rights does not make that sale a sham.

Example: Blue Bell and Farrah, two clothing manufacturers, asserted conflicting claims to the mark TIME OUT for men's clothing. On July 3rd, Farrah sent one pair of slacks bearing the new mark to each of its 12 regional sales managers. On July 5th, Blue Bell shipped several hundred pairs of its old Mr. Hicks brand slacks with new "Time Out" labels also attached, to customers. Farrah shipped substantial quantities of Time Out clothing to customers in September. The court held that neither the July 3rd, nor the July 5th uses gave rise to trademark rights. The July 3rd use was merely an intra-corporate transfer, not a sale to consumers. The July 5th use was not in connection with the actual goods destined to ultimately bear the trademark in question. Thus the first *bona fide* use was the one which occurred by Farrah in September, and it was held to have superior rights in the mark. *Blue Bell, Inc. v. Farah Mfg. Co.,* 508 F.2d 1260 (5th Cir.1975).

b.   Amount of Use Required

For the purpose of establishing a right to register under the Lanham Act, a minimal number of sales will suffice to satisfy the use requirement, provided they are bona fide transactions and the seller has an intention to continue using the mark. Thus, even mere "token" sales are adequate to create a right to register if the proper intent can be demonstrated. Where the issue is which of two competing common law claimants made first use of the disputed mark some courts will require a more significant number of sales than would be required to establish an entitlement to federal registration. These common law courts may dismiss a token use as strictly "de minimis" and hence inadequate to confer any rights.

c.   Priority of Use Determines Trademark Rights

The first merchant to use a mark in the United States will be deemed to be the owner of that mark, provided its use has been continuous and uninterrupted. It will be able to enjoin others from using the same or similar marks on the same or similar goods in its own local area of trade, and will have a superior claim for federal registration if a dispute emerges over who is entitled to register the mark. Moreover, Lanham Act registration will be denied to a trademark that closely resembles a mark that has been previously used by another firm, or that resembles a previously used "trade name" (i.e. the name of a business) if registration would give rise to a likelihood of confusion, 15 U.S.C.A. § 1052(d) (1984). However, if two firms each made their first use of a mark at about the same time and in good faith, courts will not determine ownership rights in the mark based strictly on chronology, but will instead attempt to balance the equities. *Manhattan Industries, Inc. v. Sweater Bee By Banff, Ltd.,* 627 F.2d 628 (2d Cir.1980). If a firm has filed a trademark registration in a foreign country before using the mark in the United States, and thereafter files for Lanham Act registration, the firm will be given a constructive date of first use as of the date of its foreign filing. *See SCM Corporation v. Langis Foods Ltd.,* 539 F.2d 196 (D.C.Cir.1976).

3. THE MECHANICS OF FEDERAL REGISTRATION
a. Types of Marks Recognized by Statute
The Lanham Act recognizes four different types of marks that may be federally registered. A "trademark" is any word, name, symbol or device used to identify and distinguish a merchant's goods. A "service mark" is a similar type of device used to identify and distinguish the services of one person from those of others. A "certification mark" is a mark used by one party to indicate that the goods or services of another party meet certain standards or are made in a certain way. A "collective mark" is a mark used by the members of an organization or association.

Example: In Lanham Act terminology, COCA–COLA is a trade mark for a carbonated soft drink, UNITED AIRLINES is a service mark for air transportation services, the GOOD HOUSEKEEPING SEAL OF APPROVAL is a certification mark for household goods and BRAZIL NUT ASSOCIATION is a collective mark used by sellers of Brazil nuts.

b. Application for Registration
A party desiring a federal trademark registration must file an application with the U.S. Patent and Trademark Office. The application must disclose the mark, the goods on which it is used and indicate when it was first used. A trademark examiner reviews the filing and determines if the mark meets the requirements for registration. If the examiner concludes that registration should be denied, the applicant may submit further information and ultimately appeal the decision, first to the Trademark Trials and Appeals Board, and then to the U.S. Court of Appeals for the Federal Circuit. Such proceedings are often referred to in trademark cases as "ex parte" and the caption of the case will reflect the name of only one party. If the examiner concludes that registration is permissible, the mark will be published in the Official Gazette of the Trademark Office, and if no comment is received within 30 days, a certificate of registration will be issued. This certificate is valid for a period of 20 years and the registration may be renewed indefinitely.

c. Opposition Proceedings

If any party feels that they will be injured by the applicant's registration, they may file an "opposition" after learning of the pending registration in the Official Gazette. Such an opposition must specify the reasons why the applicant is not entitled to federal registration. The merits of the opposition will be determined by an "inter partes" (i.e., two-party) hearing before the Trademark Trials and Appeals Board with appellate review by the Federal Circuit. 15 U.S.C.A. § 1063 (1984).

d. Cancellation Proceedings

After federal registration has been granted, any party who believes that he is or will be damaged by the continuation of this registration may file a petition to have the registration cancelled. During the first five years after registration, any grounds that would have initially barred registration may be asserted as a basis for cancellation. Thereafter, only certain specified grounds may be asserted. A cancellation petition is treated as an inter partes proceeding in the Trademark Office and is handled in the same fashion as an Opposition. 15 U.S.C.A. § 1064 (1984).

e. Advantages of Registration

Federal trademark registration affords numerous advantages to a merchant, by strengthening certain rights provided by common law and by affording some unique additional rights as well. These advantages are the reason why so many firms incur the expense and inconvenience of registration.

1) The Registration Symbol

Only federally registered marks may be designated with the "r in a circle" symbol. This designation calls attention to the mark and alerts other merchants that the mark is protected and should not be used without authorization. 15 U.S.C.A. § 1111 (1984).

2) Constructive Notice

The Lanham Act provides that a federal registration provides nationwide constructive notice of the registrant's claim of ownership of the mark. 15 U.S.C.A. § 1072 (1984). Thus a merchant can rely on this provision to assert superior rights even in portions of the country where it does not actually do business.

3) Incontestability

Five years after a mark has been registered, the registrant may apply to have the mark declared "incontestable". 15 U.S.C.A. § 1065 (1984). Possession of an incontestable mark is conclusive evidence of the registrant's exclusive right to use that mark on the type of goods in question, subject only to certain defenses that are itemized in the statute. 15 U.S.C.A. § 1115(b) (1984). Thus, *incontestability* has two practical implications. First, it *immunizes the registrant from certain claims that the mark is invalid when a third party seeks to have the mark cancelled.* Second, when the holder of federal registration files suit for infringement, *incontestability will also preclude the infringing defendant from asserting certain defects in the mark as defenses. Park 'N' Fly, Inc. v. Dollar Park and Fly, Inc.,* ___ U.S. ___, 105 S.Ct. 658 (1985). The most important challenges to the mark that are cut off by incontestability are (1) that the registrant is not the senior user of the mark and (2) that the mark itself is merely descriptive and lacks secondary meaning.

D. DISTINCTIVENESS

The first step in the analysis of any trademark problem is to determine if the mark is valid. Not every symbol that a merchant might want to use as a trademark is legally available for that purpose. Many potential marks are not acceptable because they will not perform the key function of a trademark—identification and distinction of goods. *Thus, in order to be valid, a trademark must be distinctive—that is, capable of identifying one firm's goods and distinguishing them from those of another.* Some marks are considered to be inherently distinctive, and thus are valid trademarks from the moment they are adopted. Others, although not distinctive initially, may become so over time. These types of marks will normally be protected only after sufficient time has passed so that distinctiveness can be demonstrated. Still other putative marks may be incapable of ever achieving distinctiveness, and thus can never be appropriated by one firm for exclusive use. In addition, a mark that was distinctive at one point, may lose its distinctiveness and consequently its right to protection

1. INHERENTLY DISTINCTIVE MARKS

Arbitrary, fanciful, and suggestive trademarks are considered to be sufficiently distinctive to warrant full protection at common law from the time of first use, and to be eligible for immediate registration under the Lanham Act as soon as they are used in interstate commerce.

a. Fanciful Marks

If a merchant decides to coin a brand new word to serve as a trademark for its product, such a trademark is known as a "fanciful" mark. A fanciful mark has no other meaning besides its implication as the identifying symbol for a particular brand of goods. It is thus inherently distinctive. At common law, it will be protected from the time it is first used as a "technical trade mark." Under the Lanham Act, it may be federally registered as soon as the merchant has used the mark on goods involved in interstate commerce.

Example: The trademark KODAK for photographic film is fanciful because it is a made up word.

b.   Arbitrary Marks

Instead of inventing a wholly new word to serve as a trademark, a merchant may choose to use one or more existing words to serve as its trademark. Such a merchant may opt for words which bear no relationship to the product involved. A consumer encountering them would not be able to use the trademark to determine what kinds of goods are being sold or to make any inference about their quality or composition. Such a mark is denominated an "arbitrary" mark. Like fanciful marks, arbitrary marks are considered inherently distinctive. They too are classified as "technical trade marks" under the common law and are protectable from the time of first use. Similarly, they may be registered as soon as goods bearing the arbitrary mark are first sold in interstate commerce.

Example: The mark FOUR ROSES for blended whiskey is an arbitrary trademark because it bears no relationship to, and does not describe, the product.

c.   Suggestive Marks

If the mark selected provides some hint about the nature or attributes of the product it identifies, but interpreting it requires a degree of imagination on the part of the consumer, the mark is considered to be "suggestive." Like fanciful and arbitrary marks, suggestive marks are considered inherently distinctive and thus "technical trade marks" under the common law. They are thus afforded protection and are eligible for registration from the time of first use.

Example: The mark COPPERTONE for sun tan oil is suggestive because, although the mark suggests some of the features of the product, it requires imagination to connect the two.

2.   MARKS THAT MAY BECOME DISTINCTIVE

Words that do not fall into one of the preceding categories of "inherently" distinctive marks will be protected only after they have been in use long enough to have acquired distinctiveness. When there is evidence of acquired distinctiveness, the mark has achieved "secondary meaning." Types of marks that are valid only upon proof of secondary meaning include those that are descriptive and misdescriptive, geographic terms, surnames, and slogans. .

a.   Descriptive Terms

1)   General Principles

Marks which merely describe the product to which they are affixed will not be protected automatically. The law assumes that consumers will not view such terms as trademarks, but only as narrative explanations of the product's features and qualities. Moreover, competing merchants may want or need to describe their products in much the same words. However, if a descriptive term is associated with one product exclusively over a long period of time, it may come to identify that brand specifically in the minds of consumers. If and when it has done so, it deserves to be protected as a trademark. Thus, *the law requires a showing of secondary meaning before descriptive terms can receive trademark protection*.

> ***Example:*** The mark CHAP STICK for chapped lip balm is merely descriptive because it narrates the basic purpose and feature of the product. It is protected as a trademark because, over time, it has come to identify one particular brand of lip balm.

2) Terminology

At common law, a descriptive mark that had achieved secondary meaning was labeled a "trade name"—not a "trademark"—and was protected in a suit for "unfair competition" rather than in a suit for "trademark infringement." The Lanham Act uses the same terms for different concepts. Under the federal statute, the term "trade name" is used to designate the name of a business, *not* a descriptive mark with secondary meaning. Moreover, the Lanham Act does not refer to a mark achieving "secondary meaning", but uses instead the synonymous expression that the mark "has become distinctive" of the merchant's goods. (This outline will follow the practice of most trademark lawyers and courts, and use the phrase "secondary meaning" in both the Lanham Act and common law contexts). In Lanham Act parlance, a descriptive term is considered a "trademark", just like an inherently distinctive term and is registerable if the applicant can prove distinctiveness (i.e., secondary meaning). Under a specific statutory provision, evidence of five years of continuous use prior to the date of application for registration is prima facie evidence of secondary meaning. 15 U.S.C.A. § 1052(f) (1984).

3) Proof of Secondary Meaning

Secondary meaning exists only if consumers mentally associate or recognize the words of the mark as denoting a single source for the product. The existence or absence of secondary meaning is thus a question of fact, dependent on how consumers actually understand the mark. The issue is whether most buyers recognize the mark in question as a brand name. Consumer survey evidence is often useful in proving secondary meaning, as is evidence concerning aggregate advertising expenditures.

4) The Suggestive/Descriptive Distinction

Determining if a mark is suggestive or descriptive is important because a suggestive mark, being inherently distinctive, is afforded trademark protection without further inquiry, while the owner of a descriptive mark must prove secondary meaning before it can assert trademark rights. Nonetheless, the line between these two types of marks is "often a difficult distinction to draw and is, undoubtedly, often made on an intuitive basis rather than as the result of a logical analysis susceptible of articulation." *Union Carbide Corp. v. Ever-Ready, Inc.,* 531 F.2d 366 (7th Cir.1976). The principal tests used to make the distinction involve (1) the degree of imagination required to deduce a description of the product from the mark (a great deal of imagination means the mark is suggestive; little imagination means it is descriptive); (2) the degree to which the words in question would be needed by competing firms to describe their goods (if they would be needed the mark is descriptive, if not, it is more likely suggestive); and (3) the degree to which other merchants have actually been using the words in question to describe their goods (actual use implies descriptiveness).

b. Deceptively Misdescriptive Terms

If a mark seemingly describes features or attributes of the product, but the product does not actually possess those traits, than the mark is misdescriptive. If the nature of the misdescription may significantly influence the consumer in deciding to buy the product than the mark is deceptively misdescriptive. Under the Lanham Act, *a deceptively misdescriptive mark cannot be registered without a showing that it has become "distinctive" (i.e. has achieved secondary meaning) with respect to the goods in question.* 15 U.S.C.A. § 1052(e), (f) (1984).

Example: The mark GLASS WAX for a glass cleaner and polisher that did not contain any wax was held to be deceptively misdescriptive, and the case was sent back to the Patent Office for a determination of whether there was proof that the mark had become distinctive (i.e., whether there was "secondary meaning"). *Gold Seal Co. v. Weeks,* 129 F.Supp. 928 (D.D.C.1955).

c. Geographic Terms

Numerous products are associated with specific regions, cities or countries. If a merchant applies a mark to such a product describing where the product was made or grown, the mark is considered geographically descriptive. If a merchant uses a geographic term as a mark that is a plausible place of origin for the type of product involved, but is actually inaccurate, than the mark is "geographically deceptively misdescriptive." Both of *these types of marks may only be protected at common law if secondary meaning can be proven, and are only registrable under the Lanham Act if there is proof that the marks have become distinctive* . 15 U.S.C.A. § 1052 (e), (f) (1984). If a geographic term used as a trademark has no connection with products of the type sold, the mark is "arbitrary", and thus protectable without secondary meaning.

Examples: The mark DENVER WESTERNS for shirts from Denver, Colorado is primarily geographically descriptive. *Re Handler Fenton Westerns, Inc.,* 214 U.S.P.Q. 848 (T.T.A.B.1982). The mark ITALIAN MAIDE for canned vegetables from the United States is primarily geographically deceptively misdescriptive. *Re Amerise,* 160 U.S.P.Q. 687 (T.T.A.B.1969). The mark HOLLAND for ink is arbitrary, and thus protectable without secondary meaning. *Re Van Son Holland Ink Corp.,* 147 U.S.P.Q. 292 (T.T.A.B.1965).

d. Surnames

1) General Principles

The most obvious trademark for many merchants is simply to use their own surname, or the surname of someone else associated with their business, in order to identify their goods. Because many persons share the same surname, however, it would be undesirable to permit the first Johnson, or Smith to preclude all others of the same name from using their name to identify their goods or services. Consequently, *the common law courts refuse to protect a surname as a trademark unless there is proof that it had achieved secondary meaning. The Lanham Act follows the same approach, providing that a mark that is "primarily merely a surname" will not be registered unless it has become distinctive.* 15 U.S.C.A. § 1052 (e), (f) (1984).

2) Identifying Surnames

It is not always clear whether a given mark is a surname. Many common adjectives are also popular American surnames, creating an immediate source of confusion. *Courts have determined that the essential inquiry is "What is the primary significance of the mark to the purchasing public?" Application of Standard Elektrik Lorenz Aktiengesellschaft,* 371 F.2d 870 (C.C.P.A.1967) (SCHAUB–LORENZ held not primarily merely a surname). If the mark in question is actually the surname of someone affiliated with the seller, courts are more likely to conclude that the public will interpret the mark as primarily a surname.

3) Right to Use One's Own Name

In most instances, when a merchant has valid trademark rights in a particular mark all others are forbidden from using the same mark on the same type of goods. This principal would work an undue hardship in the area of surname-marks, however, as it would prevent certain people from identifying themselves with their trade or business. Thus, *courts will usually not absolutely forbid parties from making use of their own surname, even if someone else has valid trademark rights in that name. Instead, the courts will enter a qualified injunction,* requiring that the junior user of the name make disclaimers when using the common name, to insure that the public understands that the two firms are not affiliated. If, however, someone is making use of his own surname in bad faith, the court will enter an absolute injunction.

Example: Plaintiff sold wines under the well-known mark TAYLOR, a surname which had achieved secondary meaning. The defendant, named Taylor, began to market his own wines under the TAYLOR brand name. Initially, the court indicated that defendant could not use the name Taylor as a trademark but could place his name on the labels, provided it appeared with a statement that he was not affiliated with the plaintiff. When defendant thereafter continued to use his name without the required disclaimers, he was found in contempt and absolutely forbidden from using his name in connection with his product. *Taylor Wine Co. v. Bully Hill Vineyards, Inc.,* 569 F.2d 731 (2d Cir.1978), *contempt found,* 208 U.S.P.Q. 80 (W.D.N.Y.1979).

e. Slogans

Although there was initially some question as to whether a slogan could function as a trademark to identify a particular brand of goods, it now appears clear that it may do so. Because most slogans, however, are descriptive phrases about the products they purport to identify, courts have been demanding in requiring a showing of distinctiveness or secondary meaning before such marks receive protection.

Example: The phrase HAIR COLOR SO NATURAL ONLY HER HAIRDRESSER KNOWS FOR SURE was held to have achieved secondary meaning as a trademark for Clairol brand hair coloring products, and thus to be properly registrable under the Lanham Act, because of its extensive use in both advertising and product displays. *Roux Laboratories, Inc. v. Clairol, Inc.,*   427 F.2d 823 (C.C.P.A.1970).

3.   WORDS INCAPABLE OF DISTINCTIVENESS

Some words are considered legally incapable of ever achieving the distinctiveness required of a trademark, and thus may never be appropriated by one merchant for its own exclusive use. These words are the basic names by which categories of products are known. At common law, such terms are called the "generic" name for a product, while the Lanham Act uses the terminology "common descriptive name." *A generic term can never achieve secondary meaning and consequently can never be used as a trademark.*

Example: The term TEE SHIRT is a generic or common descriptive name for a type of undershirt. Thus no merchant can claim trademark rights in this term, even if one merchant has been making exclusive use of it for many years.

4.   LOSS OF DISTINCTIVENESS

A word that at one time functioned as a trademark may, over time and because of changes in the way consumers use and understand the word, cease to serve a trademark purpose. Instead, the word may come to be the generic term for all products of a certain type. When that happens, the courts will cease to afford trademark rights to the party who first made use of this word, and allow any merchant who wishes to do so to use the word without liability. Among the many former trademarks that have been held to have lapsed into genericness and may now be used by all merchants are "zipper", "thermos", "aspirin", "brassiere", "escalator" and "yo-yo".

a.   Tests to Determine Genericness

1)   Buyer Understanding

The traditional test to determine if a mark has lost its distinctiveness and become generic is based on how the majority of consumers understand the word in question. If they perceive it as a brand name, the word is a trademark. If they perceive it as the name of a type of product, the word is generic. As the Supreme Court has said, to show that a word is a trademark, there must be a demonstration that the "primary significance of the term in the minds of the consuming public is not the product but the producer." *Kellogg Co. v. National Biscuit Co.,* 305 U.S. 111, 59 S.Ct. 109 (1938).

2)   Buyer Motivation

One recent case seemingly adopted a different test to determine if a mark had lost its distinctiveness. *Anti-Monopoly, Inc. v. General Mills Fun Group, Inc.,* 684 F.2d 1316 (9th Cir.1982) indicated that a word would be deemed generic if, in using it to request a product, consumers did not care who made the product but merely sought goods with particular attributes. The word would only qualify as a trademark if consumers, by using it, were expressing a desire to receive the goods of a particular producer. Thus, the *motivation* of consumers in using the word, rather than their *understanding*, would be determinative. This test was immediately criticized for casting doubt on the validity of numerous famous trademarks, and in 1984 Congress passed legislation amending the Lanham Act by adding the following language to § 14(c): "The primary significance of the registered mark to the relevant public rather than purchaser motivation shall be the test for determining whether the registered mark has become the common descriptive name of goods or services in connection with which it has been used." As a result, *the buyer motivation test is no longer a legitimate way to determine genericness.*

b.   Avoiding Genericness

Merchants may take a number of steps to prevent their trademarks from losing distinctiveness and becoming generic. First, if a wholly new (and patented) product is at issue, it is wise to coin two names, one to serve as the product name and the other to serve as the brand name. Second, the use of the word "brand" after the trademark can be used to educate consumers that the word is not a generic product name (e.g. Sanka brand decaffeinated coffee). Third, the use of the word on a variety of related products rather than one single item may prevent consumers from using the mark as a generic term.

E. UNUSUAL TRADEMARK TYPES

The overwhelming majority of trademarks consist of one or more words or some form of picture or logo. However, many firms have sought trademark protection for other formats of trademarks. Of particular concern are alleged trademark rights in the shape of either the product or its container, in the color of the product, and in the appearance of a building. Such *unconventional trademarks will generally be afforded protection if they are both distinctive and non-functional.*

1. PRODUCT OR CONTAINER SHAPES
a. Distinctiveness

For a shape to serve as a trademark, consumers must associate the shape with a particular brand of goods. Consumers will not initially view most product or container shapes as devices by which they can identify the product. However, the shape may come to represent the product over time. Thus, *at common law, the party alleging trademark rights in a shape will have to show secondary meaning. Under the Lanham Act, certain shapes may be sufficiently novel to be inherently distinctive, and thus entitled to immediate registration as a trademark from the time of first use, but this is rare. Most attempts to register product or container shapes as trademarks will require the applicant to prove secondary meaning.*

b. Non-Functionality

Not all shapes will be afforded trademark protection even if the merchant using them can prove they are distinctive. The shape must also be "non-functional". *A product or container shape is considered functional if the design improves the performance of the product and if competing firms need to be free to use the design in order to compete effectively. In re Morton-Norwich Products, Inc.,* 671 F.2d 1332 (C.C.P.A.1982).

Example: The ribbed design on top of a construction worker's hard hat was held functional, and thus not registrable as a trademark in *Mine Safety Appliance Co. v. Electric Storage Battery Co.,* 405 F.2d 901 (C.C.P.A.1969), but the well known grille of a Rolls-Royce automobile was held non-functional and thus eligible for registration in *Rolls-Royce Motors, Ltd. v. A & A Fiberglass, Inc.,* 428 F.Supp. 689 (N.D.Ga.1977).

c. Conflict With Patent Policy

One policy of federal patent laws is that inventions and product improvements that are insufficiently innovative to qualify for patent protection should be left in the "public domain"—i.e. anyone should be free to copy such developments without legal liability. On this basis, the Supreme Court held in 1964 that states could not protect, under their common law of trademarks or unfair competition, unpatented product shapes and configurations. *Sears, Roebuck & Co. v. Stiffel Co.,* 376 U.S. 225, 84 S.Ct. 784 (1964); *Compco Corp. v. Day-Brite*

Lighting, Inc., 376 U.S. 234, 84 S.Ct. 779 (1964). Language in *Compco* suggested that this would be true even if the shape in question was both distinctive and non-functional. Lanham Act protection for such shapes and configurations remained unaffected. In recent years, however, the lower federal courts have sharply limited the scope of these decisions, usually by treating the reference to distinctiveness and non-functionality as dictum. When interpreted in this fashion, the cases merely forbid state law protection of shapes that state law never purported to protect in the first place (i.e., those that are either non-distinctive or functional). Thus, the cases remain nominally still good law, but, as one leading commentator observed "it is difficult to discern what, if anything, is left of Sears-Compco policy." McCarty, *Trademarks and Unfair Competition* § 7:25A (2d ed. 1984).

2. COLORS

A merchant will have difficulty claiming trademark rights in a particular color by itself, both because the number of colors is limited and the burden on competing firms would thus often be great and because it will usually be difficult to show that a single color has become distinctive of one firm's goods. The U.S. Court of Appeals for the Federal Circuit recently held, however, that the sellers of fiberglass insulation could register the color "pink" as a trademark for its goods. *In re Owens-Corning Fiberglas Corp.*, 774 F.2d 1116 (Fed.Cir.1985) ("gradually the courts have rejected the dictum . . . to the effect that color alone is not subject to trademark . . . [T]he color of goods, as other indicia, may serve as a trademark, if the statutory requirements are met.") Combinations of colors serving alleged trademark purposes will be analyzed much like shapes, with validity turning upon the tests of distinctiveness and non-functionality. Colors may be functional because they serve a psychological purpose. Thus the soothing pink color of a stomach remedy was held functional and not protectable as a trademark in *Norwich Pharmacal v. Sterling Drug*, 271 F.2d 569 (2d Cir.1959).

3. BUILDINGS

The design of a building can be protected as a mark for services if the design meets the tests of distinctiveness and non-functionality. Such designs may also be federally registered under the Lanham Act.

F. IMPERMISSIBLE MARKS

Certain narrow categories of words and symbols may not be used as trademarks because they violate policies of commercial ethics or morality. The most significant of these are deceptive and scandalous marks.

1. DECEPTIVE MARKS

A "deceptive" term may never be protected as a trademark at common law and is not registrable under the Lanham Act. 15 U.S.C.A. § 1052(a) (1984). According to the leading case, *a mark is deceptive "when an essential and material element is misrepresented, is distinctly false, and is the very element upon which the customer relies in purchasing one product over another." Gold Seal Co. v. Weeks,* 129 F.Supp. 928 (D.D.C.1955). Such marks should be distinguished from those that are "deceptively misdescriptive", because a deceptively misdescriptive term will be accorded trademark protection upon proof of secondary meaning. Also to be distinguished are marks which are false but which no reasonable consumer would interpret as making a representation about the goods. These marks are arbitrary, rather than deceptive and hence fully protectable.

Example: The mark OLD CROW for bourbon is arbitrary, not deceptive. While it is true that the beverage is not made from old crows, no reasonable consumer would have expected that it was. The mark SOFT HIDE for an imitation leather product, however, is deceptive. *Tanners' Council of America, Inc. v. Samsonite Corp.,* 204 U.S.P.Q. 150 (T.T.A.B.1979).

2.   IMMORAL OR SCANDALOUS MARKS

The Lanham Act has a specific provision barring registration of a mark that is immoral or scandalous. This provision has been invoked to bar registration of sexually suggestive marks as well as those that are arguably sacrilegious. 15 U.S. C.A. § 1052(a) (1984).

Example: The marks MADONNA for wine and BUBBY TRAP for brassieres were refused registration on the grounds that they were immoral or scandalous.

3.   OTHER IMPERMISSIBLE MARKS

The Lanham Act forbids the registration of a mark which so closely resembles (1) a previously registered mark, (2) a previously used common law mark, or (3) a previously used trade name (i.e. the name of business) that confusion is likely. 15 U.S.C.A. § 1052(d) (1984). Similarly, a mark which falsely suggests a connection with any person, living or dead, or with any institution or business organization cannot be registered. *Id.* § 1052(a). It also bars registration of marks consisting of the flag or coat of arms of the United States, any State, or any foreign nation, *Id.* § 1052(b), or the name, portrait or signature of any living person, except with that person's consent. *Id.* § 1052(c).

G.   USING ANOTHER MERCHANT'S TRADEMARK

1.   THE CONCEPT OF TRADEMARK INFRINGEMENT

If a merchant has selected a valid mark and taken the necessary steps to obtain rights in that mark, the junior use of that mark by another who sells the same goods in the same area constitutes trademark infringement and may be enjoined. In this clearest of infringement scenarios, the public will almost surely be misled into thinking that the junior user's good were produced by the senior user. *Even if the marks used by the two parties are not identical, however, or if the goods are not the same, or if the two do not do business in the same area, infringement may still be found if the use by the junior user creates a "likelihood of confusion."*

a. Passing Off

The terms passing off, and the synonymous "palming off", are frequently encountered in trademark cases. Typically, they are used to refer to situations where the junior user is deliberately trying to sell its goods as those of the senior user. They also encompass situations where one brand of an item is called for, but another is supplied without the knowledge of the buyer—such as when a customer orders "Coke" but is given another type of cola in a restaurant. The terms also cover a variety of situations that do not technically constitute trademark infringement, such as when one firm deliberately duplicates the packaging (or "trade dress") of its better known competitor. Historically the terms were reserved for flagrant or intentional cases of trademark or trade dress infringement, but today, many courts use the terms loosely to refer to any situation where there is a likelihood of confusion.

b. Likelihood of Confusion

Likelihood of confusion is the test for trademark infringement both at common law and under the Lanham Act, 15 U.S.C.A. § 1114 (1984). The confusion spoken of is that of any significant number of buyers with respect to either the source or sponsorship of the product. The senior user need not prove that confusion has actually occurred to prove infringement—a probability or likelihood of confusion is sufficient.

1) Rationale of Likelihood of Confusion Test

It is only when a likelihood of confusion as to the source or sponsorship of a product exists that consumers will be misled into unintended commercial transactions by the junior user's unauthorized use of a trademark. By definition, if no risk of confusion is present, consumers are able to obtain the products they want without difficulty. Thus, the likelihood of confusion test protects consumers' interests by insuring that they can rely on the trademark of an item to identify products that have previously performed satisfactorily. Moreover, when buyers are likely to be confused about the source or sponsorship of goods, the senior user of a trademark may lose sales that it otherwise would have made or experience other forms of economic harm. Thus, the likelihood of confusion test also protects the trademark owner's investment in goodwill and brand identification. Consequently, in trademark infringement litigation, once the plaintiff demonstrates that it has acquired rights in a valid mark, the chief issue is whether the defendant's conduct will give rise to a "likelihood of confusion."

2) Harms From Likelihood of Confusion

The cases have recognized three principal kinds of injuries that may be experienced by a trademark owner when another party engages in unauthorized trademark use giving rise to a likelihood of confusion. The plaintiff in a trademark infringement case need not show that these specific harms are present in order to prove liability and an entitlement to an injunction, but they are relevant to the appropriate remedy and are usually present in most infringement cases.

a) Diversion of Sales

Where a likelihood of confusion exists some consumers who intend to buy the senior user's brand will mistakenly purchase the junior user's instead. As a result the senior user is deprived of profitable sales it otherwise would have made, and is thus harmed.

b) Limitation of Expansion

If the junior user sells a different product than the senior user, but uses the senior user's mark in doing so, and the public is confused as to the true source of the product, it will be difficult for the senior user to enter the new field of business at a later point in time. This limitation on the future business opportunities of the senior user is another type of harm noted by some of the cases.

c) Harm to reputation

If the junior user's goods are shoddy and customers are confused about the source or sponsorship of these goods, erroneously believing they were really manufactured by the senior user, they may react by declining to make future purchases of any goods from the senior user. The unauthorized use of the mark has thus damaged the trademark owner's goodwill.

3) Factors Probative of Likelihood of Confusion

When any merchant makes use of a trademark, there are three variables involved in that use—the mark, the goods, and the geographic area where the firm does business. *When a junior user affixes the identical mark to the identical goods and sells them in the same geographic area as the senior user, confusion is almost sure to result and infringement will be found. However a perfect identity of these three variables is not required to make out a case of trademark infringement.* Thus, where infringement has been alleged, but different marks are involved, the court must determine if the marks are similar enough to engender a likelihood of confusion. Objective evidence in the form of consumer surveys demonstrating confusion will, of course, be highly probative. The courts will also engage in a subjective comparison of the appearance, sound, and implications of the marks involved, in what has been called the "sound, sight and meaning" test.

a)   Sound

Marks consisting of words that sound alike when pronounced will be deemed capable of causing confusion even if they are not identical.

Example: The mark Coca-Cola was held infringed by the mark Cup-O'-Cola and the mark Savings Shop was held infringed by The Savings Spot.

b)   Sight

If the overall visual impression created by two marks is similar, they will be deemed capable of creating confusion, and thus infringing.

Example: Two marks consisting of logos based on the human eye and two marks involving a teardrop shaped cartoon character were held confusingly similar.

c)   Meaning

If two marks convey the same idea or meaning to consumers, they will be held infringing even if they do not look or sound alike.

Example: The mark TORNADO on wire fencing was held confusingly similar to the famous CYCLONE mark for the same product. *Hancock v. American Steel & Wire Co.,* 203 F.2d 737 (C.C.P.A.1953).

c.   Intent

Under the modern cases, the plaintiff in a trademark infringement case need not prove that the defendant acted intentionally. This is the rule in both common law and Lanham Act suits. The older common law cases distinguished between suits for "trademark infringement", which involved "technical trade marks (i.e. inherently distinctive symbols) and those for "unfair competition" which involved secondary meaning marks. Intent was not an element of the former, but had to be proven in the later category of cases. Most jurisdictions have abandoned this distinction. Intent does continue to be relevant, however, both as a factor probative of a likelihood of confusion and as a factor bearing on what type of relief is appropriate.

2.   NON–COMPETING GOODS

A junior user may adopt a mark identical to one previously used by another merchant, but place that mark on different goods than those sold by the senior user. (e.g. a firm may begin marketing Kodak Shoes or Coppertone Paint). In such a situation, the most obvious harm of trademark infringement—diversion of sales from the senior user—cannot occur, because the senior user does not make the kind of item the consumer wanted to buy. Historically, this led courts to deny relief for trademark infringement unless the defendant sold goods directly competitive with those sold by the plaintiff. The modern cases, both at common law and under the Lanham Act, have abandoned that approach. Recognizing that a trademark owner can be harmed in ways other than through a direct diversion of sales, *courts will now prevent the use of a trademark on non-competitive goods if they are sufficiently related to those sold by the senior user so that there is a likelihood of confusion as to sponsorship or source.*

a. Related Goods

Goods are considered "related", despite the fact that they are non-competing, if the consuming public would reasonably think that they come from the same source or that there is some connection between them. It is sufficient if the buying public thinks that the trademark owner is licensing and supervising the goods being sold by the junior user. Consequently, because licensing arrangements have become so prevalent in our modern economy, there can be a likelihood of confusion even when the junior user uses the mark on vastly different goods than those sold by the trademark owner, provided that the trademark owner has objective proof (usually consumer surveys) documenting the claim of likelihood of confusion. Other relevant factors bearing on whether different types of goods are "related" include whether the two kinds of goods are sold in the same type of stores, have a group of common or overlapping purchasers, or are plausible lines of expansion for firms engaged in selling one of the two items. A strong or famous trademark will be given a broader scope of protection against use on non-competing goods than is afforded to a weak or lesser known mark.

> ***Examples:*** The mark LIFE on television sets was held to infringe the mark LIFE on the well-known magazine of the same name, but the mark T.I.M.E. for trucking services was held not to infringe TIME for magazines. The mark LLOYD'S OF LONDON for men's after shave was held to infringe the same mark for insurance, while the mark CHUCKLES for dolls was held not to infringe the same mark for candy.

b. Aesthetic Functionality

Some defendants in trademark infringement litigation have argued that they were entitled to use the senior user's mark on non-competing goods because they were using it in an "aesthetically functional" way. In other words, they claimed that the trademark was being used merely to decorate the goods, or was being sold for its artistic value, and that consumers did not assume that the goods in question were licensed or sponsored by the trademark owner. This contention was accepted by the court in *International Order of Job's Daughters v. Lindeburg & Co.,* 633 F.2d 912 (9th Cir.1980), where the defendant was selling jewelry bearing the trademark symbol of the plaintiff fraternal organization, but was rejected in *Boston Professional Hockey Asso. v. Dallas Cap & Emblem Mfg.,* 510 F.2d 1004 (5th Cir.1975), where the defendant was selling cloth patches bearing the trademark symbol of the plaintiff hockey teams. Trademark licensing for use on unrelated products and for decorative purposes has become increasingly common in recent years. For instance, there is now a line of Coca-Cola clothing, with the garments prominently featuring that famous trademark. This type of licensing is so widespread and consumer awareness of it so great, that in most cases the aesthetic functionality argument would likely fail even in those courts that recognize the doctrine, because the owner of the mark will be able to prove a clear likelihood of confusion as to the sponsorship of the goods.

c. Dilution

Numerous states have passed statutes to protect trademark owners against the unauthorized use of their marks on non-competing goods even when the goods are not "related" and are so different that there is no likelihood of confusion. Such statutes are known as dilution statutes. There is no federal dilution statute and no such protection is provided by the Lanham Act. Generally, only the owner of a strong (i.e. famous and highly distinctive) trademark may invoke these provisions, which are designed to prevent a gradual erosion of the distinctiveness of the mark.

Example: The famous POLAROID mark for photographic equipment and optical devices was held entitled to protection under the Illinois Anti-Dilution Statute, against defendant's use of the mark POLARAID on heating and refrigeration systems. *Polaroid Corporation v. Polaraid, Inc.,* 319 F.2d 830 (7th Cir.1963).

3. GEOGRAPHICALLY REMOTE USERS
a. Common Law

Because many firms do business solely on a local level, it is possible for two merchants to adopt the identical mark for the same goods in different parts of the country without knowing about each other's existence or use of the mark. *Since common law trademark rights only extend to the area in which a mark is actually used, so long as each of these geographically separated users confines its activities to its region, no conflict exists and the two uses can logically and legally co-exist.* However, if either or both firms chooses to expand territorially, there is the risk that one will come into contact with the other, thus causing confusion. The courts resolve the potential conflict by ruling that *the first firm to use the mark in each market has superior common law rights in that market and may enjoin others attempting to enter its market.* Thus the senior user nationwide cannot prevent a junior user from continuing to use a mark in a remote geographic area, if that junior user was the first to have appropriated the mark in that area.

1) Good Faith
The rule protecting a junior user in its own area of trade only applies if that user adopted the mark in good faith—that is, without knowledge of the senior user's prior use of the identical mark. (Such a user is referred to as an "innocent junior user" to reflect the good faith with which it adopted the

mark in question). If the junior user had notice of the earlier use of the mark, it is in bad faith and will be enjoined when the senior user seeks to enter its market.

2)   Remoteness

Two geographic markets are "remote" in trademark law if the disputed mark is associated with a different producer in each of the two areas. There need not be a real separation of any significant number of miles so long as "the mark means one thing in one market and an entirely different thing in another." *United Drug Co v. Theodore Rectanus Co.*, 248 U.S. 90, 39 S.Ct. 48 (1918). Consequently, if a mark is being used in only one market, but has attained national prominence, there can be no "remote" markets. This might be the case if there were national advertising for a product only available in one city. Any use of the same mark elsewhere in such a situation is likely to cause confusion and should be enjoined.

Example: In 1929 plaintiff adopted STORK CLUB as its mark for a night club in New York City. The club thereafter became a prominent gathering place for celebrities and achieved national fame when it was the subject of a movie by the same name. In 1945 the defendant opened a small bar in San Francisco using the same name and the New York firm filed suit for trademark infringement. In the ensuing litigation, the use by the defendant was enjoined because the court felt that the fame of plaintiff's establishment meant that there was risk of likelihood of confusion. *Stork Restaurant v. Sahati,* 166 F.2d 348 (9th Cir.1948).

b.   Lanham Act

When a trademark owner secures federal registration of its mark, *the Lanham Act provides that the registration constitutes nationwide constructive notice of the claim of ownership, 15 U.S.C.A. § 1115 (1984). Thus, any party adopting that mark after the date of registration is not an innocent junior user.* Its claim of good faith is destroyed by the constructive notice provisions of the statute. However the senior user with federal registration may only enjoin the junior user if it can demonstrate a likelihood of confusion at the time of trial. *Dawn Donut Co. v. Hart's Food Stores, Inc.,* 267 F.2d 358 (2d Cir.1959). It will be able to do so if its mark is nationally famous. If not, it may have to wait until it is ready to actually enter the junior user's market before securing an injunction.

1)   Junior Use Pre-dating Registration

For the constructive notice provision to defeat the claim of an otherwise innocent junior user, the senior user must have secured registration before the junior user adopted the mark. *If the junior user began using the mark in good faith in a remote market after the senior user's first use but before the senior user registered, than that junior user will be permanently protected in its area of trade.* 15 U.S.C.A. § 1115(b)(5) (1984); *Burger King of Florida, Inc. v. Hoots,* 403 F.2d 904 (7th Cir.1968). However, a junior user in this situation will be "frozen" into the market area it had at the time of registration, and cannot expand into other markets.

2)   Junior User Registers First
If the junior user secures the first federal registration, it cannot thereby defeat the rights that the senior user has already accrued in its market area. It will, however, be granted exclusive rights in all portions of the country where neither party has yet expanded. *Weiner King, Inc. v. Wiener King Corp.,* 615 F.2d 512 (C.C.P.A.1980).

4.   PERMISSIBLE COLLATERAL USES
Certain uses of trademarks belonging to others have been held by the courts to be legitimate even where the goods and geographic markets are identical. These situations generally involve a user who is selling the original trademarked goods in some altered form, or who is performing some services in connection with such goods. Such activities are denominated "collateral use" of the trademark and do not constitute infringement.

a.   Imported Goods
Foreign manufacturers of trademarked goods will often exclusively license one firm to import and sell their products in the U.S. and to secure U.S. registration for their trademarks. Other firms, however, may buy the genuine trademarked goods abroad and seek to sell them in the U.S. in competition with the American trademark owner. Such goods are sometimes referred to as "gray market" goods, since the importer does not have authorization to sell them in the U.S. The courts have struggled with the question of whether such sales constitute trademark infringement, and the related question of whether such imports may be excluded at the border, under provisions of the Tariff Act of 1930. In *A. Bourjois & Co. v. Katzel,* 260 U.S. 689, 43 S.Ct. 244 (1923), the Court held that such sales by the unauthorized importer did constitute trademark infringement. Some recent cases, however, have declined to find infringement where the peculiarities of the facts made likelihood of confusion or injury to the plaintiff less likely. *Bell & Howell: Mamiya Co. v. Masel Supply Co.,* 719 F.2d 42 (2d Cir.1983); *El Greco Leather Products Co. v. Shoe World, Inc.,* 599 F.Supp. 1380 (E.D.N.Y.1984). *But see, e.g., Weil Ceramics & Glass, Inc. v. Dash,* 618 F.Supp. 700 (D.N.J.1985) (finding gray market sales of genuine Lladro ceramics infringing).

b.   Rebottled and Repackaged Goods
If a firm buys the trademarked goods of another and rebottles or repacks those goods, it may use the original manufacturer's trademark, provided its labels make clear its own identity and lack of affiliation with the trademark owner. Prestonettes, Inc. v. Coty, 264 U.S. 359, 44 S.Ct. 350 (1924).

c. Repaired or Reconditioned Goods

If a firm buys the trademarked goods of another and reconditions them, in order to sell them in a second-hand market, *it may also use the original manufacturer's trademarks,* provided, again, that it makes full disclosure of its identity, lack of affiliation with the trademark owner, and the fact that the goods are used. *Champion Spark Plugs v. Sanders,* 331 U.S. 125, 67 S.Ct. 1136 (1947).

d. Dealerships, Service Outlets and Replacement Parts

Similar to the above rules, *a firm may use the trademark of another to indicate that it sells the goods of that firm, that it makes replacement parts for its items, or that it repairs that manufacturer's goods,* without obtaining the consent of the trademark owner, so long as it does not falsely represent that it is an authorized dealership or service outlet.

e. Comparative Advertising

It is now well settled that a firm may make reference to its competitors' trademarks in advertising without committing trademark infringement, so long as the statements in the disputed ad are truthful. *Smith v. Chanel, Inc.,* 402 F.2d 562 (9th Cir.1968).

5. OTHER FORBIDDEN PRACTICES

A merchant may attempt to deceive the public or take a free ride on another firm's goodwill without actually using another firm's trademarks. This can be done by imitating the trade dress of a well regarded firm, or by using photographs of a competitor's products in a catalogue or advertisement but supplying your own brand when customers place orders. It can also be done by adopting as your trademark the trade name (i.e. business name) of a rival firm that does not use its corporate name in a trademark sense. All of these practices constitute palming off or unfair competition, regardless of whether a trademark is involved. They all may be enjoined in suits at common law. Moreover, Lanham Act, section 43(a), makes this behavior actionable in federal court as well. 15 U.S.C.A. § 1125(a) (1984).

H. TRADEMARK ABANDONMENT

1. NON–USE

If the owner of a trademark ceases to use that mark and there is some evidence of intent to relinquish it, the mark will be deemed abandoned. Thereafter, the mark is available to any other firm that wishes to adopt it. The Lanham Act provides that non-use for two consecutive years is prima facie evidence of abandonment. 15 U.S.C.A. § 1127 (1984).

2. FAILURE TO SUPERVISE LICENSEES

A trademark must be distinctive of the owner's goods or services. Consequently, *if a trademark owner licenses others to make goods or provide services under its name, but fails to supervise these licensees to see that they adhere to standards of quality control, the mark may be deemed abandoned* because consumer will not receive a comparable product every time they encounter the mark. *Dawn Donut Co. v. Hart's Food Stores, Inc.,* 267 F.2d 358 (2d Cir.1959).

I. REMEDIES

1. INJUNCTIVE RELIEF

The traditional and most common relief for trademark infringement is for the court to enjoin the junior user from continuing its unauthorized use of the mark, 15 U.S.C.A. § 1116 (1984). If the circumstances of the case suggest that an absolute prohibition of use of the mark would be unfair to the defendant, the court may enter a qualified injunction designed to balance the equities.

2. MONETARY RELIEF

A successful plaintiff in a trademark infringement case may be awarded monetary relief measured either by the amount of its own injury, or by the amount of profits earned by the defendant, along with the cost of suit, 15 U.S.C.A. § 1117(a) (1984). The defendant may be obliged to pay an award including profits even if the plaintiff cannot demonstrate that it lost any sales due to the infringement. *Maier Brewing Co. v. Fleischmann Distilling Corp.,* 390 F.2d 117 (9th Cir.1968). The courts have also endorsed damages in the amount of the sum the plaintiff would need to spend on corrective advertising to overcome the confusion which had been created by the defendant's infringement. *Big O Tire Dealers v. Goodyear Tire & Rubber Co.,* 561 F.2d 1365 (10th Cir.1977). Recent amendments to the Lanham Act provide that if the defendant is found to have engaged in intentional trademark infringement, the plaintiff shall be awarded three times its damages or the defendant's profits, whichever is greater. 15 U.S.C.A. § 1117(b) (1984).

3. DESTRUCTION OF INFRINGING ARTICLES

The Lanham Act provides that the court may order the destruction of any "labels, signs, prints, packages, wrappers, receptacles, and advertisements" in the defendant's possession which bear the infringing mark. 15 U.S.C.A. § 1118 (1984).

4. CRIMINAL PENALTIES

Under the recently adopted Trademark Counterfeiting Act of 1984, 18 U.S.C.A. § 2320, certain forms of trademark infringement are defined as "trafficking in counterfeit goods," and are made punishable by up to 5 years imprisonment and a $250,000 fine. The government may also secure an order for destruction of the counterfeit goods.

REVIEW QUESTIONS

1. **T or F** The only product shapes and containers that may be protected as trademarks are those that are functional.

2. **T or F** If trademarked goods are repacked into new containers by someone other than the trademark owner, the party doing the repacking may use the original manufacturer's trademark.

3. **T or F** A trademark may be reserved for up to 1 year prior to the time a manufacturer plans to use it.

4. **T or F** In order to make out a case of trademark infringement, the plaintiff and the defendant must be competitors.

5. **T or F** Only the holder of a federal trademark registration may use the "r in a circle" device after its trademark on packages and in advertising.

6. **T or F** A trademark is presumed abandoned under the Lanham Act if it has not been used for 5 years.

7. **T or F** A suggestive word or term will be protected as a trademark without a showing of secondary meaning.

8. **T or F** A mark that most buyers have come to understand as meaning a type of product has lost its distinctiveness and will no longer be protected.

9. **T or F** A deceptive term may be federally registered as a trademark if the applicant can show secondary meaning.

10. **T or F** The mark YELLOW PAGES for the classified telephone directory is a fanciful mark.

11. **T or F** To show liability, the plaintiff in a trademark infringement action must show the defendant acted intentionally in adopting the disputed mark.

12. **T or F** A trademark infringement plaintiff can only recover if it demonstrates that defendant's acts will cause a diversion of sales from it.

13. **T or F** An intra-corporate transfer of goods marked with a new trademark is insufficient to create common law trademark rights.

14. **T or F** A geographically descriptive term will only be protected as a trademark if it has secondary meaning.

15. **T or F** The Lanham Act permits the registration of "collective" and "certification" marks.

16. Alpha Corporation began using the mark ZING for chocolate candy bars in New York and New Jersey in 1978. It obtained a federal registration for the ZING mark in 1979. In 1980, without any knowledge of Alpha's prior use, Beta, Inc. began using the mark for chocolate candy in Los Angeles. Alpha, which still does business only in the Northeast, has learned of Beta's use and seeks to enjoin it. In the ensuing lawsuit

   a.   No injunction will issue because Beta is a good faith junior user

   b.   An injunction will issue because Beta had constructive notice of Alpha's claim of ownership of the mark

   c.   No injunction will issue because there is no likelihood of confusion

   d.   An injunction will issue because the ZING mark has secondary meaning.

17. Which of the following is not a permissible collateral use of another firm's trademark?

   a.   The manufacturers of Coca-Cola run an advertising campaign stating "Coke tastes better than Pepsi." Pepsi is the registered trademark of a competing brand of soft drinks.

   b.   Ralph runs a garage specializing in the repair of Honda automobiles. He is not affiliated with the Honda Corporation. He puts up a large sign saying "Ralph's Garage—Our speciality—Hondas."

   c.   Acme Filters makes filters for air conditioners. Its cartons state "This filter for use in Fedders Air Conditioners" or "This filter for use in Carrier Air Conditioners."

   d.   Delta Garment Company markets a line of Tee Shirts under its own Delta brand, decorated with large colorful reproductions of the trademarks of Coca-Cola, Pepsi, Seven-Up and Doctor Pepper.

18. Which of the following may be registered as a trademark without a showing of secondary meaning?

   a.   Slogans

   b.   Surname Marks

    c.   Arbitrary Marks

    d.   Geographically Descriptive Marks

19. The National Conference of Bar Examiners (NCBE) is a non-profit organization consisting of representatives of the Bar Examining authorities in each of the 50 states. Twice each year, NCBE prepares a 200 question objective multiple choice test. This test may be used by any American jurisdiction as part of its bar examination. NCBE calls this test the MULTISTATE BAR EXAMINATION or the MBE. Since its inception in 1972, this test has been taken by over 400,000 bar applicants, and the name Multistate Bar Examination is almost universally known by both lawyers and law students.

Martini Bar Review Inc. is one of several firms engaged in the sale of intensive bar examination preparation courses. As part of its course, Martini administers a 200 question objective multiple choice test under exam conditions. It calls this the PRELIMINARY MULTISTATE BAR EXAMINATION or the PMBE. Martini's advertising makes prominent reference to its PMBE, claiming that this is one aspect of the Martini course that makes it superior to others.

The NCBE views these actions of Martini with concern, and has filed suit for common law trademark infringement. Is Martini guilty of trademark infringement? Why or why not?

III

COPYRIGHT

Analysis

Copyright law today revolves entirely around the federal copyright statute, which was substantially revised in 1976. State protection in the areas covered by the statute has been explicitly pre-empted. Prior to 1976, common law protection for unpublished works co-existed with federal statutory copyright. While many of the important principles of copyright law remained largely unaltered by the 1976 revisions, and many of the earlier cases are still good law, you should note the date of all the copyright cases you read to make certain that the opinion does not refer to statutory provisions that are no longer in force, or to doctrines that have been abandoned.

Material not protected by copyright is said to be in the "public domain." Most public domain material consists of subject matter than does not qualify for copyright protection, or of material the copyright of which has expired. Thus much literature and art from the past—such as the plays of Shakespeare and the music of Mozart—is in the public domain.

Like other areas of unfair trade practices law, copyright involves a legal balancing act. On the one hand, we seek to provide protection to those who have already exerted effort—in this case creative or artistic effort—to encourage other authors and artists to engage in creative activity. On the other hand, we do not want to provide so much protection that we create impenetrable monopolies that defeat the social interests in the dissemination of knowledge, art and culture and the enhancement of competition that flow from permitting the copying of good ideas for which there is a public demand.

A. COPYRIGHTABLE SUBJECT MATTER

The initial inquiry in any copyright problem is whether the thing that plaintiff seeks to protect is eligible for protection under the copyrights laws. If the answer is no, the plaintiff may have a remedy under some other theory but copyright remedies will be unavailable. Under present law, copyright is available for any "original work of authorship fixed in any tangible medium of expression."

1. THE CONSTITUTIONAL BASIS
The Constitution empowers the Congress to pass legislation protecting the "writings" of "authors" for limited times. The language of the constitutional provision thus imposes an outer limit on the subject matter of copyright. *The constitutional language is not interpreted literally, however. Consequently, a wide variety of works that would not be considered "writings" in the colloquial sense are within the constitutional concept for the purposes of copyright protection.*

2. NON–UTILITARIAN ORIGINAL EXPRESSION PROTECTED
The statutory definition of copyrightable subject matter can be seen as imposing 4 tests. The work in question must be "original", it must be a particularized "expression" of an author, it must be "non-utilitarian" and it must be "fixed".

This subsection considers the first three of these requirements, while fixation is considered in the subsection which follows.

a. Originality

In order to qualify for copyright protection a work must be "original." Originality, however, merely means that the work was created through the independent effort of the author, and does not imply any requirement of artistic or intellectual merit. Bleistein v. Donalson Lithographing Co., 188 U.S. 239, 23 S.Ct. 298 (1903). Thus the originality requirement precludes copyright protection for something that was merely copied verbatim from another, pre-existing, work, but does not preclude protection for reproductions of works of art that require individual effort on the part of the reproducer. *Alfred Bell & Co. v. Catalda Fine Arts, Inc.,* 191 F.2d 99 (2d Cir.1951). It also precludes copyright for works consisting entirely of public domain information such as calendars or height and weight charts.

Example: The amateur movies capturing the events of the assassination of John F. Kennedy were held to be sufficiently original to deserve copyright protection in *Time, Inc. v. Bernard Geis Associates,* 293 F.Supp. 130 (S.D.N.Y.1968), despite the fact that the "creativity" involved in making the movies was minimal, consisting of merely recording the unfolding of a real world event.

b. Only Expressions, Not Ideas

Copyright protection is not available for abstract ideas, processes, methods of operation or facts, even if they are original. Only the manner in which an idea is expressed can be protected under the copyright laws. This is one of the oldest and most fundamental distinctions in copyright law. *Baker v. Selden,* 101 U.S. (11 Otto) 99 (1879); 17 U.S.C.A. § 102(b) (1984). Consequently, a work that communicates ideas that can only be expressed in one way is not eligible for copyright protection. *Morrissey v. Proctor & Gamble Co.,* 379 F.2d 675 (1st Cir. 1967) (sweepstakes rules held non-copyrightable). This distinction between protected forms of expression and freely copiable ideas preserves both freedom of expression and the competitive interests in duplication and dissemination of concepts that are not sufficiently inventive to qualify for patent protection.

Examples: Although the creators of the character Superman have copyright protection for the specific plots, words and images in the many comic books and films portraying his exploits, they do not have copyright in the concept of a superhuman crusader who battles the forces of evil, and others may thus freely use that idea. *Warner Brothers, Inc. v. American Boradcasting Cos.,* 523 F.Supp. 611 (S.D.N.Y.1981). Similarly, if one conceives of a new way to wash automobiles and summarizes the technique in a pamphlet, the words used in the pamphlet are protected, but others are free to describe the identical process of car washing in other words without infringing any rights of the first party.

c.   Utilitarian Objects Not Protectable

Creators of three dimensional objects (e.g., sculptors) often seek copyright protection for their creations. Such protection is usually available. However, *if an object looks the way it does solely because of utilitarian considerations, it is not proper subject matter for copyright.* Advances of this sort are to be protected, if at all, under the patent laws. However, if an object combines both utilitarian and decorative features, the decorative features can be protected by copyright assuming they meet the other relevant tests.

Example: If a firm produces statuettes of male and female dancing figures, and uses them as bases for table lamps, the figures may be copyrighted as works of art, because although they serve a utilitarian function, they also have non-utilitarian aspects and could exist apart from lamps of which they are a part. *Mazer v. Stein,* 347 U.S. 201, 74 S.Ct. 460 (1954). However, the artistic design of a lighting fixture cannot be copyrighted as a work of art since it has no existence independent of its utilitarian attributes. *Esquire Inc. v. Ringer,* 591 F.2d 796 (D.C.Cir.1978).

3.   FIXATION REQUIRED

An author's original expression is not eligible for copyright protection unless it is "fixed in any tangible medium of expression," 17 U.S.C.A. § 102(a) (1984). *Evanescent expressions such as improvised live performances or impromptu speeches that are not recorded, are consequently, not protectible under the federal copyright statute,* although, as is discussed below, various forms of state common law protection may be available for them. A work consisting of sounds or images that is simultaneously transmitted and "fixed" (by being video or audiotaped), qualifies for protection. 17 U.S.C.A. § 101 ¶ 13 (1984). Thus, professional sporting events that are broadcast live but simultaneously "fixed" on videotape are protected by copyright.

4.   CONVENTIONAL SUBJECT MATTER

The most frequently encountered copyrightable materials are the traditional forms of literary, visual and performing arts, such as books, plays, movies, paintings and sculptures. Their protectability rarely is an issue in modern copyright litigation, although the status of some of these materials was less certain in earlier versions of copyright statutes.

a.   Itemized Subject Matter

Section 102 of the current federal copyright statute lists 7 types of works as being within the definition of "original works of authorship fixed in any tangible medium of expression"—(1) literary works; (2) musical works; (3) dramatic works; (4) pantomimes and choreographic works; (5) pictorial, graphic and sculptural works; (6) motion pictures and other audiovisual works; and (7) sound recordings. 17 U.S.C.A. § 102(a) (1984). These categories, however, do not constitute a closed list of copyrightable works. Any other work that is "original", an "expression" and "fixed" also qualifies for protection.

b. Note Regarding Sound Recordings

Under the current statute, sound recordings may simultaneously involve different copyrightable works created by different "authors." If the recording is of music, the composer of the music and lyrics has copyright protection in the song itself. The parties who create the sound recording—namely the entertainers who play the musical instruments and sing the words and the recording company that blends the sounds—have a discrete copyright interest in their performance of the work, embodied in the sound recording. Sound recording made before February 15, 1972, however, are not protected by federal copyright, although the musical compositions used in such recordings are protected.

5. TROUBLESOME SUBJECT MATTER

Individuals have historically sought copyright protection for a wide variety of items whose status as proper subject matter of copyright has been ambiguous. Almost always, the source of the ambiguity is either that the item is arguably merely an "idea" rather than a specific "expression," or a contention that there is insufficient "originality" to trigger protection. Following are some examples of subject matters whose copyrightable status is (or in some cases was) less than clear.

a. Computer Programs

Unlike most copyrightable subject matter, a computer program cannot be used or enjoyed by itself. It only functions in conjunction with a machine. Moreover, it is often one of only a limited number of ways to express a set of instructions, although that is less and less true as the program becomes more and more complex. In addition, computer programs are often written in highly abstract programming languages or embodied in silicon chips, as opposed to more conventional languages and media of expression like paper, canvas, or magnetic tape. For these reasons, many courts struggled with the suitability of computer programs for copyright protection. Today, however, *the copyrightability of computer programs, regardless of the programming language in which they are written, is clear. Apple Computer, Inc. v. Franklin Computer Corp., 714 F.2d 1240 (3d Cir.1983). Congress added explicit copyright protection for semiconductor chips in 1984. 17 U.S.C.A. § 901 et seq. (1984).*

b. Compilations

While the assembly of large amounts of data in the forms of directories, compilations and lists is often laborious, the amount of creativity in such a project is minimal. Anyone setting out to produce a given type of compilation should arrive at the same result. Notwithstanding this arguable lack of originality, *compilations are specifically mentioned as copyrightable subject matter in the federal statute.* 17 U.S.C.A. § 103 (1984). The requisite "originality" is supplied by the labor of the compiler in putting the data together in usable form. It should be noted, however, that anyone else who independently compiles the same information does not infringe the copyright of the first compiler.

c.   Titles, Trademarks, Commercial Prints and Labels

The titles of books, movies and plays are not protected by copyright. Similarly, copyright protection is not afforded for trademarks, no matter how creative they may be. 17 C.F.R. § 202.10(c) (1984). *However product labels embodying trademarks, instructions, artistic decorations and other textual and visual material can be protected by the copyright laws. Drop Dead Co. v. S.C. Johnson & Son, Inc.,* 326 F.2d 87 (9th Cir.1963). Of course, trademarks and titles are protected under other forms of unfair trade practices law, and therefore cannot be appropriated with impunity.

d.   Translations

While some very early cases concluded that translations lacked sufficient originality to justify copyright, the current statute includes translations within its definition of "derivative works." 17 U.S.C.A. § 101, ¶ 10 (1984). Since derivative works are specifically listed as proper subject matters for copyright in 17 U.S.C.A. § 103 (1984), *translations are fully eligible for copyright.*

e.   Architecture

Blueprints or other materials generated by architects are clearly proper subject matters for copyright. *Imperial Homes Corp. v. Lamont,* 458 F.2d 895 (5th Cir. 1972). *Buildings themselves, however, are not considered "works" of "authorship" and hence are not protected under the copyright statute.* Thus, it is not copyright infringement to carefully observe and then duplicate the appearance of a building.

f.   Typefaces

Regardless of the degree of artistry involved, *type styles have generally been denied copyright protection.*

B. PUBLICATION

For much of the history of American copyright law, the concept of publication marked a crucial dividing line between state and federal protection. The present federal copyright statute makes the event of publication considerably less significant, but an understanding of the concept is an important aid to interpretation of many older copyright opinions that are still important today.

1.   HISTORICAL SIGNIFICANCE OF PUBLICATION

a.   Common Law Copyright for Unpublished Works

Prior to the Copyright Act of 1976 federal law did not apply to any work that had not been published. Such *unpublished material was protected,* instead, *by so-called "common law" copyright.* Common law copyright was perpetual in duration, and permitted an author to prevent any unauthorized exploitation of his or her work. It was sometimes described as the "right of first publication." However, since common law copyright ended on the occasion of first publication, it did not help an author secure the true economic reward for his or her work. Post-publication protection was only available if steps were taken to preserve one's rights under the federal statute.

b.   Pre–1976 Definition of Publication

Prior to 1976, the legal definition of "publication" bore only a slight resemblance to the ordinary meaning of the word in every day speech. Under the relevant cases, only a "general publication" resulted in termination of common law protection. A variety of activities were characterized as "limited publications" and these did not affect the common law copyright. *General publication only occurred if tangible copies of the work in question were made available to the public.* Thus, the delivery of speech, performance of a play, broadcast of a radio script or exhibition of a painting were all held to be merely limited publications regardless of the number of persons who were exposed to the work.

> ***Example:***   In 1963 Dr. Martin Luther King gave his famous "I have a
> dream" speech to a throng of 200,000 people at the Lincoln
> Memorial during the March on Washington. Thereafter, 20th
> Century Fox began selling recordings of the speech that they had
> made at the scene. Dr. King was held to have retained the
> common law copyright in the text of his speech, which had not
> been extinguished by his oral delivery of it in public or his limited
> distribution of written copies to the press. *King v. Mister Maestro,
> Inc.,*   224 F.Supp. 101 (S.D.N.Y.1963).

2.   CURRENT SIGNIFICANCE OF PUBLICATION

a.   Common Law Copyright Abolished

Under the 1976 Act common law copyright for works fixed in a tangible medium of expression *no longer exists.* Thus, if a novelist prepares a typed manuscript, federal protection attaches from the minute the words are placed on the page. State law remedies against someone who secretly inspected the manuscript and then began selling unauthorized copies are pre-empted. Publication remains significant, however, in a number of technical respects. The most important of those is that once a work is published, it must have a visible notice of copyright appearing on it, or else federal statutory rights may be lost. In addition, the duration of copyright rights may be measured from the date of publication rather than the date of creation in some circumstances.

b.   Current Definition of Publication

The 1976 Act contains the following definition of publication: "the distribution of copies or phonorecords of a work to the public by sale or other transfer of ownership or by rental, lease or lending. . . . A public performance or display of a work does not of itself constitute publication." 17 U.S.C.A. § 101 (1984).

C. COPYRIGHT FORMALITIES

1.   NOTICE

Prior to the 1976 copyright statute, the failure to include a copyright notice on a published work lead to a forfeiture of all statutory rights. Under the current act, inclusion of copyright notice on all published copies is still required. The present statute, however, provides some latitude for copyright owners who inadvertently omit the notice.

a.   Form of Notice

A copyright notice must consist of three components. First, either the word "copyright", the abbreviation "copr." or the "c in a circle" symbol. Second, the name of the copyright owner. Third, the date of first publication. The date, however, may be omitted in certain limited circumstances itemized by the statute. 17 U.S.C.A. § 401(b)(2) (1984).

b.   Significance of Notice

The 1976 copyright statute provides that *whenever a work is "published" it must bear the statutorily described copyright notice.* 17 U.S.C.A. § 401 (1984). This requirement is significant because the public distribution of copies of a copyrighted work lacking notice invalidates any subsequent claim of copyright, except in 3 limited cases.

1)   Only Few Copies Lack Notice

If the requisite notice is missing from only a small number of publicly distributed copies of the work, the copyright in the work is *not* invalidated. 17 U.S.C.A. § 405(a)(1) (1984).

2)   Registration Plus Correction

If the work in question was registered either before, or within 5 years after publication, and the author makes a reasonable effort to add notice to all domestically distributed copies after he or she becomes aware of the omission, the copyright in the work is *not* invalidated. 17 U.S.C.A. § 405(a)(2) (1984). What constitutes a "reasonable effort" to cure an inadvertent omission of notice is determined on a case by case basis. *Florists' Transworld Delivery v. Reliable Glassware and Pottery Co.,* 213 U.S.P.Q. 808 (N.D.Ill.1981).

3) Publisher's Omission

If the copyright owner authorized another party to publicly distribute the work and obtained a written commitment from that party that notice would appear on the copies, should the other party fail to include the notice, the copyright in the work is *not* invalidated. 17 U.S.C.A. § 405(a)(3) (1984).

c. Innocent Infringers

If any alleged infringer can prove that he or she duplicated material from a copy of the work that lacked the required notice, and that he or she was misled by the absence of notice, that person will not be liable for any infringement occurring before he or she receives actual notice that the work has been registered. 17 U.S.C.A. § 405(b) (1985).

2. REGISTRATION
a. Registration Optional

The present copyright statute explicitly states that *registration is permissive and is not a condition of copyright protection.* 17 U.S.C.A. § 408 (1984). That statement, however, must be considered in conjunction with the protections that are sacrificed if no registration has been made.

b. Registration Required for Infringement Suit

The chief importance of *registration* under the current statute is that it *is a pre-requisite to suit for copyright infringement.* The registration, however, need not be accomplished before the infringing acts. The owner of the copyright may register after learning of the infringement and then proceed to immediately file suit. 17 U.S.C.A. § 411 (1984).

c. Registration Required for Certain Remedies

Certain remedies are not available to a copyright plaintiff who has delayed in securing registration until after infringement has commenced. Specifically, "statutory damages" and attorney's fees are not available if (a) the plaintiff's work is unpublished and the infringement took place before registration or (b) the plaintiff's work is published and infringement took place before registration unless registration was accomplished within three months after first publication. 17 U.S.C.A. § 412 (1984). It should be stressed, however, that a plaintiff in this position can still register, and secure the other remedies for infringement, such as actual damages and injunctive relief.

d. Registration Procedure

Registration is accomplished by completing a prescribed application form and forwarding it, along with the required fee and deposit copies of the work involved to the Copyright Office of the Library of Congress. If the work involved is unpublished, only one copy is required for deposit. Two copies of published works must be submitted. 17 U.S.C.A. §§ 408, 409 (1984). If registration is refused, the normal rule that registration must precede an infringement suit is relaxed, and the owner of the copyright may file suit, provided that a copy of the complaint is also served on the Register of Copyrights.

3. DEPOSIT

The deposit of copies of a copyrighted work with the Copyright Office of the Library of Congress is part of the process of copyright registration. In addition, however, *all copyright owners are required to deposit two copies of their work within three months after publication, even if they do not seek registration.* 17 U.S.C.A. § 407 (1984). (There is no deposit requirement for unpublished works.) The deposit requirement insures that the collection of the Library of Congress includes copies of every work published in the United States. The mandatory nature of this requirement is qualified, however, by statutory language providing that deposit is not a condition of copyright protection. Moreover there are no sanctions for failure to deposit copies until they have been demanded by the Register of Copyrights. Thereafter, failure to deposit within three months subjects the offender to a $250 fine or, if the refusal is willful and repeated, a fine of $2500.

D. THE RIGHTS OF A COPYRIGHT OWNER

1. THE STATUTORY EXCLUSIVE RIGHTS

The federal copyright statute confers five rights on the owner of copyright in a work. Those rights are exclusive—the owner may prevent other parties from exercising these rights vis-a-vis his or her work unless permission has been granted. Not all of the rights apply to all types of works, however.

a. Reproduction

Only the copyright owner, or one acting with his or her permission, may make "copies" or "phonorecords" of the protected work. Copies are defined statutorily as "material objects, other than phonorecords, in which a work is fixed by any method now known or later developed, and from which the work can be perceived, reproduced or otherwise communicated, either directly or with the aid of a machine or device," 17 U.S.C.A. § 101 ¶ 7 (1984). Phonorecords are defined as "material objects in which sounds . . . are fixed by any method now known or later developed, and from which the sound can be perceived, reproduced or otherwise communicated." *Id.* ¶ 19. Thus, making a single copy of a book or a single unauthorized tape recording of a record constitutes infringement, unless done with the consent of the copyright holder, or excused under some other statutory provision. The exclusive right to make copies is qualified by several statutory provisions conferring limited rights on libraries, broadcasters and the owners of computer programs, among others, to make single copies of copyrighted works. 17 U.S.C.A. §§ 108, 112, 117 (1984).

b. Adaptation

Any transformation of a work into another form, such as a dramatization, translation, condensed version, or musical arrangement, is considered a "derivative work." The owner of the copyright in the orginal work has the sole right to *create a derivative work.* The preparation of such a work by any other party without the creator's permission constitutes infringement.

c. Distribution

Only the owner of the copyright is empowered to distribute copies or phonorecords of the protected work to the public, whether by outright sale, or by rental or loan. Because this right involves distribution to the public, it gives the copyright owner the power to determine when and how the work should be published. Once a given copy (or phonorecord) of the work has been transferred to another party, however, the copyright owner loses control over that particular copy (or phonorecord). Thus, the buyer may resell the copy without infringing the copyright. This is sometimes referred to as the "first sale" doctrine. 17 U.S.C.A. § 109 (1984). Of course, the buyer may not make additional copies without violating the copyright owner's reproduction rights, discussed above.

d. Performance

1) Scope of Right

Only the copyright owner may "perform" the protected work publicly. To perform a work is defined as "to recite, render, play, dance, or act it, either directly or by means of any device or process . . ." 17 U.S.C.A. § 101 ¶ 18 (1984). A performance is public if it occurs at "a place open to the public or at any place where a substantial number of persons outside of a normal circle of a family and its social acquaintances is gathered" or if it involves a public transmission. *Id.* ¶ 23. Several limitations on the performance right are codified in the statute. They permit various charitable, religious, non-profit and educational performances of copyrighted works notwithstanding the exclusive performance right. 17 U.S.C.A. § 110 (1984).

2) Covered Works

By their very nature, visual arts such as paintings, sculptures and graphic works cannot be performed, as that term is defined in the statute, and thus the exclusive performance right does not extend to them. While sound recordings can be performed, by playing them on a turntable or tape player, or similar machine, Congress made an explicit decision that the owner of a copyright in a sound recording should not have an exclusive performance right. 17 U.S.C.A. § 114(a) (1984). Thus, any party who possesses a record or tape—including a radio or television station— may play it publicly without violating the rights of the owner of the copyright in the sound recording. Playing the record, however, is also a "performance" of any underlying musical composition contained on the record. Since the composer of a musical work does have an exclusive performance right, the composer is entitled to a royalty each time the record is played, unless the work is in the public domain.

e. Display

For all types of copyrighted subject matter except sound recordings, *the copyright owner has the exclusive right to display the work.* Display is statutorily defined as being the showing of "a copy of it, either directly or by means of a film, slide, television image, or any other device or process or, in the case of a motion picture or other audiovisual work, to show individual images nonsequentially." 17 U.S.C.A. § 101 ¶ 12 (1984). However, the owner of a copy of a copyrighted work may display that copy to viewers present at the place where the copy is located, *Id.* § 109(b), and the copyright owner's exclusive right to display the work is limited by a provision permitting display for charitable, religious, non-profit and educational purposes. *Id.* § 110.

2. TRANSFER AND LICENSING
a. Voluntary Transfers and Licenses

Copyrights have all the attributes of personal property. Consequently they are fully transferable in whole or in part. 17 U.S.C.A. § 201(d) (1984). Such a transfer of rights can even be made before the work has been created, which frequently occurs in the publishing industry. A copyright owner may also grant other parties a license, permitting them to make specified uses of the work upon payment of a royalty. An outright assignment of a copyright or the grant of an exclusive license must be in writing. *Id.* § 204(a). This document can be recorded in the Copyright Office, *Id.* § 205(a), and recordation is a pre-requisite to an infringement suit on the part of the transferee. *Id.* § 205(d). In the absence of a written transfer of copyright rights, the conveyance of a physical object (such as a manuscript, or pages of sheet music, or a tape recording) does not convey any of the exclusive rights in the work itself. *Id.* § 202. Thus, the purchaser of a manuscript of a brand new novel may not make and sell copies of the work or distribute them to the public, unless the purchaser has also obtained a transfer of the copyright itself.

b. Termination of Transfers

It is often impossible, when a work is first created, to assess its commercial significance. Thus, copyright owners may enter into transfers or licenses that subsequent events reveal to have been unwise. To protect copyright owners, *transfers and licenses (other than those effected by will) are made terminable by statute.* This termination right may be exercised by the author of the work, or by various surviving heirs specified in the statute. *The termination may only be effected, however, during the five year period beginning at the end of thirty-five years from the date of execution of the grant.* 17 U.S.C.A. § 203 (1984). Such a termination must be by written notice to the transferee or licensee, and causes all rights in the work to revert to the author or the author's heirs.

Example: In 1980 Jones prepares the manuscript of a novel. In 1985 Jones executes an unqualified transfer of copyright in favor of Acme Publishing Co. in return for a payment of $1000. Thereafter the book became a smash hit, selling hundreds of thousands of copies.

Notwithstanding the original transfer, Jones (or Jones' heirs, if Jones is dead) may serve a written termination on Acme at any time from the year 2020 to the year 2025. If such a notice is served, all rights in the novel will revert to Jones or the heirs.

c. Compulsory Licenses

As was noted at a number of points above, the exclusive rights of copyright owners are limited in a variety of situations. Those previously discussed limitations consisted largely of provisions specifying that certain parties (e.g. libraries or charities) could use copyrighted material in certain limited ways for free, without being guilty of infringement. Other provisions permit certain acts without the express consent of the copyright owner, but require the payment of a royalty. These arrangements are known as "compulsory licenses." Three of the more important compulsory license provisions are discussed below.

1) Phonorecord Reproduction of Musical Compositions

If the copyright owner of a musical composition has publicly distributed phonorecords of a sound recording of that composition, any other person may secure a compulsory license permitting him or her to also make phonorecords of the work. Such a license does not, however, permit the making of "copies" of the musical work, such as sheet music. It also does not permit direct copying of previously made sound recordings, unless the owner of the copyright in those sound recordings also consents. This compulsory license is obtained by serving a written notice on the owner of the copyright in the musical composition. The copyright owner will receive royalties for this use of his or her composition in an amount fixed by the Copyright Royalty Tribunal. 17 U.S.C.A. § 115 (1984).

Example: In 1978 Smith wrote music and lyrics for a new song, "Born in the U.S.S.R." In 1979, Smith published sheet music of this song. In 1980, Gotown Records, acting with Smith's consent, hired Ruth Springsheen to make a sound recording of the song. Phonorecords of the Springsheen performance were placed on public sale. In 1984, Omega Records wishes to hire Barry Maninose to record his version of "Born In the U.S.S.R." and to sell phonorecords of that recording to the public. They are permitted to do so under the compulsory license described above, and will have to remit the required royalty to the original composer, Smith. Omega may not duplicate and sell sheet music to this song, however, and it may not duplicate and sell phonorecords of the Springsheen recording unless Gotown and Springsheen consent.

2) Jukebox Performance of Musical Compositions

As noted above, the author of a sound recording does not have an exclusive right to "perform" the recording. Anyone is free to play a record or tape of the performance publicly. The composer of a musical work, however, does have an exclusive performance right. Thus the public playing of a sound recording will infringe the rights of the composer unless advance permission has been obtained. However, the operator of a coin-operated phonorecord player (i.e. a jukebox) can obtain a compulsory license from the composer of the musical work, permitting performances of the composition on that jukebox without liability. The composer in such a case will receive royalties, in an amount calculated by the Copyright Royalty Tribunal. 17 U.S.C.A. § 116 (1984).

3) Noncommercial Broadcasters

Noncommercial educational broadcast stations may secure a compulsory license permitting them to perform published musical compositions for a royalty to be calculated by the Copyright Royalty Tribunal. 17 U.S.C.A. § 118 (1984).

d. Blanket Licenses

Radio and television broadcasters who use musical recordings face a situation similar to the one confronting jukebox operators insofar as performance rights are concerned—they may play recorded music without violating the rights of the parties who created the recording, but they risk infringing the rights of the composer of the music if they act without permission. Because most broadcasters play an enormous amount of music it is difficult or impractical for them to secure individual licenses from hundreds of composers. To facilitate licensing in this situation, performing rights societies came into existence. The two most significant societies are the American Society of Composers, Authors and Publishers (ASCAP) and Broadcast Music, Inc. (BMI). These societies act as clearing houses, obtaining licensing rights from individual composers, and then granting "blanket licenses" to broadcasters. These blanket licenses permit them to perform any composition within the repertoire of the society for a flat fee.

3. DURATION OF RIGHTS

Copyright protection runs for the life of the author, plus fifty years. 17 U.S.C.A. § 302(a) (1984). If the work in question is a work for hire (i.e. a work prepared by an employee for an employer within the scope of employment, or a work specially commissioned with a written agreement that the item is a "work for hire") or if it is anonymous or pseudonymous, the term of the copyright will be either 100 years from the date of creation or 75 years from the date of publication, which ever comes first. *Id.* § 302(c). There is a statutory presumption that, after 75 years from publication or 100 years from creation, which ever comes first, the author has been dead for fifty years and that the copyright has thus expired. This presumption can be defeated if anyone with an ownership interest files a statement providing relevant information about the status of the author. *Id.* § 302(e).

E. INFRINGEMENT

Copyright infringement is the unauthorized exercise of one of the rights that the statute reserves exclusively for the copyright owner. Usually, the infringement will involve unauthorized copying of the work, although it may involve unauthorized adaptation, vending, performance or display. In cases involving unauthorized copying, it will often be difficult to prove copying directly. Thus, in the typical case, the plaintiff will attempt to show that the defendant had access to the protected work and that the infringing item bears a substantial similarity to that protected work. This showing gives rise to an inference of unauthorized copying.

1. SUBSTANTIAL SIMILARITY

Only the "expressions" contained within a work are protected by copyright—anyone is free to copy the ideas. Copiable "ideas" include such things as historical facts or discoveries revealed by the author of a non-fictional work, or standard fictional ideas and characters used by a novelist. If an ordinary lay person would conclude that the defendant has appropriated non-trivial amounts of the plaintiff's expression, however, that establishes the type of similarity that is probative of copying and thus of infringement. Professor Nimmer, the author of the leading Copyright Treatise, has identified two types of substantial similarity— "comprehensive nonliteral similarity" and "fragmented literal similarity"—both of which suggest that copying has occurred.

a. Comprehensive Nonliteral Similarity

If the overall structure of the defendant's work has been copied from that of the plaintiff, the two works will be considered substantially similar, even though the exact same words are not used. Thus paraphrasing a protected work will not save the plagiarist from a finding of copyright infringement. Of course the copied structure must be sufficiently specific to constitute the particular expression of the author, not merely the general idea of the book. Whether that is true in any given case will require a subjective judgment. *Nichols v. Universal Pictures Corp.,* 45 F.2d 119 (2d Cir.1930).

Example: If an author chooses to premise a work on the notion of a wise cracking police officer who travels to a distant city to solve a difficult case, he would not infringe the copyright in the movie Beverly Hills Cop. However, if that author places the wise cracking police officer in Detroit, depicts him as a young black man, gives him a friend who is mysteriously killed during a visit to Detroit, has the cop travel to California to find his friend's murderer, has this cop initially challenged by, but then ultimately in alliance with, the local police who come to admire his ingenuity and are themselves relatively incompetent against serious criminals, makes the villain an extremely wealthy and well protected art dealer who is secretly involved in importing drugs, and closes the work with a shoot out at the villain's mansion, some courts might conclude that the work is a substantial copy of the movie Beverly Hills Cop. That is so even if not a single line of dialogue from the original has been appropriated.

b. Fragmented Literal Similarity

If some of the actual words (or notes, or images) of the copyright owner's work have been taken by the alleged infringer, similarity is clear. The sole question in such a case is the substantiality of that similarity. Substantiality is assessed by considering the importance of the part taken to the plaintiff's work as a whole, an obviously subjective standard.

c. Common Errors

Substantial similarity is important because it is circumstantial evidence of copying. Another indication of copying is the fact that the works of both the plaintiff and the defendant contain "common errors." Thus, if the protected work is factual in nature and contains a misstatement, a demonstration that the same misstatement appears in the defendant's work makes it highly likely that copying has occurred.

2. ACCESS

If the degree of similarity between the protected and allegedly infringing works is overwhelming, an inference of copying will be drawn without any demonstration that the defendant had access to the protected work. Where a lesser degree of similarity is involved, the plaintiff must prove that the defendant has some opportunity to view the protected work, in order to negate the inference that the similarity is due to coincidence. Where plaintiff's work has been published that may be adequate evidence of access by itself. A more specific showing of access will be required for an unpublished work.

3. INTENT

There is no intent requirement for copyright infringement. Thus inadvertent or even subconscious copying is actionable.

F. FAIR USE

Not every copying of a copyrighted work constitutes infringement. *The fair use doctrine immunizes certain conduct that would otherwise violate the copyright laws,* when allowing the conduct is deemed socially useful, consistent with the First Amendment and unlikely to undermine the economic interest of authors in their creations.

1. RELEVANT FACTORS

Prior to the 1976 copyright statute, the fair use doctrine was a common law concept, based on criteria identified in the cases. While the fair use doctrine continues to require ad hoc determinations about the equities of each particular case, the current statute sets out four factors that bear on the inquiry. 17 U.S. C.A. § 107 (1984).

a. Purpose and Character of Use

If the defendant's use of the work is commercial in nature, it is less likely to be classified as fair use. On the other hand, if the use of the work is private and non-commercial, it is much more likely to be considered fair use. Thus, home taping of copyrighted television programming for "time shifting" purposes was held to be fair use in *Sony Corp. of America v. Universal City Studios Inc.,* 464 U.S. 417, 104 S.Ct. 774 (1984), in part because it is private, non-commercial activity. Similarly, use of a work for purposes of scholarship or criticism makes a finding of fair use more probable.

b. Nature of the Copyrighted Work

When it is customary for the users of a given type of work to copy portions of it as part of the process of using it, the copying involved is likely to be classified as fair use. A book of forms is an example of such a work. Similarly, if a work is difficult to obtain from an authorized source—such as an out of print book—that might also make copying portions of the book "fair use." On the other hand, if a work is still in manuscript form and the author has publication plans that have not yet come to fruition, that would suggest that unauthorized uses of the work should not be considered fair. *Harper & Row Publishers v. Nation Enterprises,* ___ U.S. ___, 105 S.Ct. 2218 (1985).

c. Amount and Substantiality of Portion Used

The more of a protected work that is copied by an unauthorized user, the less likely it is that the copying is fair use. If the most important part of the work has been taken, that also points against a conclusion of fair use, even if the actual percentage involved is small.

d. Effect on Market for Copyrighted Work

In situations where defendant's copy either substitutes for, or destroys the value of, the plaintiff's work, the copying does not constitute fair use. For example, the copying of material from textbooks for distribution to students is not fair use because the author's intended market was the very same students who now have no need to buy the book. This factor has been described as the single most important aspect of the fair use inquiry.

Example: After leaving the White House, President Ford contracted with Harper & Row to publish his memoirs. Time magazine was also granted limited rights to publish excerpts from the forthcoming book. The most interesting aspect of the manuscript was

President Ford's analysis of the Nixon pardon. Prior to publication Nation magazine obtained a copy of the manuscript without authorization, and published a news story with numerous quotations about the pardon from the manuscript. Thereafter, Time cancelled its agreement to publish excerpts. When Harper & Row brought suit for infringement the Supreme Court rejected Nation's fair use defense, noting that the publication of the excerpts substantially undermined the value of the serialization rights that had been sold to Time. *Harper & Row Publishers v. Nation Enterprises*, ___ U.S. ___, 105 S.Ct. 2218 (1985).

2. PARODY AS FAIR USE

A satirist of literary, musical or dramatic works must obviously allude to the original in some way. Hence courts must consider whether and when use of copyrighted material for purposes of parody is fair use. In one famous case, where parallels with the original were close and numerous, the court concluded that the satirical or comedic purpose of the copying did not excuse the defendant and refused to find fair use. *Benny v. Loew's Inc.*, 239 F.2d 532 (9th Cir.1956) (Comedy sketch based on movie "Gaslight" held infringing). More recent cases, however, have allowed a fairly wide latitude for parody, permitting enough copying so that the satirist is able to "recall or conjure up" the original.

Example: During a skit on the television program Saturday Night Live satirizing the public relations efforts of New York City, actors purporting to be the civic leaders of the Biblical village of Sodom performed the copyrighted song "I Love New York" with the altered lyrics "I Love Sodom." This was held to be a fair use of the original musical composition and not actionable. *Elsmere Music, Inc. v. National Broadcasting Co.*, 482 F.Supp. 741 (S.D.N.Y.1980), *aff'd*, 623 F.2d 252 (2d Cir.1980).

G. REMEDIES

1. INJUNCTIVE RELIEF

An owner of a copyrighted work who proves infringement is entitled to an injunction that is "reasonable to prevent or restrain infringement." 17 U.S.C.A. § 502(a) (1984).

2. MONETARY RELIEF

A successful plaintiff may recover his or her own actual damages. If the defendant made a profit from the infringement of copyright, the plaintiff may also recover those profits to the extent that they are not included in computing the damages. The plaintiff has the option to seek "statutory damages" instead of actual damages and profits. Such damages will be an amount not less than $250 and not more than $10,000, as the court considers just. If the infringer is proven to have acted willfully, the statutory damage award may be as high as $50,000, and if the infringer can prove that he or she acted innocently, the statutory damage award may be reduced to not less than $100. The court may also award costs and attorney's fees to the prevailing party. 17 U.S.C.A. §§ 504, 505 (1984).

3. IMPOUNDMENT

The court may order all unauthorized copies, phonorecords, and manufacturing materials to be seized at any time during the pendancy of an infringement suit, and the final decree can provide for the destruction of such material. 17 U.S.C.A. § 503 (1984).

4. CRIMINAL SANCTIONS

If infringement is willful and for the purposes of "commercial advantage or private financial gain," the infringer may be subjected to criminal prosecution and punishment by imprisonment of up to one year and a maximum $10,000 fine. The criminal penalties for record and tape piracy are even more severe. The fraudulent use of, or removal of, a copyright notice are also criminal offenses. 17 U.S.C.A. § 506 (1984).

REVIEW QUESTIONS

1. **T or F** The term of a copyright is normally the life of the author plus fifty years.

2. **T or F** Copyright protects an author only against the literal copying of his words.

3. **T or F** Computer programs are copyrightable.

4. **T or F** Copyright registration is mandatory.

5. **T or F** The inadvertent omission of copyright notice from any copies of a work sold to the public will result in a forfeiture of all rights in that work.

6. **T or F** It is an infringement of the copyright of a composer of music to play a sound recording of the work on the radio without a license or other permission.

7. **T or F** Willful copyright infringement for commercial gain is a crime.

8. **T or F** Prior to the publication of a work, it is protected under state law by common law copyright.

9. **T or F** It is fair use for a book reviewer to quote brief passages from a novel that is protected by copyright.

10. **T or F** At common law, the performance of a play before a live paying audience did not constitute a publication.

11. **T or F** A playwright cannot create a play based on a copyrighted novel without the permission of the novel's author.

12. **T or F** A merchant may secure copyright protection for the trademarks used on its goods.

13. **T or F** If the defendant's work is a verbatim copy of plaintiff's copyrighted work, the plaintiff need not show access to its work in a copyright infringement suit.

14. **T or F** The plaintiff in a copyright infringement suit must prove that the defendant acted intentionally.

15. For which of the following could the creator *not* obtain copyright protection

   a. An abstract sculpture that does not depict a real world object.

   b. A novel way to build bookshelves, described in an article in a Home Repair Encyclopedia.

   c. A printed listing of all persons living within Chicago organized by the name of the street on which they live.

   d. A tape recording of the sounds made by a variety of different song birds.

16. Assuming each of the following activities is unauthorized by the creator of the work involved, which is most likely to be characterized as "fair use?"

   a. The author of a history of the American space program has quoted extensively from an unpublished diary kept by John Glenn when he was an astronaut that was secretly obtained from Glenn's housekeeper.

   b. A high school teacher has supplemented the reading for his course by distributing a photocopy of a chapter of a college text in the subject to his 30 students.

   c. A law professor preparing a law review article has reproduced verbatim a 6 page excerpt from a 20 page article previously written by another professor, the thesis of which he then goes on to attack.

d.   A comedy troupe has written new, vulgar lyrics to all the songs in the musical Fiddler On the Roof, and performs the work to paying audiences at a Greenwich Village nightclub in New York.

17.   Samuel Johnson admired the works of Shakespeare ever since he was a student.   As a hobby, he wrote "updated" versions of a number of Shakespeare's plays in the form of novels.   One of these, written in 1982, was based on Macbeth, but set in contemporary Glasgow, Scotland.   This novel followed the action of Shakespeare original exactly, but the dialogue was contemporary and the roles of the characters were changed to reflect modern times.   Thus, Macbeth was an ambitious member of Parliament from Scotland, the three witches were made over into three lobbyists, the King of Scotland was the Prime Minister of the modern day United Kingdom, etc.   Johnson never published this novel.

In 1984, Johnson inadvertently left a copy of his Macbeth novel on a plane while returning from a business trip.   This copy had Johnson's name and address typed plainly on the cover but did not bear any notice of copyright. It was found by Helen Smith, a high school English teacher.   She had always found it difficult to interest her students in Shakespeare and was fascinated by the Johnson work.   Over the next few weeks she wrote a play based on the Johnson novel.   The dialogue in the play was largely but not entirely copied from the Johnson novel.   A month later, she had her senior English class perform the play.   The performance was reported in a newspaper story. Thereafter, she received inquires from a number of teachers around the country who also wanted to put on the play.   She responded by offering to sell them copies of the play for $5 each.

The same newspaper story also came to Johnson's attention.   He is upset and has come to you for advice.   He wants to know if Ms. Smith is guilty of copyright infringement.   Is she?

*

IV

MISAPPROPRIATION

Analysis

A. Protection for Business Schemes
B. Protection for Intangible Stock in Trade
C. Protection for Celebrity's Fame
D. Pre-emption Problems

Many businesses or individuals create and own valuable intangible assets. Other firms may attempt to use these intangibles for their own benefit without the owner's consent. If the intangible involved is a trademark or copyright there are, as we have seen, detailed rules regulating use by other parties. As we shall see, the same is true for patents and trade secrets. Many intangibles, however, do not fall into one of these clearly defined categories. Where that is so, protection against an unauthorized taking of the intangible must be sought under the relatively amorphous heading of "common law misappropriation" or, in cases where the facts permit, some other contract or property theory. Because cases of this sort are heavily influenced by notions of proper commercial ethics, there is a significant subjective component to the decisions. Nonetheless, certain clear themes do emerge.

A. PROTECTION FOR BUSINESS SCHEMES

Creative individuals frequently have notions about how others could improve their business. Such concepts may consist of plot outlines for show business firms, themes for future advertising campaigns, or specific ideas as to how a manufacturing firm could improve product design and performance. Often the individuals with these ideas will approach the relevant business and try to convince it to "buy" the idea. The firm may be reluctant to do so, however, for a variety of reasons. Nonetheless, it may later wind up using what looks like the very idea that was offered to it. Many cases have thus addressed the question of when a business has "appropriated" an outsider's idea, and is thus obligated to pay for it.

1. ELEMENTS OF A PROTECTABLE BUSINESS SCHEME
Not every "idea" is entitled to judicial protection. Normally, *courts will only protect those ideas that are "concrete," "novel" and "useful."*

a. Concreteness
Disclosure of a general idea normally will not give rise to any obligation of payment on the part of the recipient. On the other hand, an idea need not be reduced to a completely detailed proposal in order to warrant protection. For instance, if an individual conceives of a new format for a radio program, he or she need not prepare a script for each show in order to render the idea concrete. *Hamilton National Bank v. Belt*, 210 F.2d 706 (D.C.Cir.1953).

b. Novelty
No matter how detailed it is, an idea that is already well known in a given field of business will not qualify for protection. Only novel ideas are protected, and novelty is a factual question for the jury. If the defendant can show that it independently generated the same idea prior to being told about it by the plaintiff, that will defeat plaintiff's claim that the idea was novel. *Downey v. General Foods Corp.*, 31 N.Y.2d 56, 334 N.Y.S.2d 874, 286 N.E.2d 257 (1972).

c.   Usefulness

An idea must be useful before courts will impose a duty to pay for it.   In most cases, however, the defendant will have actually used the idea in question, thus usefulness will be assumed.   Some courts do not require a showing of usefulness as a separate element of a protectable idea on the theory that any concrete and novel idea is necessarily useful.

2.   THEORIES FOR IMPOSING OBLIGATION TO PAY FOR IDEAS

When an idea meets the above tests and the defendant has used it, the remaining question is whether the defendant is liable to pay for the idea.   Analysis of that question differs depending on the legal theory asserted by the plaintiff.   A variety of different theories have been invoked by plaintiffs in this situation.

a.   Contractual Theories

Where the parties have entered into an explicit contract governing disclosure and use of the idea, the agreement will usually be enforced.   Where there is no express agreement, the most common judicial approach is to determine if the facts are such that a contract should be implied. Minniear v. Tors, 266 Cal.App. 2d 495, 72 Cal.Rptr. 287 (1968).   If the defendant received the idea without having solicited it and without any advance notice that the submission would be made—as is often true with suggestions mailed to large corporations—it is unlikely that an implied contract to pay for the idea will be found.

b.   Quasi-Contract

In many idea submission cases, no agreement to pay for use of the idea appears in an express contract, and none can be implied from the conduct of the parties.   Nonetheless, *some courts will impose a duty to pay if the equities of the situation require it to prevent unjust enrichment. Matarese v. Moore-McCormack Lines, Inc.,*   158 F.2d 631 (2d Cir.1946).

c.   Confidential Relationship

If the relationship between the party disclosing the idea and the party making use of it is such that the later has gained the confidence of the former and purports to act with his or her benefit in mind, the relationship will be considered confidential. *Where a confidential relationship is found, the party using the idea will be obliged to pay compensation for it.*

d.   Property

If a business scheme is classified as "property" no one else may use it without the owner's permission. A few courts have found that certain ideas constituted property, and that consequently businesses using them owed compensation to the individual who initially conceived of them.

3.   CORPORATE PRACTICE WITH UNSOLICITED IDEAS

Many corporations have adopted procedures to avoid inadvertent liability for idea appropriation with respect to unsolicited suggestions received in the mail.   One usual procedure involves segregation of such ideas in a separate part of the company, so that a claim of independent development of the idea by the company can be documented if necessary. Another common strategy is the use of standard "idea disclosure" forms in which the corporation states that compensation, if any, is in its sole discretion.

B. PROTECTION FOR INTANGIBLE STOCK IN TRADE

The idea appropriation scenario discussed above involves a situation where the intangible asset in question—the idea—is voluntarily disclosed by its creator to a limited audience who, it is expected, will make commercial use of it. The sole question is whether there should be a duty to pay for the idea. A different situation exists for the many businesses whose chief occupation is the creation of intangible items (such as information or entertainment) that are then sold to the public at large. Here, the exposure of the intangible is much more widespread, but it assumed that each party receiving it will only make private use of it. We can think of this situation as one where the intangible is the "inventory" or "stock in trade" of the creator, who makes money by selling it on a widespread basis. Of course, other parties may attempt to reproduce the intangible themselves and sell it in competition with the creator. The "misappropriation" doctrine attempts to define when such behavior will result in legal liability.

1. HISTORICAL FOUNDATIONS: THE *INS* CASE

The misappropriation doctrine derives from the Supreme Court's famous opinion in *International News Service v. Associated Press,* 248 U.S. 215, 39 S.Ct. 68 (1918).

a. Facts

The Associated Press was a wire service whose reporters gathered news and prepared stories that were printed in member newspapers. Copies of these newspapers were often posted on bulletin boards for the public to read. The defendant INS, a competing new service, regularly sent its employees to read these stories and then rewrite the information in their own words. INS then transmitted these stories to INS member papers throughout the U.S. Often, INS papers published important news stories before their competitors who subscribed to AP because of these practices, even though AP had expended the effort to get the story. AP was unable to allege copyright infringement since INS was careful not to use any of the actual "expressions" contained in the AP stories. Instead, they brought suit under the common law for "piracy" of "hot news." The Supreme Court held that the behavior was actionable, thus giving birth to the new tort of misappropriation.

b. Legal Status of *INS* Case

The *INS* case was a diversity case, decided before the decision in *Erie R.R. Co. v. Tompkins,* 304 U.S. 64, 58 S.Ct. 817 (1938). Thus it was based on "federal common law." With the decision in *Erie* federal common law ceased to have any vitality. Thus the *INS* case lacked any binding authority after 1938. Thereafter its importance was its persuasive value in convincing state courts to recognize misappropriation as a form of unfair competition.

2. ELEMENTS OF THE TORT

The general language of the *INS* opinion makes reducing it to a list of elements a difficult task. It appears, however, that *to recover for the tort of misappropriation, a plaintiff would have to show three elements: (1) that it created an intangible asset through the expenditure of effort and with the expectation of profit; (2) that defendant took that asset at comparatively little effort and made commercial use of it; and (3) that the taking by the defendant economically harmed the creator either by depriving it of a profit or otherwise.* (It should be noted that the sum expended by the defendant to *exploit* the intangible is irrelevant—the sole inquiry under the second element mentioned above is whether the defendant exerted *creative* effort to further develop or modify the intangible or merely took it as is). Some courts have held that the plaintiff and the defendant need not be competitors in order for a misappropriation remedy to lie, e.g., *Board of Trade v. Dow Jones & Co.,* 98 Ill. 2d 109, 74 Ill.Dec. 582, 456 N.E.2d 84 (1983), but other courts require it, *United States Golf Ass'n v. St. Andrews Systems,* 749 F.2d 1028 (3d Cir.1984) (applying New Jersey law). Many courts consider the key issue in misappropriation cases to be whether the defendant's activities are likely to destroy the incentives for plaintiff and others in its position to engage in the relevant productive or creative activities.

3. COMPARISON OF MISAPPROPRIATION AND PASSING OFF

Prior to the *INS* case, the typical form of unfair competition was "passing off"— that is, the sale of one's *own product* in such a way as to deceive the public into thinking that it was manufactured by someone else. *INS* represented the reverse of this pattern. There the defendant took and sold *a product created by its rival,* but did so under its own name. The case thus establishes that this variant of commercial behavior is also unfair. Note that this situation is unlikely to come up where a tangible product is involved. If a merchant takes its rival's tangible products without paying for them, it is a case of simple theft. It is because intangible assets can be simultaneously sold by many people that the *INS* situation seem unusual when first encountered. Nonetheless it, too, is nothing more than theft.

4. APPLICATIONS OF THE DOCTRINE

In the years immediately following the *INS* opinion, several opinions—notably those from the Second Circuit—gave the misappropriation doctrine a very limited effect. For instance, relief was denied for the unauthorized duplications of dress and hat designs. However, after the *Erie* decision, when misappropriation became a state law problem, the concept was treated more expansively by various jurisdictions in a wide variety of contexts. For instance, producers of live musical, dramatic and operatic performances used it to obtain relief against parties who made unauthorized recordings of performances and sold them in competition with official versions. Similarly, professional sports teams have successfully relied on the doctrine to enjoin unauthorized play-by-play broadcasts originating from buildings overlooking the stadium. Two recent cases found misappropriation where commodity exchanges created new types of futures contracts based on well known security indices such as the Dow Jones and the Standard & Poor's 500 Index. *Board of Trade v. Dow Jones & Co.,* 98 Ill.2d 109, 74 Ill.Dec. 582, 456 N.E.2d 84 (1983); *Standard & Poor's Corp. v. Commodity Exchange, Inc.,* 683 F.2d 704 (2d Cir.1982) (New York law).

C. PROTECTION FOR CELEBRITY'S FAME

Identification with, or evocation of, celebrities such as popular entertainers or athletes often assures a product's commercial success. This connection can be accomplished in a variety of ways. The celebrity's name or likeness can be used to identify the product. Alternatively, the product may prominently display the name or picture of the celebrity, as a tee-shirt or poster. The product might even consist of some or all of the celebrity's act, such as a videotape or sound recording. When merchants sell such products without permission of the celebrity involved, they may undermine that celebrity's marketing efforts and deprive him or her of economic rewards. Consequently many celebrities have sought to forbid such uses of their names, likenesses and performances.

1. RIGHT OF PUBLICITY: A "CONCLUSION" OR A SEPARATE TORT?
a. Elements for Publicity Claims
It is often said that a celebrity who is successful in preventing unauthorized use of his or her fame has vindicated his or her "Right of Publicity." While some courts have purported to recognize a new and discrete Right of Publicity, celebrities in this situation often must prove facts identified with one or more of three well established legal theories—(1) trademark infringement or passing off; (2) misappropriation; or (3) violation of privacy. Consequently, some have argued that even where "right of publicity" terminology is used by the courts, the right of publicity should be thought of as a "conclusion" that a famous plaintiff has proven a right to recover on some established theory and not as an independent doctrine. Goldstein, *Copyright, Patent, Trademark and Related State Doctrines,* 255 (2d ed. 1981). Others, however, view the right of publicity as independent of other unfair competition theories and distinct from conventional privacy claims. In this view, the Right of Publicity is violated if another makes "unpermitted use of plaintiff's name, likeness, persona or identity for commercial purposes." McCarthy, *Trademarks and Unfair Competition* § 10.21(A) (2d ed. 1984).

b. Relationship of Privacy and Publicity
In some jurisdictions, privacy principles flow from the common law, while elsewhere, such as in New York, they are statutory. The range of behaviors condemned under the rubric of "invasion of privacy" varies from state to state.

Some states include the "appropriation of names or likenesses" without consent as a privacy invasion while other do not. Where a state has historically followed a narrow definition of the right of privacy, its courts are more likely to speak in terms of a right of "publicity" when they grant relief to a celebrity who has challenged the unauthorized use of his or her name or likeness. On the other hand, in those states where this type of behavior is considered a species of invasion of privacy, the courts are likely to grant relief without using "publicity" terminology. *Stephano v. News Group Publications,* 64 N.Y.2d 174, 485 N.Y.S.2d 220, 474 N.E.2d 580 (1984) (No right of publicity in New York independent of statutory right of privacy).

> ***Example:*** When football player Elroy "Crazylegs" Hirsch learned that a cosmetics company was marketing a shaving gel under the trademark "Crazylegs," he brought suit under two theories— appropriation of his name for commercial purposes and common law trademark infringement. Although Wisconsin did not recognize any common law privacy rights at the time of the case, the Supreme Court of that state held that Hirsch had stated a valid cause of action on both theories. In sustaining the first cause of action the court indicated that, in its view, the Right of Publicity was separate from the traditional Right of Privacy. *Hirsch v. S. C. Johnson & Son,* 90 Wis.2d 379, 280 N.W.2d 129 (1979).

2. THE "HYBRID" NATURE OF PUBLICITY CLAIMS

Publicity claims often proceed simultaneously under several of the theories identified above because, in most situations, the case has aspects of passing off, of misappropriation and of invasion of privacy at the same time. The passing off occurs because the use of the celebrity's name may serve as an (inaccurate) identification of source or sponsorship to consumers. Misappropriation occurs because the defendant is capitalizing on the fame that the celebrity has built up through great effort. Invasion of privacy is implicated because the defendant may be using an intimate aspect of the plaintiff's personality without permission. Thus, the defendant simultaneously violates several interests of the celebrity.

> ***Example:*** When a merchant sells a John Travolta poster without permission consumers may believe that it is sponsored or licensed by Travolta, and buy it because they view that fact as some representation of product authenticity or quality. Second, the poster is valuable only because Travolta has, through his talents, such as they are, developed a loyal following of fans who want Travolta memorabilia. The popularity of Travolta is an intangible asset created by him, but being sold without permission by the defendant. In addition, the poster violates a privacy interest of Travolta because he may not wish to have his likeness vended in this fashion.

3. WHO MAY ASSERT A "PUBLICITY" CLAIM

Most cases involving the unauthorized use of some aspect of a famous individual's personality have involved entertainers or athletes. Thus claims have been pursued by parties representing Elvis Presley, Groucho Marx, Bela Lugosi, Muhammad Ali, Arnold Palmer and football player "Crazylegs" Hirsch. However, celebrated individuals from all walks of life may be able to prevent others from using their name, likeness or other attributes on commercial products, if they can satisfy the elements of one of the theories identified above. Of course, non-famous persons can usually prevent the use of their name and likeness for commercial purposes by relying on the right of privacy.

Example: Representatives of Martin Luther King brought suit to prevent the sale of souvenir busts of the civil rights leader by an unauthorized seller. Stating that there was no reason "why a public figure prominent in religion and civil rights should be entitled to less protection than an exotic dancer or a movie actress," the Supreme Court of Georgia held that the plaintiffs had a valid cause of action. *Martin Luther King, Jr., v. American Heritage Products,* 250 Ga. 135, 296 S.E.2d 697 (1982).

4. FIRST AMENDMENT LIMITS ON CELEBRITY'S RIGHTS

The right of a celebrated person to prevent unauthorized use of aspects of his personality is not unlimited. If the defendant's activities implicate First Amendment values, the celebrity will not be permitted to interfere. Thus, several courts have held that the preparation of an unauthorized biography does not violate any "publicity" interest of the subject of the biography. On the other hand, the First Amendment will not shield a party—even the news media—from liability where that party takes the entirety of an entertainer's act without consent and thereby destroys its economic value. *Zacchini v. Scripps-Howard Broadcasting Co.,* 433 U.S. 562, 97 S.Ct. 2849 (1977).

5. DESCENDABILITY

One of the most difficult aspects of suits brought by the heirs of famous persons against parties engaged in unauthorized activities has been whether the rights of the celebrity survive death. Different courts have resolved the questions differently.

a. Narrow View—Rights Terminate on Death

Some courts have held that the right to preclude others from capitalizing on the fame of a celebrity ends when the celebrity dies. This is the result that would be expected if the theoretical basis of protection for the celebrity is held to be principally the law of privacy, because privacy rights are generally viewed to terminate on death. One of the leading cases appearing to take this view is *Lugosi v. Universal Pictures,* 25 Cal.3d 813, 160 Cal.Rptr. 323, 603 P.2d 425 (1979).

b. Intermediate View—Descendable If Exploited

Other courts have held that the heirs of a celebrity may be able to prevent others from capitalizing on his or her fame IF the celebrity took steps to exploit that fame during his or her lifetime. This approach is consistent with a trademark theory of protection, since the exploitation requirement is analogous to the requirement of secondary meaning, required before certain trademarks will be protected. The amount and nature of exploitation demanded by different jurisdictions varies, and the law on this point is still in a formative stage. However, more exploitation is likely to be required where the deceased party's fame did not derive from profit making activities—such as where he or she was a famous military hero or astronaut—than where he or she was an entertainer or athlete.

c. Broad View—Descendable Regardless of Exploitation

Still other courts have taken the position that the right to preclude unauthorized commercial uses of the famous attributes of a deceased person will survive that person's death regardless of whether or not the fame was exploited during life. This approach is consistent with viewing the "publicity" claim as a species of misappropriation, since once the valuable intangible of "fame" has been created, it is a property right that is transferable on death just like any other property.

d. Duration Of Rights After Death

Those courts that recognize some rights as enduring after the celebrity dies have not suggested precisely how long those rights last. One dissenting opinion suggested borrowing the copyright statute's provisions on duration, which would mean terminating the protection 50 years after death, *Lugosi v. Universal Pictures,* 25 Cal.3d 813, 160 Cal.Rptr. 323, 603 P.2d 425 (1979) (Bird, C.J. dissenting), but that remains merely a suggestion. No clear rule has emerged on this point. As one leading treatise notes: "At the moment, state law on duration of the right of publicity is a fuzzy patch-work quilt of conflicting and confusing decisions." McCarthy, Trademarks and Unfair Competition § 10:21(E) (2d ed. 1984).

D. PRE-EMPTION PROBLEMS

To the extent that state law attempts to protect intangible business assets that have intrinsic value, it resembles federal copyright law. If the states provide a broader scope of protection than the federal statute, there is a question of whether Congress intended to leave certain intangibles unprotected, and thus freely copiable. If so, the state law—whether embodied in a statute or in cases—is pre-empted and must give way under the Supremacy clause of the Constitution.

1. SECTION 301 OF THE COPYRIGHT STATUTE

Congress explicitly addressed the question of pre-emption in preparing the revised copyright statute enacted in 1976. Section 301 of that statute spells out what types of state remedies are no longer allowed. Under that section, a state doctrine is pre-empted if it grants rights equivalent to one of the five exclusive rights provided by the copyright statute to intangible assets that are within the statutorily defined subject matter of copyright. *If the intangible protected by the state is not within the subject matter of copyright OR if the rights conferred are different than those itemized by that statute, the state law is not pre-empted and may co-exist with the copyright statute.*

a. Protection of Subject Matter Not Within Copyright

The subject matter of copyright includes all works of authorship fixed in tangible media of expression. (See Section A of Chapter III above). States may protect any intangibles *not* within this definition. Thus, since the misappropriation doctrine is usually invoked to protect ephemeral intangibles that have not been "fixed," such as live performances, it is not pre-empted by federal law. There is language in the legislative history of Section 301 indicating that this was the result intended by the Congress, although that history is somewhat ambiguous.

Example: Assume that under the common law of State X, it would be actionable misappropriation to make a videotape of a high school basketball game (not being broadcast to the general public) and sell that tape for profit. Because the game itself is not within the subject matter of copyright (i.e. it is not a work of authorship fixed in a tangible medium of expression), the state remedy is not pre-empted. The "thing" being protected is not a copyrightable thing, and thus section 301 does not apply.

b. Granting Rights Not Provided by Copyright

The copyright statute confers five types of exclusive rights on the creator of a work of authorship fixed in a tangible medium of expression. (See Section D of Chapter III above). If a state remedy gives the creator of an intangible some *other* right, different from those five itemized in the federal statute, it is not pre-empted.

Example: Assume State Y enacts a statute granting painters the right to enjoin anyone who exhibits their work in public from altering or changing the work in any way. The right to prevent alteration of artistic works is *not* one of the rights granted by the federal law. Consequently this statute is not pre-empted. Note that this is true even though the subject matter involved—paintings—is clearly within the subject matter of copyright.

c. Practical Effect of Section 301

The principal effect of the pre-emption provision of the copyright statute is to abolish so called "common law copyright." If a work is of the type that could be protected by federal copyright, the only way for the creator to protect against copying or unauthorized performance or exhibition is to observe the requirements of the federal statute.

Example: Author has just completed the manuscript of a new novel, which he has left on his desk. Sneak, the cleaning person at Author's office, makes a photocopy of the novel and immediately thereafter publishes it. Author sues Sneak under state law for misappropriation. Sneak defends by claiming that the state cause of action is pre-empted. Sneak will win. The subject matter here—a novel—is within the scope of copyright. The rights involved—the exclusive privileges to make and sell copies—are also within the rights guaranteed by the copyright statute. Thus, the state remedy is pre-empted. If Author desires any relief he must seek remedies against Sneak by obtaining a federal copyright registration and then bringing suit under the federal statute. Note that Sneak's behavior here would have been actionable under state law *prior to 1976* as a violation of Author's common law copyright.

2. PRE-EMPTION ANALYSIS BEFORE THE 1976 STATUTE

a. 1964 to 1972

Prior to 1976, the Copyright statute did not have a provision dealing explicitly with the scope of federal pre-emption. In the face of this legislative silence, some courts assumed that Congress desired individuals to be free to copy any intangible that was not protected by the copyright statute. This was an "either/or" approach to pre-emption—either the item in question was protected by the federal law or it was designed by Congress to be available for all. There was no middle ground left for state law. *Columbia Broadcasting System v. DeCosta*, 377 F.2d 315 (1st Cir.1967). This approach was patterned on the Supreme Court's opinions in *Sears, Roebuck & Co. v. Stiffel Co.*, 376 U.S. 225, 84 S.Ct. 784 (1964) and *Compco Corp. v. Day-Brite Lighting, Inc.*, 376 U.S. 234, 84 S.Ct. 779 (1964), which used a similar type of "either/or" analysis in holding that state trademark protection for shapes and configurations was pre-empted by the federal patent statute.

b. The *Goldstein* opinion

In *Goldstein v. California*, 412 U.S. 546, 93 S.Ct. 2303 (1973), the Supreme Court rejected the "either/or" approach to pre-emption analysis insofar as the copyright act was concerned. In that case, the Court held that some items not within the scope of copyrightable subject matter were intangibles about which Congress did not have strong feelings. As to these kinds of creations, the Court concluded that the states were free to provide such protection as they each saw fit. Thus, a California "record piracy" statute forbidding the duplication of sound recordings that, at the time, were not protected by copyright, was upheld. This approach to pre-emption was effectively codified in § 301 of the copyright law, discussed above.

REVIEW QUESTIONS

1. **T or F** The misappropriation doctrine of the *INS* case is applicable in all jurisdictions as binding Supreme Court precedent.

2. **T or F** There is no judicial consensus on the duration of a celebrity's so called "right of publicity."

3. **T or F** The news media enjoy an absolute First Amendment privilege to report and depict the acts of celebrities and performers without incurring any liability for misappropriation.

4. **T or F** Misappropriation is likely to be found if the defendant's conduct destroys the incentive for persons in the plaintiff's position to engage in creative activity.

5. **T or F** A party conceiving a new business scheme and revealing it to another may only be compensated if an express contract for payment exists.

6. **T or F** Mother Teresa would not have any valid causes of action against a novelty company selling buttons with her likeness because her fame does not derive from profit making activities.

7. **T or F** The duration of the rights of a celebrity to prevent unauthorized uses of name and likeness will probably be longer in a jurisdiction relying on a privacy theory to protect such rights than in a jurisdiction relying on a misappropriation theory.

8. **T or F** A firm may not recover for misappropriation in any jurisdiction unless it and the defendant are direct competitors.

9. **T or F** A party is unlikely to be compensated for revealing a business scheme or idea to another unless the idea is novel, concrete and useful.

10. **T or F** Businesses can minimize the risk of liability for use of unsolicited ideas by routing all such ideas to their research and development departments.

11. In which of the following situations is a state cause of action most likely to be pre-empted by the copyright statute?

a. Alpha attends an outdoor rock concert given by several well known musical groups. This concert was not broadcast. While at the concert, Alpha takes several dozen photographs, and thereafter, without permission of the musicians, publishes a "souvenir book" where many of these photographs are reproduced. Some of the musicians have filed suit under state law.

b. Beta is a sculptor living and working in State X. Beta sells a work to an art gallery for $1000, which thereafter resells it to a collector for $2000. State X has a statute providing that an artist shall receive 10% of the profit on the resale of a work of art by a gallery. Beta brings suit in state court to recover $100.

c. Gamma operates a store leasing video cassettes. There is a small 50-seat auditorium in the store where patrons may "preview" cassettes. An admission fee of $1.00 is charged and different movies are played throughout the day. Customers may remain in the auditorium as long as they like. A movie studio has invoked state misappropriation theory to enjoin this practice.

d. Delta approached executives of a television network and told them that she had an idea for a new television series. They promised to consider the idea if she put it in writing and indicated that they would pay her if they used the concept. Thereafter she prepared a 6 page memorandum detailing the features of her proposed new show and mailed it to the network. Although she has heard nothing further from the network, a new show introduced this season bears a strong resemblance to the one outlined in her memorandum. Delta has filed suit for breach of an implied-in-fact contract under state law.

12. Which of the following parties is least likely to be able to prevent the described use of his name or likeness?

a. A minor league baseball player, upset that a local merchant is selling beer under a trademark resembling the player's name.

b. A U.S. Senator, upset that a leading merchant has published a critical pamphlet about him containing a number of pictures of the Senator alongside well known organized crime figures.

c. A Roman Catholic archbishop, upset that a souvenir shop across from the cathedral is selling picture post-cards bearing his portrait.

d. A law school professor, upset that the student government is selling cup-cakes with her name written in icing on the tops.

13. The Cleveland World's Fair Corp. (or CWF) was formed in 1980 by civic and business leaders to organize and put on a world's fair in Cleveland in 1984. The theme of the fair was to be "The Joys of Lesser Known Cities." CWF began contacting numerous mayors around the world to solicit their participation, and secured participation commitments from some 28 cities, including Manchester, England; Rouen, France; Mannheim, Germany; Gudalajara, Mexico; and Bratislava, Czechoslavakia. Each city undertook to build a unique and architecturally interesting pavillion on the fairgrounds in suburban Cleveland, and by 1982 construction had begun.

To insure the financial success of the project, CWF granted numerous exclusive licenses and concessions to a variety of firms. Included among these licenses was one granted to Acme Publishing, giving it the sole rights to make picture postcards of the Fair's buildings and grounds and to sell those at the Fair. The Fair opened as scheduled in 1984 and even with steep ticket prices of $12 for adults and $8 for children, it was a big hit. A strong demand for memorabilia and souvenirs of all sorts developed almost immediately after the Fair opened.

Louie Lenscap, an accomplished amateur photographer, visited the fair on opening day and was struck with the interesting appearance of the buildings. He returned on each of the next 5 days and took many hundreds of pictures of the various pavillions in various lighting conditions. He then selected the 15 most attractive snapshots and used them to make picture postcards, which he sold to a variety of downtown and suburban Cleveland stores with a considerable degree of success.

CWF has learned of Louie's activities and has consulted you. They would like to file a suit in Ohio state court for common law misappropriation, but first want your assessment of their chances for success. Is Louie guilty of misappropriation?

V

PATENTS

Analysis

Patents, like copyrights, seek to encourage desirable creative activity by rewarding the creators of certain types of valuable intangibles with limited monopolies. Patent law assumes that the prospect of this reward acts as an incentive to inventors. Patent law also seeks to increase society's level of knowledge by demanding disclosure of inventions as the price for the valuable exclusive rights that are conferred by a patent. Like copyright law, patent doctrine derives exclusively from federal statute, which in turn implements a direct constitutional provision. Unlike copyright law, which merely forbids copying, patent law guarantees the holder of a patent the exclusive right to make, use and sell his or her invention for the statutory period of 17 years.

Patents are available for only specified categories of subject matter that meet the three statutory tests of novelty, non-obviousness and utility. Moreover, patents will only issue if the inventor observes a variety of procedural requirements imposed by the statute. Even after a patent issues, it may be judicially challenged and held invalid.

A. TYPES OF PATENTS

The patent statute provides for three types of patents—utility patents, design patents, and plant patents. Each has different requirements and different attributes. The three types are briefly explained below. The balance of this chapter focuses exclusively on utility patents.

1. UTILITY PATENTS

A utility patent is the type of patent most laypersons are likely to envision when they think of patent law. The great bulk of patents issued are, in fact, of this type. A utility patent is granted to an *invention* falling within the subject matter and meeting the standards that are discussed in the following sections. Because of space limitations, this chapter deals solely with utility patents.

2. DESIGN PATENTS

The patent law also provides for protection of certain designs for articles of manufacture. 35 U.S.C.A. § 171 (1984). The subject of protection here is the unique *appearance* of the object involved. Some material that is eligible for design patent protection may also be copyrightable. The term of a design patent is only 14 years, not 17 years as in the case of a utility patent.

3. PLANT PATENTS

The inventor of a new variety of asexually reproducing plant may also secure patent protection. 35 U.S.C.A. § 161 (1984). If the new plant is sexually reproduced—in other words, grows from seeds—protection similar to that of a patent is available under the Plant Variety Protection Act of 1970, 7 U.S.C.A. § 2321 (1984).

B. PATENTABLE SUBJECT MATTER

The federal patent statute specifically itemizes the types of patentable subject matter. Generally, *utility patents may be obtained on three categories of products— machines, articles of manufacture, and compositions of matter—as well as on processes. They may also be obtained on any new and useful improvement on an item falling into one of these four categories.* 35 U.S.C.A. § 101 (1984). It is important to note two points at the outset, however. First, not all items within these categories are patentable. Any particular item must also satisfy the further requirements of novelty, utility, and non-obviousness, that are discussed in the following sections of this chapter. Second, these categories have been limited by judicial interpretations that declare certain things to be unpatentable subject matter.

1. MACHINES
A machine is any device or apparatus consisting of a multitude of parts that function together to achieve a particular result. Both automatic and hand operated devices are comprehended within this category. Moreover, the category of machines includes both wholly new devices and sub-units designed to work together with larger, pre-existing machines.

2. COMPOSITIONS OF MATTER
Compositions of matter are mixtures or combinations of naturally occurring substances that have properties different from those of their ingredients. The most obvious examples are new chemicals, pharmaceutical drugs, or metallic alloys. Even unstable, transitory intermediate chemical products are within this category. *In re Breslow,* 616 F.2d 516 (C.C.P.A.1980).

3. MANUFACTURES
Any item that is "man-made" and not naturally occurring and is neither a machine nor a composition of matter is considered an article of manufacture. Thus, this is a residual category. The identifying attribute of an article of manufacture is that it is made by human action and consequently the term has been interpreted to include even items such as bridges and buildings.

4. PROCESSES
The U.S. Supreme Court has defined a process as "a mode of treatment of certain materials to produce a given result. It is an act, or a series of acts, performed upon the subject-matter to be transformed and reduced to a different state or thing." *Cochrane v. Deener,* 94 U.S. (4 Otto) 780 (1877). In other words, a *process is a way of doing something. The patentable subject matter here is not the result of the process, but the actual method or steps involved in achieving that result.*

5. UNPATENTABLE MATERIAL

A number of items that, at first blush, appear to fall within one of the four foregoing categories, have been held by the courts to be outside the scope of patentable subject matter.

a.   Printed Material

Although arguably within the concept of an "article of manufacture," *printed matter, such as a business form, is not eligible for patent protection.* There is an exception, however, if printed matter is involved in an invention that derives its chief creative value from its physical arrangement or structure rather than from the content of the printing.

Example: A novel arrangement for a book of tickets is patentable even though it incorporates printed material (the tickets) because its inventive elements flow from how the tickets are arranged rather than from what is printed on the tickets.

b.   Products of Nature

Since *a naturally occurring substance is* not a machine, manufacture, or composition of matter, it is *not patentable.* Thus, the first individual to discover a new element or micro-organism cannot obtain patent protection. In *Funk Bros. Seed Co. v. Kalo Inoculant Co.,* 333 U.S. 127, 68 S.Ct. 440 (1948), the Supreme Court denied patent protection for a new mixture of bacterial cultures to be used as a plant inoculant because the ability of the various strains in the combination to co-exist without inhibiting the effects of each other was merely the "work of nature." This result has been criticized as carrying the definition of a "product of nature" too far. Of course, human-made elements and even human-engineered living organisms are proper subject matters for patents. *Diamond v. Chakrabarty,* 447 U.S. 303, 101 S.Ct. 2204 (1980).

c.   Laws of Nature and Natural Phenomena

Just as the discovery of a naturally occurring substance does not entitle the discoverer to patent protection, *the unravelling of a mystery of nature does not permit the genius who unlocks the secret to apply for a patent.* Thus, it is often pointed out that Einstein could not have patented the formula $E = mc^2$ nor Newton the laws of gravity. A mere idea is not patentable, just as it is not copyrightable. On the other hand, a process that incorporates a recently discovered natural principle remains patentable.

Examples: When Samuel B. Morse sought a patent for his telegraph, one of the claims in his application appeared to seek exclusive rights for *any* device using electromagnetism to communicate over distances. To grant a patent on such a claim would have been tantamount to giving Morse a patent on electro-magnetism. Consequently, this claim was disallowed. *O'Reilly v. Morse,* 56 U.S. (15 How.)

62 (1854).   However, when an inventor incorporated the discovery that fatty substances could be separated into their component elements through the use of water alone under high heat and pressure, into a specific new *process* for treating fats and oils, the patent was upheld. *Tilghman v. Proctor,* 102 U.S. 707 (12 Otto) (1880).

d.   Mathematical Formulas and Computer Programs

Mathematical formulas or algorithms, as they are sometimes called, *are similar to natural principles and hence not proper subject matter for patents.*   Because computer programs operate on mathematical bases but are often used to implement industrial processes, the courts have struggled with their patentability.   While noting that the "line between a patentable 'process' and an unpatentable 'principle' does not always shimmer with clarity," the Supreme Court denied a patent for a mathematical method for updating "alarm limits" in *Parker v. Flook,* 437 U.S. 584, 98 S.Ct. 2522 (1978) (Alarm limits are numbers indicating maximum safe levels of temperature, pressure, etc. during a chemical process.   During phases of the process, the limit may need to be recalculated, or "updated.").   However, where a process for molding and curing synthetic rubber utilized mathematical equations and computer programming in several of its steps, *Parker* was distinguished and patent protection was allowed.   *Diamond v. Diehr,* 450 U.S. 175, 101 S.Ct. 1048 (1981).   Thus, while computer programs by themselves are not patentable inventions, new methods of manufacturing that use programs will be patentable.   As the copyrightability of computer programs has become increasingly clear, the unavailability of patent protection for programs unrelated to processes has become a less significant issue for both the courts and the computer industry.

e.   Business Methods

Methods of carrying out business and systems of bookkeeping or record keeping have been held to fall outside the scope of patentable subject matter.

Example: A system to prevent fraud by hotel and restaurant waiters and cashiers is not patentable even if never before used by others in the field. *Hotel Security Checking Co. v. Lorraine Co.,*   160 F. 467 (2d Cir.1908).

f.   The "Function of an Apparatus"

The inventor of a new machine that produces a new and useful result cannot claim patent protection for the result. However, if the only way of achieving a particular result is through a series of steps that will be executed by a patentable machine, the series of steps is potentially also patentable—as a process—despite the "function of an apparatus" doctrine. *In re Zoltan Tarezy-Hornoch,* 397 F.2d 856 (C.C.P.A.1968).

Example: If one invented a machine that, when placed against the body, eliminated cancerous cells, that machine would surely be patentable. However, the inventor could not secure protection for all methods of curing cancer (i.e., the function of his apparatus here). The patent would be solely for this particular machine.

g.   New Uses of Old Products
One cannot secure a patent for discovering that an already existing product has new uses that were previously unrecognized. Thus, if one were to discover that a roof sealing compound used to repair leaks will, when rubbed on the scalp, cure baldness, this discovery is not patentable.

C.   THE REQUIREMENT OF NOVELTY

The Constitution empowers the Congress to grant patents for inventions. The term "inventions" naturally implies that the item in question is new, different, and a departure from what has come before. If patent applicants did not have to demonstrate that their inventions were previously unknown, they would actually be able to withdraw information from the public domain by securing patents on previously known objects and processes. This notion is carried forward into the patent statute by its requirement that a patent will only issue if the applicant can demonstrate the novelty of his or her invention. 35 U.S.C.A. § 102 (1984).

1.   NOTE ON TERMINOLOGY
Section 102 of the patent statute itemizes a number of events that will defeat patentability. Some of those (subsections (a), (e), and (g)) are events that may have occurred before the applicant invented the item in question. This outline refers to those events as raising problems of "novelty" and deals with those issues in this section. Other portions of section 102 (subsection (b) and (d)) deal with events that occur after the date of invention but prior to the date of filing of a patent application. This outline refers to those events as raising problems of "statutory bar" and treats them in the following section. Some judicial and academic writers, however, refer to *both* types of events as raising issues of "novelty." Similarly, some writers use the term "anticipation" to refer only to events that defeat novelty, while other writers and most courts use the term "anticipation" to refer *both* to events that defeat novelty and to events that trigger statutory bar. The best guide to how a writer is using a certain term is to note which subsection of section 102 is at issue.

2.   DOMESTIC EVENTS DEFEATING NOVELTY
If someone conceived of the invention in question before the patent applicant did so, and shared that new conception with the world, the invention has been "anticipated." This will defeat the applicant's claim of novelty and preclude a patent from issuing because something is not "novel" or an "invention" if someone else already thought of it and began to publicize it. The occurrence of any of four

events *in this country* will destroy the applicant's showing of novelty: *If the invention was (1) patented, (2) described in a printed publication, (3) known by others or (4) used by others before it was invented by this applicant it is not novel.* 35 U.S. C.A. § 102(a), (1984).

Example: On March 1, 1984, Prof. Pepperwinkle, a noted scientist living in Bangor, Maine, invented a type of eyeglasses that gives the wearer "X-ray vision." Unbeknownst to him, however, an article appeared in the January, 1984 issue of Hawaiian Optometrist magazine describing how to make the same type of glasses. Consequently, Prof. Pepperwinkle's invention lacks novelty and he may not secure a patent.

3.   FOREIGN EVENTS DEFEATING NOVELTY

If the invention in question was either patented abroad, or described in an available printed publication abroad, that will also destroy the required showing of novelty. Note that both of these foreign forms of anticipation are "documentary" in nature. Where foreign activity is at issue, only a written revelation of the principles of the invention will destroy the applicant's claim of novelty—conduct abroad is not considered.

4.   SINGLE SOURCE WITH AN ENABLING DISCLOSURE

For an invention to be anticipated by a documentary source, that single source must disclose all of the elements of the claimed invention. Shanklin Corp. v. Springfield Photo Mount, 521 F.2d 609 (1st Cir.1975). In other words, the reference in question must, by itself, enable one skilled in the relevant art, to make the invention. This same notion is also captured by the observation that "that which infringes, if later, anticipates, if earlier." *Shields v. Halliburton Co.,* 667 F.2d 1232 (5th Cir.1982). Mere speculation in print about a hypothetical new product or machine, however, without any indication of how it might be made or built, is not an anticipation.

5.   USE OR KNOWLEDGE ACCESSIBLE TO THE PUBLIC

If the alleged anticipation of an invention flows from the use of or knowledge about it by another party in this country, the use or knowledge must be publicly available. An earlier secret use by another of the item the applicant seeks to patent does not constitute anticipation. *Gayler v. Wilder,* 51 U.S. (10 How.) 477 (1850); *Gillman v. Stern,* 114 F.2d 28 (2d Cir.1940). However, so long as there were no affirmative steps to conceal the earlier use of the item, ordinary use of the device is sufficient to constitute anticipation even if that ordinary use does not result in the item being very widely publicized. *Rosaire v. Baroid Sales Division,* 218 F.2d 72 (5th Cir.1955). Use or knowledge of the invention in a foreign country does *not* constitute anticipation.

6.   ACCIDENTAL RESULTS DO NOT DESTROY NOVELTY

If novelty is challenged on the grounds that the invention was previously used by others, the parties engaged in that prior use must have been consciously aware of the invention and its merits. *Accidental and unappreciated use of the technology will not defeat novelty,* largely because there is no guarantee that casual results of this sort can be duplicated. In effect, the process that achieves the result remains undiscovered so long as those using it are unaware of it and how to replicate it. The key factor is that the earlier result was unintended and unappreciated.

7. PRIORITY AND DILIGENCE

The patent statute provides that a patent will not issue if "before the applicant's invention thereof the invention was made in this country by another who had not abandoned, suppressed, or concealed it." 35 U.S.C.A. § 102(g) (1984). *The right to a patent is thus limited to the first party to invent* —the senior inventor (who is not necessarily the first person to file for a patent). When there is a dispute over who is the senior inventor and two parties both claim that status, the patent office will declare an "interference" to resolve that factual question. The strict chronological approach to priority of invention is modified in one respect, however. If the junior inventor can show that, although he or she did not think of the invention first, he or she was the first to reduce it to practice, and can also demonstrate that the senior inventor failed to act with continuous diligence to perfect and patent the invention, then the junior inventor will be entitled to the patent.

D. STATUTORY BAR

The patent laws seek to encourage inventors to promptly patent their inventions. The sooner the patent is issued, the sooner the technology revealed by the invention will become available to the public. To implement this objective, the patent statute has provisions designed to encourage prompt application. The chief effect of these provisions is to deny a patent to any party who has delayed for more than one year between the time of invention and time of filing of a patent application if certain events have occurred outside of the one year grace period. 35 U.S.C.A. § 102(b) (1984).

1. EVENTS GIVING RISE TO STATUTORY BAR

Several events will bar the inventor from securing a patent regardless of whether other conditions for patentability have been satisfied. *A patent will be denied if (1) the invention was patented here or abroad more than one year before the present application was filed; (2) the invention was described in a printed publication here or abroad more than one year before the present application; (3) the invention was in public use or on sale more than one year before the present application; (4) the applicant for the patent has, at any time, abandoned the invention.* Note that the first three penalize delay in filing a patent application. The first and the fourth of these grounds are largely self-explanatory. The following material highlights some important aspects of the second and third itemized grounds.

a.   Description in Publications

If a device or process was described in a printed publication after applicant invented it but more than a year before applicant filed for the patent, the right to the patent has been lost. The publication, however, must be an "enabling disclosure." In other words, just like a source that destroys novelty, *a written source that creates a statutory bar is one that, by itself, permits one skilled in the art to make the invention.*

b.   The Concept of Public Use

Although the statute speaks in terms of "public use," relatively little publicity is required to trigger this provision. A use may be "public" even if only one of the patented articles has actually been used and even if the invention is hidden from public view while being used, provided that is the natural and intended way for the product to be used.

Example: In 1855 Barnes invented new, unbreakable corset springs, which he gave to two female friends, one of whom he eventually married. The ladies thereafter used these corset springs regularly, and in 1863 Barnes actually demonstrated the corset springs to another individual. Barnes finally secured a patent in 1866. The patent was thereafter held void on the grounds that the invention had been in "public" use for more than the permissible time. *Egbert v. Lippmann,* 104 U.S. (14 Otto) 333 (1881).

c.   Secret Use By the Patent Applicant

An inventor may make secret use of a new device or process for a considerable time before seeking patent protection. Such activity constitutes a "public use," for purposes of applying the statutory bar provisions of the patent act. Thus the inventor must apply for a patent within one year after beginning his or her own use of the invention or else all rights will be lost.

Example: An inventor who conceived of a new process to build up the metal on worn machine parts applied for a patent in August 1942. The patentee had been making use of this process in his shop under secret conditions from a date prior to August 1941. This was held to be a "public use" of the process (occurring more than one year before the application) rendering the patent invalid. *Metallizing Engineering Co. v. Kenyon Bearing & Auto Parts Co.,* 153 F.2d 516 (2d Cir.1946).

d.   Experimental Use

If the inventor engages in acts that constitute public use as part of genuine efforts to conduct experiments designed to develop or perfect the invention, statutory bar will not be predicated on those acts. Use of the invention to determine if it has sufficient commercial value to justify applying for a patent is also considered "experimental" and thus not a basis for statutory bar. *Cali v. Eastern Airlines, Inc.*, 442 F.2d 65 (2d Cir.1971). However, market testing of the invention to determine consumer preference is not within the concept of an "experimental" use and thus will bar a patent if it took place more than one year before the inventor files an application. *In re Smith,* 714 F.2d 1127 (Fed.Cir.1983).

2. DIFFERENCES BETWEEN STATUTORY BAR AND LACK OF NOVELTY

Many of the events giving rise to statutory bar closely resemble those that defeat the applicant's attempt to show novelty. Nonetheless, the two concepts are distinct, principally because novelty concerns events that occurred before the applicant *invented* the item in question, while statutory bar concerns events that occurred after invention but more than one year before the inventor *applied* for a patent. Consequently, statutory bar can arise because of acts committed by the very person who is now seeking a patent, while anticipation necessarily arises only through the acts of a third party.

Example: On January 1, 1980 Jane Smith invents a mind reading helmet. On June 1, 1980 Claude deBoeuf, a French citizen, also invents a mind reading helmet and promptly files for a French patent, which is issued on July 1, 1980. Smith finally applies for a U.S. patent on January 1, 1982. Smith's application should be denied on the grounds of statutory bar. Although the invention was novel—because no one patented it, made it, or described it before Smith did—Smith delayed too long in seeking patent protection. The invention was patented abroad more than one year before her application date. Note that the result is the same if deBoeuf had not secured a patent, but instead had published an article fully revealing how to make the helmet on July 1, 1980. The result also would be the same if deBoeuf was not involved, and Smith herself had begun selling or making non-experimental public use of the helmet in 1980, without filing for the patent until 1982.

E. THE REQUIREMENT OF NON–OBVIOUSNESS

Although a device may not yet have actually been produced or written about, the need for it and the method of making it may be self-evident to those schooled in the relevant craft or science. In such a case, there is no need to encourage creativity by holding out the reward of a patent. Should the demand for the object become more pressing, any number of people will be able to make the object and society will avoid the price of the 17 year monopoly that comes with a patent. For this reason, *a patent applicant must prove that his or her invention is not obvious before a patent will issue.* 35 U.S.C.A. § 103 (1984).

1. DIFFERENCE BETWEEN NON–OBVIOUSNESS AND NOVELTY

Although closely related, the concepts of non-obviousness and novelty are distinct. It is possible that a particular machine or device has never been identically made or identically described in any one documentary source, but that almost anyone skilled in the relevant craft could make it if necessary. In a case like this, if one sought a patent on the item, we could not deny the patent on lack of novelty grounds because there has been no anticipation in print or in practice of the precise invention at issue. Nonetheless, the item in question is "obvious" and thus not patentable. Note that the question of novelty is essentially an objective inquiry (i.e., has anyone made or described this before?), whereas the inquiry as to non-obviousness is, as is developed below, largely subjective.

2.   HISTORY OF NON–OBVIOUSNESS REQUIREMENT

The non-obviousness requirement was not added to the patent statute until 1952. For over 100 years prior to that, however, the courts essentially required non-obviousness by requiring a patent applicant to demonstrate the "inventiveness" of the material for which a patent was sought. In other words, the subject matter had to be a considerable advance over what had gone before, not a mere incremental or obvious improvement. Where the product or process in question "is the work of the skillful mechanic, not that of the inventor," patent protection was to be denied. *Hotchkiss v. Greenwood,* 52 U.S. (11 How.) 248 (1851).

a.   The Flash of Genius Requirement

In deciding, in 1941, that a cordless cigarette lighter was not sufficiently inventive to qualify for patent protection, the Supreme Court stated that, to be patentable, "the new device, however useful it may be, must reveal the flash of creative genius, not merely the skill of the calling." *Cuno Engineering Corp. v. Automatic Devices Corp.,* 314 U.S. 84, 62 S.Ct. 37 (1941). There was some concern that this language precluded patents for new devices developed through laborious experimentation and required instead that the invention have been the product of the insight of an ingenious mind.

b.   Section 103

To eliminate any inference that the manner in which a product or process is invented has any bearing on its patentability, Congress included the following sentence in Section 103, when that provision was added in 1952: "Patentability shall not be negatived by the manner in which the invention was made." The legislative history makes it clear that this provision was designed to negate any "flash of genius" requirement for patentability.

c.   The *Graham case*

In 1965 the Supreme Court indicated that the statutory requirement of non-obviousness added in 1952 codified the judicial requirement of "invention" which had been reflected in the cases since the mid-nineteenth century. The court then indicated that the *non-obviousness or inventiveness test should be resolved through a three-step process: (1) "the scope and content of the prior art are to be determined;" (2) "differences between the prior art and the claims at issue are to be ascertained;" and (3) "the level of ordinary skill in the pertinent art resolved." Graham v. John Deere Co.,* 383 U.S. 1, 17, 86 S.Ct. 684, 693 (1965).

3. THE CONCEPT OF THE "PRIOR ART"

Obviousness is tested by reference to the prior art in the relevant field. Therefore, as the Supreme Court commanded in *Graham,* identification of the prior art is the logical first step in disputes over obviousness.

a. Sources of the Prior Art

The principal references constituting prior art are those that are also consulted to determine if an invention lacks novelty or is subject to statutory bar— namely, prior patents, prior publications, or prior knowledge or use. (Of course these references are consulted for different purposes depending on the issue). Other materials, such as the patent applicant's own prior work can be considered prior art under certain circumstances. Material contained in U.S. patent applications filed by others, that were not public at the time of the disputed invention but which became public thereafter when a patent was granted, are considered to be prior art, available as of the application date. *Hazeltine Research, Inc. v. Brenner,* 382 U.S. 252, 86 S.Ct. 335 (1965).

b. Topical Scope of Prior Art: Analogous Prior Art

The subject matter constituting "prior art" is that bearing on the same technological problem as is purportedly addressed by the invention at issue. This is so even if that material comes from a different commercial field of endeavor. References from analogous fields are also included. The question of scope turns on whether a skilled party grappling with the same problem as the patentee would have consulted the source whose inclusion or exclusion is at issue.

Example: An inventor sought a patent for a system designed to improve the flow of low temperature rocket fuel. The patent office held the matter obvious because it was similar to a process that had been described in a published article involving Japanese techniques for making knives. On appellate review, however, the court concluded that material relating to cutlery was not from an "analogous" art and thus should not be considered in determining the obviousness of the invention. *In re Van Wanderham,* 378 F.2d 981 (C.C.P.A. 1967).

4. FACTUAL TESTS FOR DETERMINING "OBVIOUSNESS"

In determining if an invention is obvious the Patent Office and the courts must put themselves in the place of artisans skilled in a wide variety of crafts, and try to determine what would be relatively apparent to such persons given the body of material identified as the relevant "prior art." To sharpen that inquiry, certain tests of obviousness have developed in the case law.

a. Negative Tests of Invention

Certain kinds of alterations of existing items are self-evident and would probably be tried by anyone tinkering with an object in an attempt to improve it. *If one of these straightforward alterations results in a novel product, the courts are likely to deny patent protection on the grounds that the result was obvious.* Examples of these negative tests include (1) substituting a new or superior material for a component of an existing item; (2) enlarging or shrinking a device; (3) omitting an element of a device; (4) changing the proportions of ingredients in a composition of matter; and (5) making a known product adjustable.

b. Combinations and the Requirement of Synergism

Where an invention consists of a combination of pre-existing elements or ingredients, a new and useful result must be demonstrated before it will be found non-obvious. *Sakraida v. Ag Pro, Inc.,* 425 U.S. 273, 96 S.Ct. 1532 (1976). If elements, when combined, yield only a predictable result, it can be concluded that the combination was obvious to those skilled in the art. Therefore many cases state that "the whole must be greater than the sum of the parts" in order for the object to be patentable. This is sometimes referred to as a "synergism" requirement. Several courts and commentators have criticized the use of the term "synergism," however, as merely adding semantic confusion and not really aiding in the resolution of the fundamental question of whether the combination at issue was obvious to persons skilled in the relevant art.

c. Secondary Considerations

The question of whether a particular invention would have been obvious to a hypothetical individual skilled in the relevant art involves hindsight and subjective judgment. Thus, to minimize the risk of unfair results, the courts often rely on objective marketplace factors in resolving the issue of obviousness. These various indicia are referred to as "secondary considerations" and some of the more important of these factors are reviewed below.

1) Long Felt Need

If the invention at issue was needed for some time in an industry, but was not forthcoming until this patent applicant began selling it, that is a strong indication of non-obviousness.

2) Commercial Success

The fact that a new item is successful suggests that others had an economic incentive to try to devise, manufacture and sell it. The fact that they did not do so suggests that the new item—or at least a feasible way of making it—was not obvious to them.

3)   Professional Approval

Where others in the field express either admiration for the patentee's work or surprise at its success, that tends to suggest that the invention was not obvious to them and others skilled in the art.

4)   Widespread Licensing

A decision on the part of many or all of the firms in the industry to seek a patent license implies that they view the patent as valid, and hence that the invention is probably not void for obviousness. However, the weight of this factor varies with the circumstances under which the licenses were entered into and the amount of royalties being charged.

5)   Simultaneous Invention by Others

If a number of persons all developed the same product or process at about the same time, that is some evidence that the subject matter involved was obvious and none of the individuals is entitled to a patent.

F.   THE REQUIREMENT OF UTILITY

In addition to being novel and non-obvious, an invention must be "useful" to qualify for patent protection. 35 U.S.C.A. § 101 (1984). The utility of an invention will not be presumed. The Supreme Court has held that a patent applicant must be able to show a specific and substantial utility for the claimed invention, and the mere fact that a process works to produce an object (for which no use has been identified), or that the object so produced is the subject of ongoing scientific research, is insufficient to show utility. *Brenner v. Manson,* 383 U.S 519, 86 S.Ct. 1033 (1966). However, that opinion does not specify the type of affirmative showing that must be made to demonstrate utility. It is clear that *if the sole purpose of an invention is an illegal or immoral one, the item will be held to lack "utility" and a patent will be denied.*

G.   PATENT APPLICATION PROCEDURE

1.   DRAFTING THE PATENT

The principal parts of a patent application are the specification and the claims. If necessary for an understanding of the invention, the application must include drawings as well.

a.   Specification

The specification is the portion of the patent describing the invention. The statute requires that it contain "a written description of the invention, and of the manner and process of making and using it, in such full, clear, concise, and exact terms as to enable any person skilled in the art to which it pertains . . . to make and use the same, and shall set forth the best mode contemplated by the inventor of carrying out his invention." 35 U.S.C.A. § 112 (1984). If any information necessary to practice the information is omitted from the specification (other than information which would be possessed by a person of ordinary skill in the relevant art), the patent can be held invalid. *Flick-Reedy Corp. v. Hydro-Line Mfg. Co.,* 351 F.2d 546 (7th Cir. 1965).

b. Claims

The claims are the specific attributes of the invention described in the specification which the applicant alleges are new and inventive. In the language of the statute, there must be "one or more claims particularly pointing out and distinctly claiming the subject matter which the applicant regards as his invention." 35 U.S.C.A. § 112 (1984). *Once the patent issues the scope of protection it affords will be defined by the wording of the claims.* It follows that careful claim drafting is crucial.

2.   PATENT EXAMINATION

a.   Procedure

When a patent application is filed, it is assigned to an examiner in the U.S. Patent and Trademark Office who determines if the requirements of patentability have been met. If the examiner concludes that a patent should issue, that decision is essentially final. If the examiner rejects the patent, the applicant may apply for reexamination, and provide further information to the patent office. 35 U.S.C.A. § 132 (1984). If the patent is rejected a second time, after reexamination, the applicant may then take an administrative appeal to the Patent Office Board of Appeals. 35 U.S.C.A. § 134 (1982). If this appeal is unsuccessful, the applicant may either appeal directly to the Court of Appeals for the Federal Circuit, 35 U.S.C.A. § 141 (1984) or file a suit against the Commissioner of Patents in U.S. District Court for the District of Columbia to compel issuance of a patent. 35 U.S.C.A. § 145 (1984).

b.   Duty of Candor

Because the administrative phase of patent proceedings is *ex parte, the law imposes a duty of candor on the applicant* to make sure that all relevant information about the prior art and facts surrounding the invention are disclosed. *Any material misstatement or failure to disclose material information during the patenting process constitutes a breach of this duty, and is a ground for either denying the patent at the administrative level, or declaring it to be invalid during subsequent litigation.* Moreover, if a party secures a patent through fraud, he or she may be subject to subsequent liability under the antitrust laws.

c.   Confidentiality

Material contained in a patent application is kept confidential until such time as a patent is actually issued. 35 U.S.C.A. § 122 (1984). If no patent ever issues, the applications remain permanently confidential.

3. REISSUE

After a patent issues, the patentee may become aware that it is defective in some respect. It may not name all of the parties who should have been identified as joint inventors, it may be worded too broadly, and thus claim protection for things that are actually part of the prior art or it may be worded too narrowly, and thus fail to protect the entirety of the invention in question. Ordinarily, these defects render the patent invalid. However, if the error in question was not due to "deceptive intention" on the part of the patentee, he or she may return to the patent office and have the patent reissued in corrected form. No new matter may be introduced during the reissue proceeding. If the reissue will result in a patent with a broader scope than the original, the application for reissue must be made within 2 years from the grant of the original patent. The term of the reissued patent will be only for the unexpired portion of the original patent term. 35 U.S. C.A. § 251 (1984).

H. PATENT INFRINGEMENT

A patent is valuable because it permits the patentee to prevent others from engaging in behavior that is normally permitted as within the scope of legitimate competition. Specifically a *patent confers an exclusive right to make, use or sell the claimed invention.* This means that in the usual infringement case there are two principal issues—first, interpreting the claims of the patent to see just what types of things or processes are within its scope, and then determining whether the defendant's acts fall within the forbidden categories of "make," "use," or "sell."

1. SCOPE OF THE PATENT

a. Duration

The term of a patent is 17 years, except in the case of a design patent, where the term is 14 years. Patents are not renewable.

b. Doctrine of Equivalents

If a patent were read literally, a clever infringer could almost always avoid liability by making minor changes to differentiate his device from the device described in the patent. That would undermine the purpose of the patent laws, since it would largely destroy the value of a patent. To prevent this result, *the defendant's device may be held infringing even if not identical to the patent claims provided that the "two devices do the same work in substantially the same way, and accomplish substantially the same result. . ."* *Graver Tank & Mfg. Co. v. Linde Air Products Co.,* 339 U.S. 605, 70 S.Ct. 854 (1950). This is known as the doctrine of equivalents. The Supreme Court has noted that "the range of equivalents depends upon and varies with the degree of invention." *Continental Paper Bag Co. v. Eastern Paper Bag Co.,* 210 U.S. 405, 28 S.Ct. 748 (1908). As a result, the holder of a pioneering patent will have a broader scope of protection against potential infringers than a party whose patent covers merely a minor improvement. However, if the allegedly infringing device differs in important and substantial ways from the claims that are recited in the plaintiff's patent, the doctrine does not apply, and no infringement will be found. *General Dynamics Corp. v. Whitcomb*, 443 F.2d 630 (4th Cir.1971).

c. File Wrapper Estoppel

During the course of the patent application process, the applicant may narrow his or her claims in response to objections from the examiner. The applicant may even do so believing the examiner to be mistaken about the point at issue. Regardless of the motive involved at the time, *the patentee may not later claim infringement under the doctrine of equivalents of something that corresponds to a portion of a claim that was surrendered during the patent examination process.* Because these various concessions as to the scope of the claims are noted on a "file wrapper" at the patent office, this doctrine, limiting the rights of the patentee, is known as file wrapper estoppel.

2. DIRECT INFRINGEMENT
a. Making, Using or Selling

Patent infringement does not require intent. Even a wholly innocent subsequent inventor will be liable for infringement if he or she makes, uses, or sells a device within the scope of the claims of a previously issued patent. The making, using, or selling involved must occur within the United States to constitute infringement. Moreover, a party who does not actually make, use or sell the infringing object, but who actively induces another to do so will also be held liable as an infringer.

b. Exhaustion After First Sale

Once a patentee—or person authorized by the patentee—sells an object within the scope of the patent, the patent rights are exhausted as to that physical object. This means that it is not patent infringement for you to use your telephone or camera even though those objects are probably protected by patents. You are also free to resell these objects without incurring liability for infringement. *Keeler v. Standard Folding-Bed Co.*, 157 U.S. 659, 15 S.Ct. 738 (1895). If you bought a patented object from a seller who did not have any authorization to sell it, however, you infringe the patent every time you use the device.

c. Repair and Reconstruction

The purchaser of a patented object is free to have it repaired when necessary. However, it is considered infringement to have the object completely reconstructed after it has entirely worn out. This insures that the patentee will secure the economic benefit of replacement sales as well as original sales. Of course, the distinction between repair and replacement is not a bright line. Courts try to exercise caution to avoid giving the patentee a monopoly over parts and supplies that are not within the subject matter of the patent.

3.   CONTRIBUTORY INFRINGEMENT
a.   Sale of Non-Staples by Third Parties

One can be liable for patent infringement without actually making, selling or using the product or process described in the patent, if one provides an ingredient that permits another party to engage in those impermissible activities. This behavior will only amount to contributory infringement, however, if (1) the material sold has no other use except as a component of a patented device and (2) the selling party acts knowingly. In the words of the statute, "whoever sells a component of a patented machine, manufacture, combination or composition, or a material or apparatus for use in practicing a patented process, constituting a material part of the invention, knowing the same to be especially made or especially adapted for use in an infringement of such patent, and not a staple article or commodity of commerce suitable for substantial noninfringing use, shall be liable as a contributory infringer." 35 U.S.C.A. § 271(c) (1984).

b.   Sale of Non-Staples by Patentee

Occasionally, inventors secure patents on new processes that use previously existing chemicals for which there had formerly been no practical uses. Once the process is patented, the sale of the chemical by any other party is likely to constitute contributory infringement since, by definition, there is no other use for these chemicals except to practice the patented process and the purchasers from the third party may not have obtained patent licenses. Because the patent statute provides that a patentee may legally engage in acts which, if engaged in by others, would constitute contributory infringement, the Supreme Court held that a patentee in this position can require users of the process to buy the chemical in question from him, even though the patent itself does not cover the chemical. *Dawson Chemical Co. v. Rohm and Hass Co.,* 448 U.S. 176, 100 S.Ct. 2601 (1980). Note that if the chemical in question had a variety of other uses, it would be considered a "staple" item, and the patentee could not insist that parties purchase it solely from him.

4.   REMEDIES

The holder of a patent who proves infringement is entitled to both injunctive relief and damages. The statute indicates that damages should be "in no event less than a reasonable royalty for the use made of the invention by the infringer." 35 U.S. C.A. § 284 (1984). The statute permits the court to increase the damage award to up to three times the amount found as actual damages. In exceptional cases, the court may award attorney's fees to the prevailing party in an infringement suit.

REVIEW QUESTIONS

1. **T or F** An invention lacks novelty if two previously published articles, when read in conjunction, reveal how to make the device.

2. **T or F** The fact that a new machine was an immediate commercial success is an indication that it was obvious.

3. **T or F** If an inventor has been selling his invention to the public for 18 months before applying for a patent, he will be denied the patent.

4. **T or F** The fact that a device was developed by trial and error is a sufficient ground on which to deny a patent because of lack of inventiveness.

5. **T or F** Computer programs are patentable.

6. **T or F** For the purpose of determining obviousness, the prior art consists of material from the same technological field as the invention and material from analogous fields.

7. **T or F** Alpha has invented and patented a process for making glass unbreakable by soaking it in kerosene of a certain temperature for a specified period of time. It is contributory infringement for a party to sell kerosene to a glass manufacturer who does not have a license to use this process.

8. **T or F** A patentee is entitled to automatically recover treble damages if successful in an infringement suit.

9. **T or F** File Wrapper Estoppel is a limitation or qualification of the Doctrine of Equivalents.

10. **T or F** If a patent examiner initially rejects an application, the applicant is entitled to a re-examination.

11. **T or F** The "specification" of a patent must be sufficiently clear and detailed so as to permit a party reading it to duplicate the invention.

12. **T or F** For the purposes of invoking "statutory bar" to preclude the patenting of a device in public use for more than one year, the use in question must be sufficiently widespread to have come to the attention of the general public.

13. In which of the following situations is it most likely that the invention was "obvious" and thus not patentable?

    a.   Alpha invents a new lie detecting machine which is praised in the professional literature and widely adopted by police departments and banks.

b. Beta invents a new medicine for acne by starting with an existing preparation, eliminating one of its ingredients, and doubling the amount of another ingredient.

c. Gamma invents a new football shoulder pad that absorbs more impact than all previous devices of this type. Eight years ago, an article in the Journal of Nuclear Physics applied the same principle as Gamma utilized, to explain how to build support pads that cushion impacts within the core of nuclear reactors.

d. Delta invented a new type of orthopedic shoe by trying out several hundred different shapes and constructions on a group of people with feet problems before arriving at an effective new design.

14. Omega invented a new type of video-recorder that can record eight different TV programs at the same time. He obtained a patent on this machine and began manufacturing and marketing it through ordinary channels. Assuming none of the following parties has contacted Omega or is operating with Omega's explicit permission, which of them is most likely to be held guilty of patent infringement?

a. Alpha purchases one of these machines from a leading department store and uses it at home to make tapes.

b. Beta sells videotape over the counter in a stereo store to a variety of consumers, some of whom use the tape in the Omega device.

c. Gamma, an amateur inventor, has coincidentally stumbled on the method for building a machine just like the Omega device, which he has constructed and uses for his own purposes at home.

d. Delta owns a stereo repair outlet and both services and repairs Omega video recording devices for their owners.

15. The October 1982 issue of Cardiac Medicine magazine contained a research paper describing how the simultaneous administration of a 500mg dose of the well-known anti-motion sickness drug Alphamol and a 500mg dose of the well-known antibiotic drug Betamycin served to markedly reduce high blood pressure. The combined effect of these two drugs, neither of which was conventionally used in treating heart patients, had never before been noted.

In June of 1983, Dr. Kildare, a medical researcher at the University of The Catskills, discovered inadvertently that when a small amount (1mg) of Betamycin was added to a large quantity of Alphamol which was heated to the temperature of 132 degree Celcius, a chemical reaction took place and a new substance was formed. Dr. Kildare designated the new substance Gammadol.

After conducting a chemical analysis of the new compound, Dr. Kildare developed a suspicion that it might be useful in controlling heart palpitations. Because there were very few preparations that were effective in this regard, he spent the next several months conducting controlled clinical tests of the drug.

In September, 1983, while these experiments were still going on, an article appeared in a French medical journal, Le Sante de la Coeur, describing the same method of making Gammadol that Kildare had stumbled upon in June. The French article referred to the new drug as Coeurplacide and contained a scientific explanation of how and why the new substance would be effective in reducing heart palpitations. The author of this article was unaware of Dr. Kildare and his work.

Dr. Kildare did not see the French article. In August 1984, Dr. Kildare, convinced that his experiments were successful, applied for a patent on a composition of matter equivalent to the Gammadol/Coeurplacide drug. Is he entitled to a patent?

*

VI

TRADE SECRETS

Analysis

Not all merchants who make valuable commercial "inventions" choose, or are able, to protect them through the patent system. First, patent protection may be unavailable because the matter involved is outside the subject matter of the patent statute or is insufficiently inventive. Alternatively, the merchant may not find the patent system's trade-off between protection and disclosure to be an attractive bargain. Instead, the merchant may prefer to keep the discovery confidential and rely on state common law protection for trade secrets.

The initial issue in the study of trade secret law is what kinds of devices, processes, and information are the proper subject matter of a trade secret. If proper subject matter is involved, further inquiries concern what kinds of activities by third parties to learn the secret are forbidden and what kinds of remedies are available to the party who developed the secret.

A. MATERIAL CONSTITUTING TRADE SECRETS

Although many trade secrets involve industrial processes—in other words, manufacturing techniques—the concept of a trade secret is much broader than this.

1. UNIFORM ACT DEFINITION
The Uniform Trade Secrets Act contains the following definition: "Trade secret means information, including a formula, pattern, compilation, program, device, method, technique or process that: (i) derives independent economic value, actual or potential, from not being generally known to, and not being readily ascertainable by proper means by, other persons who can obtain economic value from its disclosure or use, and (ii) is the subject of efforts that are reasonable under the circumstances to maintain its secrecy." The definition in the Restatement of Torts is very similar. In other words, *a trade secret is any confidential information that is valuable to a firm because it provides that firm with a competitive advantage.*

Example: The formula for Coca-Cola is a trade secret, since it has commercial value to its owners and since they take serious steps to keep it confidential.

2. MINIMAL NOVELTY AND UTILITY REQUIRED
Although the subject matter of a trade secret need not be inventive in the patent law sense, "some novelty will be required if merely because that which does not possess novelty is usually known; secrecy, in the context of trade secrets, thus implies at least minimal novelty." *Kewanee Oil Co. v. Bicron Corp.,* 416 U.S. 470, 94 S.Ct. 1879 (1974). *Similarly,* because a trade secret must be commercially useful information that confers a competitive advantage, *there is a requirement that the material involved have some utility before it will be protected as a trade secret.*

3. REQUISITE DEGREE OF SECRECY

As indicated by the Uniform Act definition, *most jurisdictions demand only that the amount of secrecy be reasonable under the circumstances. Absolute secrecy is not required,* and it is not a breach of "secrecy" to permit employees to have access to the trade secret if that is necessary to enable them to do their jobs. The typical precautions required to satisfy the secrecy requirement are restrictions on visitors to the area of the factory where the secret is being practiced, and a limitation of disclosure to those with a need to know. "Confidential" stamps on documents embodying the secret are also useful precautions. Of course, if the information is available in published materials, is widely known in the industry, or is described in an issued patent, there is no secrecy, and hence no trade secret protection.

4. MATTERS HELD TO BE TRADE SECRETS

Among the types of material held entitled to trade secret protection are formulas for the preparation of food, drugs, cosmetics and industrial chemicals; manufacturing processes, methods and techniques; machines and the patterns and plans to build them; lists of customers or sources of supply; advertising and marketing plans; and knowledge of facts about real estate, such as whether it possesses mineral deposits or is located at the site of future development. Whether information is a "trade secret" is a question of fact to be determined by the jury. If material is considered a trade secret, it has many aspects of personal property, the most important of which is that the owner can license others to use the secret.

B. APPROPRIATION BY PARTIES WITH LEGITIMATE ACCESS

A firm possessing trade secrets will be protected, at common law, against misappropriation of those secrets by others. One frequent type of misappropriation occurs when a party who initially learned about the secret legitimately through voluntary disclosure by the owner, thereafter either uses the secret for his or her own commercial advantage or discloses it to others. In such cases courts will grant relief if the defendant acted in violation of a duty of trust and confidence, because where such a duty exists, there is both an obligation to keep the secret and an obligation to refrain from using it.

1. EXPLICIT DUTY TO MAINTAIN SECRECY

Firms must often reveal their trade secrets to third parties, either to make use of the secret in their business, or to serve some other legitimate commercial purpose. To protect itself in such circumstances *a firm owning trade secrets can enter into a contract* with those parties *explicitly imposing a duty* on them *to keep the secret confidential.* Such agreements are judicially enforceable and will prevent the third party from using the secret for its own commercial advantage.

a. Parties On Whom Duty May Be Imposed

Many companies use such provisions in contracts with *employees* who have access to trade secrets, especially those involved in research and development.

They are also used in contracts for the sale of a business, so that if the sale falls through, the owner of the business has protection against attempts by the *prospective buyer* to use the secrets. Because the owner of a trade secret can grant a license to other parties to practice the secret for a limited period of time, trade secret licensing agreements also may contain these provisions, to protect the owner of the secret from the *licensee's* attempt to continue using it after the license has expired.

b.   Covenants Not to Compete

To secure even broader protection against the use of trade secrets by a departing employee, the employer may include a "covenant not to compete" in the employment contract. Such a provision forbids the employee from engaging in any competition with the former employer in a specified area for a specified period of time. Similar covenants are often included in contracts for the sale of a business. Such *covenants are only permissible if they are reasonable in terms of both their scope and duration.* An over-broad covenant of this type will be held void as against public policy and might even violate the antitrust laws. In determining if the covenant is over-broad the courts are particularly influenced by the situation of the employee in question. *See Milwaukee Linen Supply Co. v. Ring,* 210 Wis. 467, 246 N.W. 567 (1933) (Covenant not to compete restricting employment opportunities of handicapped former employee with limited education held void).

2.   IMPLIED DUTY TO MAINTAIN SECRECY

Even where no specific contractual provisions exist, if a trade secret is disclosed under circumstances fairly suggesting that the parties contemplated the maintenance of secrecy, courts will imply a duty of confidentiality to protect the secret. Many courts have found such an implied duty of confidentiality in the employer-employee relationship. If the employee changes jobs and thereafter discloses the secret to a new employer or uses it in a new business, the original employer will be entitled to relief. Other relationships in which a confidential relationship has been implied include those between partners and those between parties negotiating over the sale of a business.

Example: Smith was in the cargo and freight container business. Dravo expressed an interest in buying the business and the two entered into negotiations. During these negotiations, Smith sent Dravo secret blue prints and patent applications concerning its innovative cargo containers. The negotiations fell through and thereafter Dravo began marketing freight containers similar to Smith's. Smith brought suit for trade secret theft. Although the court noted that "it is clear that no express promise of trust was exacted from defendant," it held that a relationship of trust should be implied from the facts and granted relief. *Smith v. Dravo Corp,* 203 F.2d 369 (7th Cir.1953).

C. TRADE SECRET THEFT BY STRANGERS

When a trade secret is learned in some other way than by the voluntary disclosure of the owner, the dispositive legal question is whether the secret was learned by "improper means."

1. BEHAVIOR CONSTITUTING IMPROPER MEANS

If a party learns the content of a trade secret through illegal activities, those means are clearly "improper" and provide the trade secret owner with a basis for relief in a civil suit for trade secret theft. Thus, outright theft of documents containing the secret information, as well as bribery, fraud or electronic surveillance are all unacceptable ways of learning someone else's trade secrets and will be condemned as improper. *Even if the method of learning another party's trade secret is not technically illegal, it will also be labeled improper if it is a calculated attempt to overcome reasonable efforts to maintain secrecy.* The policy of the law is to avoid a result that requires trade secret owners to undertake extravagant expense to preserve secrets. Consequently, if the precautions taken are reasonable, any industrial espionage that circumvents those precautions will be condemned as improper.

Example: A chemical company was constructing a new plant to manufacture methanol. The chemical was to be produced through the use of a new process, which was a trade secret. The process could be determined, however, by inspecting the installations within the plant. Defendants flew over the construction site in a small plane and took photographs of the plant while construction was still in progress. This flight was not in violation of any criminal law and did not even constitute trespassing. Nonetheless, the chemical company was successful in the ensuing suit for trade secret theft. The court held that it would be unfair to require the chemical company to keep the construction site covered while construction was still in progress, and that the aerial photography here constituted an improper means of learning the secret. *E.I. duPont deNemours & Co., Inc. v. Christopher,* 431 F.2d 1012 (5th Cir.1970).

2. REVERSE ENGINEERING IS NOT IMPROPER MEANS

Many products are manufactured pursuant to plans or with technologies that are trade secrets and then sold to the public at large. In some cases the method of manufacture of these items may be discovered by careful study of the object. Typical methods of discovery include taking the product apart or performing experiments on it. This process of analysis is usually called "reverse engineering." *Numerous cases hold that reverse engineering is not an improper means of learning a trade secret.* Risk of discovery by reverse engineering is a risk that a firm takes when it chooses to rely on trade secret protection for a valuable commercial asset. Note that if a firm secures patent protection for a new device or manufacturing process it is protected against "reverse engineering." This is one of the most important differences between patent and trade secret protection.

3. INNOCENT USE OF STOLEN SECRETS

A party who obtains a trade secret by improper means may decide not to make use of the secret directly. That party may not even be engaged in a line of business that permits him to capitalize on the secret. Consequently, such a party may opt, instead, to reveal the secret to another party for money or otherwise. Often the third party acquiring the secret in this fashion is unaware that it is "stolen" information. When the owner of the secret learns what has happened, it may file suit not only against the actual thief, but against the third party who is using the secret as well. Nonetheless, such *a third party will not incur any liability for using the secret so long as it did not know—and did not have any reason to suspect—that the secret was obtained improperly.* Once it learns that the secret is stolen, however, the third party must then cease using it unless that party has materially changed its position.

Example: MacIntosh was employed at Chipco, a high technology silicon chip manufacturer in Maine, for many years. He had access to all their trade secrets. In 1983 he moved to California and obtained a job with Hi-Tech-Co, another silicon chip manufacturer. He immediately suggested numerous product "improvements," which were, in substance, the trade secrets he had learned at Chipco. Hi-Tech-Co was unaware of MacIntosh's former employment or the source of his information until it received a letter from Chipco in 1985. In the subsequent trade secret suit, Hi-Tech-Co is not liable for its use of the secrets from 1983 to 1985. It will be enjoined from using them thereafter, unless it has materially changed its position in the interim—perhaps by redesigning its factory to incorporate the new technology.

D. TRADE SECRET DISCLOSURE BY GOVERNMENT

As noted above, firms owning trade secrets must be concerned about disloyal employees and competitors practicing espionage. It is also important, however, for such firms to be vigilant in their dealings with the government, lest their trade secrets be inadvertently disclosed. This is especially true of firms doing work as government contractors, but can be a problem for any firm that must comply with regulatory requirements that mandate submission of sensitive data.

1. FREEDOM OF INFORMATION ACT

Under the Freedom of Information Act (FOIA), 5 U.S.C.A. § 552 (1984) private parties may obtain copies of government records. However, that statute contains a number of exemptions, one of which authorizes agencies to decline to reveal "trade secrets and commercial or financial information obtained from a person." Consequently, if trade secret material must be submitted to a federal agency under obligation of law, it should be clearly marked as such, and accompanied by an explanation of why the material is sensitive. This will put the agency on notice to invoke this exception if the material is demanded under the FOIA. Where agencies have withheld information under this exemption, the courts have largely sustained their action.

2.   REVERSE FOIA SUITS

If an agency plans to disclose trade secret material contrary to the wishes of the party who submitted it, the owner of the secret may bring a suit under the Administrative Procedure Act, 5 U.S.C.A. § 706 (1984), to enjoin the disclosure. Chrysler Corporation v. Brown, 441 U.S. 281, 99 S.Ct. 1705 (1979). Such suits are sometimes called reverse FOIA actions, but the governing standard to determine if disclosure is forbidden is not derived from the FOIA. Instead, the plaintiff in such a case must be able to invoke some other statute, such as the Federal Trade Secrets Act, 18 U.S.C.A. § 1905 (1984), that gives it substantive protection against disclosure of the material.

E.   REMEDIES FOR TRADE SECRET THEFT

1.   DAMAGES

Plaintiffs in trade secret litigation may recover both compensatory and punitive damages, but will usually have to demonstrate that the defendant acted in bad faith.

2.   INJUNCTIONS

a.   Subject Matter Still Secret

Where the subject matter of the trade secret is still "secret" at the time of trial, court will enjoin continued use of the secret by the defendant. Such an injunction will also forbid the defendant from making further disclosures of the secret to other parties. The term of such an injunction is usually the period of time necessary for the defendant to independently develop the information in question. A court's willingness to grant an injunction as relief for trade secret misappropriation will depend, in part, on the novelty of the secret involved. The more novel or creative it is, the more likely a court will be to grant injunctive relief.

b.   Subject Matter in Public Domain

In many cases, by the time an allegation of trade secret theft comes to trial, the secret has passed into the public domain. This may be because of reverse engineering, other scientific advances by competing firms, or because the defendant or someone else has made a public disclosure of the secret. In many cases, it is because a patent has issued, containing a description of the relevant technology, and has thereafter been judicially declared invalid. In situations like these, *where the secret is public, courts differ over the availability and scope of injunctive relief.*

1) Perpetual Injunction

Some courts are not influenced by the fact that the subject matter of the secret is now out in the open, and will enjoin the defendant from using the technology in question permanently. This means that the defendant alone, among all firms in its industry, is barred from using processes or devices that all competitors may use. This is justified on the grounds of penalizing the defendant for its wrongdoing and of deterring future thefts of trade secrets. The leading case taking this view is *Shellmar Products Co. v. Allen-Qualley Co.,* 36 F.2d 623 (7th Cir.1930).

2) No Injunction

Other courts find it unacceptable to prevent a firm from using technology that is now in the public domain. These courts hold that the plaintiff's sole remedy is for damages or an accounting of profits once the secrecy has ended. *Conmar Products Corp. v. Universal Slide Fastener Co.,* 172 F.2d 150 (2d Cir.1949).

3) Head Start Injunction

Still other courts have sought to find a middle ground. These courts note that the benefit to the defendant from misappropriating the secret was the opportunity to use it from the date of misappropriation to the date it became public. After it became public, continued use by the defendant is not solely attributable to its wrongful conduct, since from that time forward, all firms in the industry had access to the information. Therefore, some courts grant injunctions running for the interval described above, which is the "head start" the defendant unfairly obtained over competitors by virtue of its theft. Thus, if the secret was misappropriated in 1982, became public in 1984, and trial of the claim of trade secret theft concluded in 1985, the term of the resulting injunction against the defendant would be two years. *See Winston Research Corp. v. Minnesota Mining & Manufacturing Co.,* 350 F.2d 134 (9th Cir.1965).

3. CRIMINAL REMEDIES

There is no general federal criminal prohibition against trade secret theft. Some courts have held that making copies of documents containing trade secrets and taking them across state lines violates the National Stolen Property Act, 18 U.S.C.A. § 2314 (1984), *United States v. Bottone,* 365 F.2d 389 (2d Cir.1966), but where no material is actually transported, that statute may be inapplicable, *United States v. Smith,* 686 F.2d 234 (5th Cir.1982). *About 20 states have specific statutes making trade secret theft a crime.*

F. PRE–EMPTION PROBLEMS

There are a number of ways in which state protection for trade secrets might be argued to conflict with federal law. By and large, however, the courts have ruled that trade secret protection may co-exist along side the patent and copyright laws.

1. CONFLICT WITH THE POLICY OF FREE COPIABILITY

The patent laws reflect a policy that material not sufficiently inventive to qualify for a patent should be left in the public domain so that all parties may copy it. That was the rationale of *Sears Roebuck & Co. v. Stiffel Co.,* 376 U.S. 225, 84 S.Ct. 784 (1964), limiting state trademark protection of unpatented shapes and configurations (*see* discussion in Chapter II above). *Trade secret protection does not conflict with that policy because, by definition, trade secrets are not in the public domain.* State trade secret law really prevents theft or misappropriation, rather than mere copying. The only theoretically difficult problem occurs when courts enter injunctions against defendants in trade secret litigation or enforce trade secret licensing agreements after the secret has already lapsed into the public domain. In such a case, the defendant is being prevented from making free use of something that is both unpatented and is public information. It has been held, however, that since such state court decrees only operate against the defendant, there is no general limitation on the right to freely copy, and thus no significant conflict with the patent laws.

> *Example:* In 1955 Mrs. Aronson devised a new type of keyholder. Treating her design as confidential information, she licensed a firm to manufacture the keyholder for a specified royalty. She also applied for a patent, which was ultimately denied. In the meantime the licensee began manufacturing the keyholder. Because it was a simple device, other firms immediately discerned how to manufacture it and began to compete with the licensee. The licensee filed suit for a declaratory judgment that the royalty agreement was unenforceable since the design of the keyholder was now in the public domain. The Supreme Court held that state enforcement of the contractual obligation was not inconsistent with the patent laws, and did not impermissibly withdraw any idea from the public domain. *Aronson v. Quick Point Pencil Co.,* 440 U.S. 257, 99 S.Ct. 1096 (1979).

2. CONFLICT WITH THE POLICY OF PROMOTING DISCLOSURE

The courts have recognized that another policy of the patent laws is the promotion of disclosure of information. They achieve this purpose by offering inventors an attractive bargain—17 years of monopoly protection in return for a full description of the invention. The existence of state trade secret protection might encourage some inventors to decline that bargain, and thereby reduce the degree to which technological advances are made publicly available. Nonetheless, the Supreme Court rejected this argument in *Kewanee Oil Co. v. Bicron Corp.,* 416 U.S. 470 (1974), explicitly holding that *state trade secret law is not pre-empted by federal patent law.* Moreover, that case noted that yet another purpose of the patent laws—creation of incentives that will encourage creative behavior—is actually advanced by state trade secret protection, since it, too, operates as an incentive to innovation.

G. TRADE SECRETS AND OTHER UNFAIR TRADE CONCEPTS

1.   TRADE SECRET AND PATENT
As the pre-emption discussion illustrates, trade secret and patent law are closely connected.   To a large degree they are alternative modes of protecting the same types of intangible assets.   Trade secret protection has several advantages over patent law: (1) it is indefinite in duration, lasting as long as the owner can keep the secret; (2) it is less expensive to obtain than patent protection, which requires a complex and expensive application procedure; and (3) it protects a broader range of material than the patent laws, such as customer lists and marketing plans.   On the other hand, patent law is superior because it protects against reverse engineering and independent discovery by others as well as against theft.

2.   TRADE SECRET AND IDEA APPROPRIATION
The principles governing trade secret law are very similar to those involved in cases involving alleged appropriation of business schemes.   In each situation, the intangible (the scheme or the secret) must be sufficiently concrete, useful and original to merit protection, and in each, liability will often turn on proof of a confidential relationship between the parties.   The difference is that in the business scheme case, the plaintiff expected the defendant to make commercial use of the information and the dispute is over the right to payment, while in the trade secret case, the plaintiff argues that the defendant's use itself is impermissible.

3.   TRADE SECRET AND INDUCEMENT TO BREACH CONTRACTS
Customer lists are frequently protected as trade secrets.   If a former employee begins contacting persons on a customer list, however, such activities may also rise to the level of an inducement to breach a contract.   Whether such a claim can be successfully asserted will naturally depend on whether the relationship between the customers in question and the former employer was contractual in nature. *See Adler, Barish, Daniels, Levin and Creskoff v. Epstein,* 482 Pa. 416, 393 A.2d 1175 (1978).   There, former associates of a law firm departed to form a new firm, and contacted numerous clients who had been previously represented by their former employers.   The court held that this activity constituted inducement to breach a contract.

REVIEW QUESTIONS

   1. **T or F** A covenant not to compete will only be enforced if it is reasonable in scope and duration.

2. **T or F** It is permissible to attempt to deduce another party's trade secrets through the use of reverse engineering.

3. **T or F** If a government agency decides to release material containing trade secrets, the party who may be adversely affected has a right to judicial review.

4. **T or F** Once a trade secret has passed into the public domain, a licensee of the secret may stop paying royalties.

5. **T or F** For behavior to constitute an improper means of learning a trade secret, it must violate some state or federal criminal statute.

6. **T or F** A machine or process need not be sufficiently inventive to qualify for a patent in order to be protected as a trade secret.

7. **T or F** A party who proves trade secret misappropriation is entitled to a perpetual injunction even if the material constituting the secret has lost its secrecy and become public.

8. **T or F** An employee will not be held to have misappropriated a trade secret by using it for his own purposes unless there is an explicit contractual obligation forbidding him from doing so.

9. **T or F** A innocent third party, who learns a trade secret under circumstances not giving rise to knowledge that the information has been stolen, may use the information without liability until being informed of its trade secret status.

10. **T or F** A "head start" injunction will prevent the defendant from using a trade secret from the date the complaint is filed until a trial on the claim of trade secret theft has been completed.

11. In 1968 the Maison D'Arome perfume house developed a formula for a new type of perfume, designated X519. They kept the only copy of the written formula in a safe to which only 3 employees had access. In 1970 Maison D'Arome licensed the X519 to Ralph's of Paris for a term of 20 years. The license required the payment of a royalty of $1 for each bottle of X519 sold by Ralph. In 1985, Fragrance Magazine published an article setting out the results of analysis by its chemists that revealed the X519 formula. Shortly thereafter, Ralph informed Maison D'Arome that it would no longer pay royalties under the license. Maison D'Arome has sued to enforce the license provisions. In the ensuing litigation

   a. Ralph will win because the license was void as being of unreasonable scope and duration.

b.   Ralph will win because any state attempt to enforce the license after the secret became public is pre-empted by the patent law policy of free copiability for unpatented formulas.

c.   Maison D'Arome will win because the secret was ascertained and disclosed by the magazine through wrongful means.

d.   Maison D'Arome will win because trade secret licenses are enforceable according to their terms even after the secret has become public.

12. Apex Tool and Die makes and sells industrial machines and equipment to purchasers in a wide variety of industries. Its manufacturing operations are conducted in two plants, one in New Jersey and one in Ohio. Apex specializes in made-to-order material and has spent considerable effort over the years in identifying customers who have a demand for made-to-order machine tools in lieu of the standard sizes and configurations that are more commonly available. It now does business with some 300 customers across the nation.

Apex maintains its customer lists by computer. Since both plants serve all customers on occasion, a set of computer diskettes containing the list of all 300 customers is kept at each plant location. In addition, the vice president for sales has made a "backup" copy of the diskettes which he keeps at home and which he sometimes reads on his own personal computer. Personnel at both plants have been instructed to treat the diskettes carefully. In Ohio they are kept in the plant safe. In New Jersey they are kept in the desk of the plant manager.

When the diskettes are used, they are placed into the computer, which reads the contents into the memory of the machine. This material is retained in memory until specifically erased by the keyboard operator, but it cannot be displayed on the screen unless the operator punches in a specified password. The password is known by the computer operators at Apex and is listed in a Computer Reference Manual which is kept on a desk next to the computer terminal.

Last year, Apex decided to close down its New Jersey operation. It arranged to sell all of its assets at that plant to Zenith Tool and Die, a competing manufacturer. Among the assets sold was the personal computer in the New Jersey plant. The New Jersey customer list diskettes and Computer Reference Manual were not sold, however.

When Hal Modem, the sales manager, at Zenith was working with the newly acquired Apex computer one day after work he inadvertently hit a button which produced a list of "Items stored in Memory." The screen display stated that one of the items was "Customer List" and indicated that this item was "password protected."

The next morning, Hal contacted Thelma Johnson, the former computer operator for Apex who had retired when the New Jersey plant was sold. He asked Ms. Johnson if she could visit him at Zenith's offices and she agreed. When she got there, he explained that he wanted her to provide the password so that he could review the customer lists. When Ms. Johnson indicated that she didn't know if that was okay, Hal said "Well they sold us the whole business, including the customer lists, so I don't know what you're so worried about." When Ms. Johnson continued to express reluctance Hal indicated that he would make it worth her while to provide the password, and then offered her a thousand dollars. At this point she agreed, typed in the crucial word ("Swordfish") and the customers names and addresses appeared on the screen.

Apex learned of these events subsequently when many of its customers indicated that they had been approached by Zenith who was soliciting their business. Apex is upset and has sued Zenith for theft of trade secrets. Is Zenith guilty? Explain.

*

VII

COMPETITOR REMEDIES FOR FALSE ADVERTISING AND DISPARAGEMENT

Analysis

Most of the unfair practices examined thus far involve appropriation of valuable intangible rights belonging to another and use of them without permission for one's own purposes. That pattern recurs with trademarks, patents, trade secrets, copyrights, and the more ephemeral intangibles protected by the misappropriation doctrine. There is another way a firm can seek unfairly to divert patronage from a rival, however—it can make direct misrepresentations to the public. Those can either be claims of false merit about its own products, or false allegations of problems and defects with the goods or services of its rival. This behavior gives rise to problems of false advertising and disparagement, respectively.

False advertising or disparagement is behavior that affects three separate constituencies. First, by diverting patronage from firms that sell superior products to firms that lie convincingly, the behavior harms efficient and honest firms. Second, by tricking consumers into buying goods that they do not really want, the behavior harms consumers. Finally, by dragging down the level of business and commercial ethics, the behavior is generally harmful to the economy.

The law provides remedies to each of the constituencies identified above. This chapter will consider remedies available to aggrieved competitors. The following chapters will consider the public remedies that can be pursued by the Federal Trade Commission, and the private remedies available to deceived consumers.

A. COMMON LAW REMEDIES FOR FALSE ADVERTISING

The early common law cases complaining of a competitor's false advertising were brought as "unfair competition" cases. In the typical unfair competition case, the defendant is accused of "passing off" its goods as those of the plaintiff, often through trademark infringement, and the plaintiff claims injury because sales are diverted from it to the defendant (*see* Chapter II). When the common law courts first confronted these false advertising cases, they looked for behavior resembling "passing off" and injury in the form of diversion of sales. Few false advertising situations fell into that pattern. As a result, the common law remedy for false advertising was sharply limited.

1. NO REMEDY IN USUAL CASE
In the usual false advertising situation the defendant advertises that its goods possess attributes that, in fact, they do not have. A number of other, honest firms, however, do sell merchandise with these attributes. These firms are usually referred to as vendors of the "genuine goods." When one vendor of genuine goods brings suit protesting the false advertising, it cannot prove that it would have gotten any of the sales unfairly garnered by the false advertiser, because even if the misled consumers had known the truth about the defendant's products, they might have purchased from a different vendor of genuine goods than the plaintiff. To be more concise, the plaintiff in such a case cannot prove economic injury. Thus, *the common law courts held that no relief was available for false advertising.*

Example: Plaintiff was a vendor of genuine aluminum washboards around the
turn of the century. The defendant was selling zinc washboards and
falsely advertising them as genuine aluminum. The plaintiff brought
suit for common law unfair competition. Noting that "[i]t is true that
in these cases . . . the public are deceived, but it is only where this
deception induces the public to buy the goods *as those of complainant*
that a private right of action arises," the court held no relief was
available. *American Washboard Co. v. Saginaw Manufacturing Co.,* 103
F. 281 (6th Cir.1900) (emphasis supplied).

2. SOLE SOURCE MAY RECOVER

Under the logic of the rule described above, there is one situation where a false
advertising plaintiff is able to recover at common law. That is when the plaintiff
can prove that it is the *only* firm selling the "genuine goods." If the plaintiff has
a monopoly of the type of goods in question, any consumer deceived by the
defendant's false advertising would necessarily have bought from the plaintiff if he
or she had known the truth. This situation is equivalent to "passing off" because
through the false advertisements, the defendant, in effect, represents its goods as
being those of plaintiff. Consequently, the courts formulated what is sometimes
referred to as the "sole source" rule—*if the plaintiff is the sole source of the genuine
goods, it has a common law remedy for false advertising.*

Example: Plaintiff claimed that it was the sole vendor of a patented safe with
an "explosive chamber" designed to thwart safe crackers. The
defendant falsely claimed that its safes also had such a device, even
though they did not, and altered their appearance to make this claim
seem truthful. In the ensuing false advertising suit, the Court of
Appeals concluded that plaintiff stated a valid common law cause of
action, because, as the court observed, "if it be true that the plaintiff
has a monopoly of the kind of wares concerned, and if to secure a
customer the defendant must represent his own as of that kind, it is a
fair inference that the customer wants those and those only." *Ely-
Norris Safe Co. v. Mosler Safe Co.,* 7 F.2d 603 (2d Cir.1925). (This case
was reversed by the Supreme Court on the grounds that, as a matter
of fact, the plaintiff did not actually have a monopoly in the field of
safes with explosive chambers).

3. MODERN CASES

Newer cases predicated on common law theories have slightly relaxed the
restrictions described in the preceding paragraphs. Thus, *if an advertisement is
clearly targeted at one specific competitor, modern courts have permitted that firm to
pursue a false advertising case even though it was not the sole source of the genuine
goods, and even though the qualities falsely claimed by the defendant for its goods
were not possessed by the plaintiff's goods.* Nonetheless, the sole source rule
continues to significantly limit the utility of common law remedies for competitors
aggrieved by false advertising. Several statutory remedies exist as alternatives,

however, so there is little pressure for common law courts to modify this restrictive approach.

> *Example:*   ECA made safety control devices for oil and gas burners. It also sold a replacement part known as a programmer. Several other firms also sold programmers, but ECA's were easiest to install and it had the dominant share of the market. Honeywell prepared a brochure falsely representing that its programmers were simple to install and suggesting that they be used instead of the ECA product. ECA filed suit for common law false advertising and was successful, even though it was not the sole source of this type of controller and even though the defendant's acts were not equivalent to passing off. *Electronics Corp. of America v. Honeywell, Inc.,* 428 F.2d 191 (1st Cir.1970).

B.   STATE STATUTORY REMEDIES FOR FALSE ADVERTISING

1.   STATUTORY PROVISIONS ARE WIDESPREAD

Every state in the union has some form of statute modelled on, or resembling, the Federal Trade Commission Act, which is discussed in Chapter VII of this outline. Many of these statutes forbid deceptive advertising and grant private rights of action to both competitors and consumers. Thus, state statutory law is a significant source of protection for honest merchants victimized by a competitor's false advertising. Many courses in Unfair Competition do not emphasize these statutes, however, because they do differ in significant respects from each other. One useful model for discussion is the Uniform Deceptive Trade Practices Act (UDTPA).

2.   NO "SOLE SOURCE" LIMITATION

Section 3 of the UDTPA provides that "A person likely to be damaged by a deceptive trade practice of another may be granted an injunction against it under the principles of equity . . . . Proof of monetary damage, loss of profits, or intent to deceive is not required." Since only a likelihood of injury need be shown, *a plaintiff does not have to demonstrate that it has a monopoly on the sale of the genuine goods to invoke this statute.* This is generally true for most state deceptive practice statutes, even those that differ from the UDTPA. Moreover, another provision of the UDTPA explicitly provides that the plaintiff and defendant need not even be competitors for a cause of action to lie.

3.   TYPES OF FALSEHOODS PROHIBITED

Some state statutes contain a general prohibition against "deceptive" acts, without any definition or itemization. This is also the approach of the Federal Trade Commission Act. General provisions of this type are, of course, plainly broad enough to include most conceivable forms of false advertising. *Other statutes,* however, including the UDTPA, *contain a more detailed listing of the forbidden behavior.* Among the specific practices barred by the UDTPA are representations "that goods or services have

. . . characteristics, ingredients, uses, benefits or quantities that they do not have;" representations "that goods are original or new if they are deteriorated, altered, reconditioned, reclaimed, used or second-hand;" and representations "that goods or services are of a particular standard, quality or grade . . . if they are of another." Either approach—general prohibition, or itemized list—tends to reach a much broader range of deceptive activities than the common law.

4.   LIMITED UTILITY OF STATE STATUTORY REMEDIES

While the statutes under discussion significantly expand the common law, many of them suffer from a significant limitation—they only provide for injuctive relief. This is true, for instance, of the UDTPA. Given the protracted timetable of most commercial litigation and the rather short life of most advertising campaigns, this means that, as a practical matter, the case will be won or lost at the preliminary injunction stage. If the plaintiff does not secure preliminary relief, the harmful ad campaign may do maximum damage and then be withdrawn before the trial on the merits even begins. Moreover the standards for preliminary relief are often quite rigorous, requiring, for example, a showing of "irreparable injury" before an injunction will be granted. The net result is that many firms will not find state statutory remedies for false advertising to be terribly useful devices for vindicating their rights. *Cf. Bally Mfg. Corp. v. JS & A Group, Inc.,* 88 Ill.App.3d 87, 43 Ill. Dec. 321, 410 N.E.2d 321 (1980).

C.   FEDERAL LANHAM ACT REMEDIES FOR FALSE ADVERTISING

1.   HISTORICAL BACKGROUND

Section 43(a) of the Lanham Act, the federal trademark statute, provides that "Any person who shall . . . use in connection with any goods or services . . . any false description or representation, including words or other symbols tending falsely to describe or represent the same, and shall cause such goods or service to enter into commerce . . . shall be liable to a civil action by any person . . . who believes that he is or is likely to be damaged by the use of any such false description or representation." The language of this provision suggests that it may be available to a competitor who wishes to prevent a rival from engaging in false advertising. Nonetheless, the provision was not initially interpreted in this fashion.

a.   Early Cases

When § 43(a) was first invoked in the false advertising context, defendants argued that the provision merely codified the "sole source" doctrine of *American Washboard* and *Ely-Norris* and did not grant any additional rights. They contended that since the provision was part of a trademark statute, it must be limited to "trademark-like" situations—in other words, cases of passing off. As noted above, a false representation only amounts to passing off one's goods as those of another when the other is the sole manufacturer of the genuine goods. The first cases to consider this argument found it persuasive and gave section 43(a) a narrow construction. *Samson Crane Co. v. Union Nat. Sales, Inc.,* 87 F.Supp. 218 (D.Mass.1949) ("the section should be construed to include only such false descriptions or representations as are of substantially the same economic nature as those which involve infringement or other improper use of trademarks."). This left the section as a federal cause of action for enforcement of state common law trademark rights, but stripped it of utility as a false advertising remedy.

b.   Modern Cases

In the landmark opinion *L'Aiglon Apparel, Inc. v. Lana Lobell, Inc.,* 214 F.2d 649 (3d Cir.1954), Circuit Judge Hastie rejected the restrictive approach to § 43(a) described above. Instead, he held that the provision should be given the broad interpretation that is suggested by its expansive language. Under this view, *a plaintiff need not analogize the situation to passing off in order to state a § 43(a) cause of action.* Virtually all the modern cases follow this approach.

2.   STANDING: WHO MAY INVOKE SECTION 43

Although the modern cases significantly broadened the scope of section 43, they did not hold that *any* firm may bring suit to stop false advertising. Despite statutory language conferring a right of action on any party who "*believes* that he is or is likely to be damaged," the courts have held that a mere subjective belief of harm is insufficient. Consequently, *there is a requirement that a plaintiff seeking an injunction demonstrate objectively that it is likely to be injured because of the false advertising engaged in by the defendant. Specifically, a section 43(a) plaintiff must show that it is likely to lose sales as a result of the defendant's behavior before an injunction will issue.* Where the plaintiff and defendant compete directly, however, many courts will find the necessary likelihood of lost sales from that fact alone. If a section 43(a) plaintiff seeks money damages, it must show an actual shift in patronage away from itself and to the defendant, before it can recover.

Example: Johnson & Johnson, a seller of baby oil, alleged in a suit under § 43(a) that the manufacturers of Nair depilatory falsely represented in television ads that a new version of Nair (with baby oil) could moisturize and soften skin, when, in fact, it could not. The circuit court required that plaintiff demonstrate "a logical causal connection between the alleged false advertising and its own sales position," before an injunction would issue. This burden was deemed satisfied by Johnson & Johnson's showing that the two firms were competitors in the hair removal market, that it had experienced an actual decline in sales and that, according to consumer surveys, users of Nair believed that they could dispense with baby oil if they used the defendant's new improved product. *Johnson & Johnson v. Carter-Wallace, Inc.,* 631 F.2d 186 (2d Cir.1980).

3. WHAT CONSTITUTES A FALSE DESCRIPTION OR REPRESENTATION

Not every falsehood is actionable under § 43(a). The plaintiff must demonstrate that the misrepresentation in question was material, that is, one which could have influenced the purchasing decision of a consumer. On the other hand, where only injunctive relief is being sought, *the plaintiff does not have to show that a specific number of consumers have actually been deceived. It is sufficient if the advertisement has a "tendency" to deceive. Black Hills Jewelry Mfg. Co. v. Gold Rush, Inc.,* 633 F.2d 746 (8th Cir.1980). The plaintiff need not prove that the defendant made the false representation intentionally.

D. COMMON LAW REMEDIES FOR DISPARAGEMENT

1. DISPARAGEMENT DEFINED

Disparagement is a falsehood that tends to denigrate the goods or services being sold by another party. While closely related to the notion of defamation, the two must be kept distinct, as the elements a plaintiff must prove differ in defamation and disparagement cases. In defamation the alleged falsehood attacks the character and injures the reputation of the seller of merchandise (or, of course, any other individual), while in a disparagement case, the statement is directed not at the seller, but at goods or services.

2. ELEMENTS OF DISPARAGEMENT

A party states a common law cause of action for disparagement if it can prove (1) that the defendant made offending statements about its products (2) that are false and (3) that resulted in so-called "special damages." The special damages requirement means that the plaintiff must be able to prove specific pecuniary losses flowing from the defendant's conduct, usually in the form of documented lost sales. (In a defamation case, by contrast, the party whose character has been attacked does not need to prove special damages).

3. FIRST AMENDMENT LIMITS ON DISPARAGEMENT ACTIONS

In order to avoid chilling the forms of debate and commentary on public issues protected under the First Amendment, the Supreme Court has held that where a defamation plaintiff is a public figure, he or she must prove the defendant acted with actual malice before recovery will be permitted. *New York Times v. Sullivan,* 376 U.S. 254, 84 S.Ct. 710 (1964). Actual malice, in this context, means that the defendant published the allegedly false statement either knowing that it was false, or with a reckless disregard for whether it was true or false. There is authority that this rule also applies in disparagement cases. Thus, *where the merits of a product become the subject of public debate, a firm asserting a cause of action for disparagement will have to show the defendant acted with actual malice. Bose Corp. v. Consumers Union of United States, Inc.,* 466 U.S. 485, 104 S.Ct. 1949 (1984). If a disparagement plaintiff is successful in showing the falsity of the statement, injury, and, where necessary, malice, there is no First Amendment obstacle to the issuance of an injunction forbidding the defendant from continuing its disparaging activities.

E. STATE STATUTORY REMEDIES FOR DISPARAGEMENT

Many state unfair practices statutes are broad enough to encompass claims of product disparagement. The Uniform Deceptive Trade Practices Act specifically includes, in its list of actionable deceptive practices, one rendering a firm liable if it "disparages the goods, services, or business of another by false or misleading representation of fact." The observations made about these statutes as remedies for false advertising in Section "B" of this chapter are also applicable when they are invoked against disparagement.

F. FEDERAL LANHAM ACT REMEDIES FOR DISPARAGEMENT

1. NO REMEDY FOR EXPLICIT DISPARAGEMENT

The language of Lanham Act § 43(a), as discussed above, forbids the dissemination of false descriptions or representations in commerce. It has been held, however, that *the statute only reaches falsehoods that concern one's own products. Thus, if a firm makes false and disparaging statements about another firm's products, those statements cannot form the basis of a § 43(a) cause of action.*

Example: One of two competing manufacturers of egg custard prepared a "comparison sheet" contrasting the virtues of the two products. This sheet allegedly said false and disparaging things about the other firm's custard. That other firm brought suit under Lanham Act § 43(a), but the court dismissed the case, noting that "the Act does not embrace misrepresentations about a competitor's product but only false or deceitful representations which the manufacturer or merchant makes about his own goods or services . . ." *Bernard Food Industries, Inc. v. Dietene Co.,* 415 F.2d 1279 (7th Cir.1970).

2. CERTAIN REPUTATIONAL HARMS ARE ACTIONABLE UNDER § 43(a)

While the rule stated immediately above prevents reliance on § 43(a) in the typical disparagement situation, there are certain limited situations, involving misrepresentations by one party that are harmful to the reputation of another, that can be reached under the section.

a. Altering Creative or Artistic Works

Some parties who buy artistic works desire to make alterations before exhibiting them. There are a number of reasons why this may occur. For instance, a sculpture may be too large to fit in the space where the owner wishes to exhibit it, so parts may be removed. The contemplated alterations, however, may be contrary to the artistic style and desires of the artist. If the work is exhibited in the altered form, but identified as the work of the original artist, that artist's reputation may be damaged. This harm is similar to disparagement in that it leaves consumers with a depreciated view of someone else's products or services. Yet there is authority for the proposition that such situations are actionable under § 43(a) because the altering party is the owner of the work and is making a false representation about his own goods—namely that it represents the (unadulterated) creative effort of the artist in question. (Such alterations are actionable in many European nations under a concept known as "droit morale").

Example: In 1973 the American Broadcasting Company obtained the rights to broadcast certain comedy performances of the British group Monty Python. Before broadcasting the material, ABC heavily edited it, both to make room for commercials and to delete offensive matter. When broadcast, it was identified as the work of Monty Python. The group sought an injunction under Section 43(a). The Circuit Court concluded that "an allegation that a defendant has presented to the public a 'garbled,' . . . distorted version of plaintiff's work seeks to redress the very rights sought to be protected by the Lanham Act, [§ 43(a)], and should be recognized as stating a cause of action under that statute." *Gilliam v. American Broacasting Companies, Inc.,* 538 F.2d 14 (2d Cir.1976).

b. Obscene Parody

Occasionally, certain firms will use a famous trade symbol of another business as part of a scandalous or obscene presentation. The harm of such activity is that it may alienate customers and cause them to think poorly of the firm whose symbol is being used. This is a harm similar to the one that underlies the disparagement cause of action. Yet, the use of the other firm's symbol within the defendant's own work has permitted courts to find the behavior actionable under § 43(a) as a false statement of sponsorship made by the defendant about his own goods. While some showing of likelihood of confusion is necessary in a case like this, some courts have shown a willingness to find that confusion based on relatively slight evidence while others have been more demanding. That has lead to a certain inconsistency in the decided cases.

Example: Defendant produced the pornographic film called "Debbie Does Dallas." At one point during this film, a woman dressed in the costume of a Dallas Cowboys Cheerleader performs various sexual acts. The Cheerleaders organization brought suit under § 43(a) claiming that the defendant had made a false representation about its product, the movie, through the unauthorized use of the uniform—namely that the movie had been sponsored by the Dallas Cowboys Cheerleaders. The plaintiffs prevailed on this theory. The court analyzed the existence of likelihood of confusion by noting that "the uniform unquestionably brings to mind the Dallas Cowboys Cheerleaders. Indeed it is hard to believe that anyone who had seen defendants' sexually depraved film could ever thereafter disassociate it from plaintiff's cheerleaders. This association results in confusion . . ." *Dallas Cowboys Cheerleaders, Inc. v. Pussycat Cinema, Ltd.,* 604 F.2d 200 (2d Cir. 1979).

Example: Defendant manufactured and distributed a poster depicting a pregnant, smiling girl, dressed in the uniform of the Girl Scouts of America and bearing the slogan "Be Prepared." The Girl Scouts filed suit under § 43(a) and a variety of other theories, but were denied relief because the court found that there was no likelihood consumers would think that the plaintiff sponsored the poster. While many persons had responded with outrage to the defendant's activities, the court remarked that "indignation is not confusion. To the contrary, the indignation of those who have called would appear to make it clear that they feel that the Girl Scouts are being unfairly put upon, not that the Girl Scouts are the manufacturers or distributors of the object of indignation." *Girl Scouts of the U.S.A. v. Personality Posters Mfg. Co.,* 304 F.Supp. 1228 (S.D.N.Y.1969).

REVIEW QUESTIONS

1. **T or F** There is no Lanham Act cause of action for explicit disparagement.

2. **T or F** Only a firm with a monopoly in the sale of goods with a particular attribute has a common law cause of action against another party who falsely claims that its goods have that attribute.

3. **T or F** A false advertising plaintiff relying on Lanham Act § 43(a) will have to make a more specific showing of lost sales if it seeks damages than will be required if it seeks merely injunctive relief.

4. **T or F** Any false statement is actionable under Lanham Act § 43(a).

5. **T or F** The earliest cases interpreting Lanham Act § 43(a) limited it to cases of passing off.

6. **T or F** State statutes providing remedies for false advertising have generally codified the sole source rule.

7. **T or F** Droit Morale is the European doctrine that provides a private remedy for competitors who allege that their commercial rivals are engaged in false advertising.

8. **T or F** A plaintiff alleging common law disparagement must prove "special damages" in order to recover.

9. **T or F** A disparagement plaintiff must prove that the defendant acted with actual malice if the merits of its product are the subject of a public controversy.

10. **T or F** A plaintiff relying on Lanham Act § 43(a) must prove that the defendant acted intentionally in order to secure injunctive relief.

11. In which of the following situations is the defendant least likely to be held liable in a suit predicated on Lanham Act § 43(a)?

    a.   The defendant, a clothing manufacturer, sells red tee shirts with white lettering in the same script as the Coca-Cola trademark, but containing the message "Enjoy Cocaine."

    b.   The defendant, a manufacturer of disposable razors, publishes a pamphlet stating that use of a competing brand of razor blades will cause skin cancer. There is no significant objective evidence that this is correct.

    c.   The defendant, a lawyer practicing as a solo practitioner, runs a television ad stating "we have personnel in our office who are expert in virtually every field of law."

    d.   The defendant, a radio station, edited certain drug related references out of a new popular song by the rock group Slam. Its disc jockeys play the song and introduce it as "the great new hit from Slam."

12. ComputerHaus is one of many retail computer outlets in Dodge City. Like many of these other stores, its staff consists of several highly trained computer experts who make themselves available to customers both before and after a purchase. Crazy Jerry is a discount retailer who just began selling computers. It does not have a staff with any technical expertise to speak of. Crazy Jerry has begun to advertise heavily on television. Its ads state "We've got personnel who can answer your every computer question. Their training and expertise in computers is unsurpassed." Which of the following statements is true?

    a.   ComputerHaus has a valid cause of action against Crazy Jerry for common law false advertising.

    b.   ComputerHaus has a valid cause of action against Crazy Jerry for common law disparagement.

    c.   If ComputerHaus can document specific sales lost to Crazy Jerry, it has a valid cause of action for damages under the Uniform Deceptive Trade Practices Act.

d. If ComputerHaus can document specific sales lost to Crazy Jerry, it has a valid cause of action for damages under Lanham Act § 43(a).

13. Phillips & Grant (P & G) is a large consumer goods company that manufactures, among other things, a hand lotion called "New Supra." Many other firms market hand lotions. The leading brand on the market is a product called Valamine Extra Care Lotion (VECL), made by Consumer Products, Inc. (CPI).

In an attempt to improve the market position of New Supra, P & G commissioned a clinical test designed to compare the effectiveness of its product against that of VECL. The test was designed and conducted by American Testing Labs, Inc., an independent firm, that received a fee of $250,000 from P & G for its efforts.

The test involved the selection of 100 consumers in each of three markets— Philadelphia, Chicago, and Boulder, Colorado. Each participant in the test was given a quantity of both New Supra and VECL. Each was told to apply New Supra, as needed to the right hand and VECL as needed to the left hand, for a period of 6 weeks. Thereafter, the participants were surveyed as to their conclusion about the merits of the two products. The results were as follows:

	Philadelphia	Chicago	Boulder
New Supra Superior	34%	30%	24%
No Difference	35%	41%	25%
VECL Superior	31%	29%	51%

Based on these results, P & G asked its advertising agency to prepare an advertising campaign touting the results. The agency developed print and television ads, the key phrasing of which was: "In two separate, independent, clinical tests over two thirds of users surveyed found New Supra as good or better than VECL at relieving dry, chapped hands."

When CPI noted these commercials they immediately conducted some tests of their own. When the consumers in those tests did not indicate a clear preference for either product, they concluded that there was something inappropriate about the P & G advertisements. They have contacted you and want to know if they have any valid cause of action against P & G. Do they?

VIII

FEDERAL TRADE COMMISSION REGULATION OF UNFAIR AND DECEPTIVE PRACTICES

Analysis

A. Overview of FTC Procedure
B. The Meaning of Unfairness
C. The Meaning of Deception
D. Advertising Substantiation
E. Remedies for Violations of Section 5
F. FTC Rulemaking

The Federal Trade Commission is both an antitrust and consumer protection agency. Its principal substantive responsibility is to enforce Section 5 of the Federal Trade Commission Act, which forbids "unfair methods of competition and unfair or deceptive acts or practices." Consistent with the scope of this outline, this chapter focuses exclusively on the consumer protection activities of the Commission.

Because the F.T.C. is an administrative agency, an understanding of its role in preventing deceptive advertising, disparagement, and related forms of unfair competition requires command of both substantive and procedural issues. Thus, this chapter will address the meaning of the crucial terms "unfair" and "deceptive," but it will also consider such procedural issues as what forms of relief the F.T.C. may impose on firms which have violated the law and the power of the Commission to proceed by rulemaking instead of case-by-case adjudication.

A. OVERVIEW OF F.T.C. PROCEDURE

The F.T.C. consists of 5 Commissioners appointed by the President to serve 7 year terms. The President also designates one Commissioner to serve as Chairman. The Chairman has principal responsibility for personnel and budgetary matters at the Commission. The following paragraphs review the chronological steps the Commission takes in identifying and prosecuting unfair and deceptive practices.

1. IDENTIFYING ILLEGAL BEHAVIOR
The F.T.C. learns of potential violations of the Federal Trade Commission Act in two principal ways—through its own investigations and through the complaints of competitors and consumers. The Federal Trade Commission has numerous investigative powers including the right to issue subpoenas and to demand that firms file "special reports."

2. NEGOTIATED DISPOSITION
When the F.T.C. concludes that legal action is warranted, the staff drafts an administrative complaint. In the usual case, however, formal administrative proceedings are not commenced immediately. Instead, the complaint—called a "proposed complaint" at this stage—is forwarded to the offending firm (referred to as the "respondent" in F.T.C. jargon) along with a notice of contemplated relief. *The firm in question can then agree to settle the dispute without further proceedings by entering into a "consent order."* Before such an agreement becomes final, however, it must be published in the Federal Register, and the public has 60 days in which to submit comments. A very significant portion of F.T.C. decisional law consists of these non-litigated consent decrees.

3. FORMAL ADJUDICATION

a. At the Agency Level

When the Commission and the respondent cannot agree on a consent decree, the F.T.C. formally serves the complaint. Thereafter, *the proceedings resemble a typical civil suit, except that they are conducted before an Administrative Law Judge (or ALJ) at the Federal Trade Commission instead of in district court.* After discovery and motion practice a hearing is held at which the Commission staff presents its proof of what the respondent did and its theory of how that behavior violates the statute. The respondent, naturally, is permitted to challenge any aspect of that showing. At the close of the hearing the ALJ prepares an Initial Decision. The losing party may then appeal to the full Commission which hears oral argument and may adopt, modify or set aside the Initial Decision.

b. Judicial Review

If the respondent prevails at the Commission level, the matter is terminated—the Commission staff may not appeal. On the other hand, *if the staff has succeeded and an order has been imposed against the respondent, that firm or individual may seek judicial review in the U.S. Court of Appeals.* The court may affirm, modify, or set aside the order.

4. RULEMAKING

Often an investigation will reveal that certain "unfair" or "deceptive" practices are being utilized on a widespread or industry-wide basis. In such cases, the Commission may choose to proceed by rulemaking. Numerous statutory provisions specify the procedures that the Commission must follow in preparing rules, and the final version of any rule is also subject to judicial review. Some of the more important details of the Commission's rulemaking powers are considered in the last section of this chapter.

B. THE MEANING OF UNFAIRNESS

1. HISTORICAL DEVELOPMENT

a. 1914 to 1938

From the adoption of the Federal Trade Commission Act in 1914 until it was amended in 1938, the Act did not contain any reference to "unfair or deceptive acts or practices." Its sole prohibition was against "unfair methods of competition." While this language clearly condemned behavior violative of antitrust norms, its utility as a tool against false advertising and other unfair trade practices was unclear. This ambiguity surfaced in cases holding that the Commission would have to demonstrate an injury to competitors in order to prove a statutory violation—that injury to consumers alone would not be sufficient. *Federal Trade Commission v. Raladam Co.,* 283 U.S. 643, 51 S.Ct. 587 (1931).

b. The Wheeler-Lea Amendment

To eliminate any uncertainty over the scope of the Act, Congress added the prohibition of "unfair or deceptive acts or practices" to the statute through the Wheeler-Lea Amendment of 1938. This made clear the Commission's power to intervene to protect consumers against unscrupulous practices regardless of the existence of harm to competing firms.

c. 1938 to 1964

In the years that followed the Wheeler-Lea Amendment, the Commission did not develop separate theories for "unfair" and "deceptive" practices. Instead, most practices were simply attacked as being *both* unfair and deceptive. In 1964, however, while the Commission was engaged in issuing rules requiring mandatory health warnings on cigarette packages, it issued a statement itemizing the factors that it would consider to determine when non-deceptive practices were illegal because they were "unfair." The factors were (1) whether the challenged practice offends public policy; (2) whether it is immoral, unethical, oppressive or unscrupulous; or (3) whether it causes substantial injury to consumers.

d. The *Sperry & Hutchinson* Case

The legal status of the Commission's list of factors remained unclear until 1972. In that year, the Supreme Court decided *Federal Trade Commission v. The Sperry & Hutchinson Co.,* 405 U.S. 233, 92 S.Ct. 898 (1972). Although that case was based on an antitrust-type violation, the Court used it as an opportunity to endorse the factors that the Commission had identified in 1964. Consequently, the case gave the F.T.C. a green light to proceed on an unfairness theory in cases where it could not prove deception. The Commission responded by using this authority in a number of contexts that many critics thought unwise. By the late 1970's there was talk of eliminating the F.T.C. authority to attack unfairness.

2. CURRENT DOCTRINE

In response to the criticism that it had been abusing its power to correct "unfair" practices, the Commission attempted to clarify its view of the unfairness concept. This clarification appeared in a letter prepared in late 1980 for submission to a Senate Committee. *The letter indicated that, in the future, behavior would only be considered unfair if it caused injury to consumers that was substantial, unmitigated, and unavoidable.* Legislation pending as this book goes to press would codify this standard.

a. Substantial Injury

According to the Commission, behavior which causes only a trivial or speculative harm to consumers is not unfair. *The harm in question must be signficant either in monetary terms or because of risk of physical injury.* The Commission did note, however, that behavior posing the risk of a relatively small harm to a large number of people should also be considered "substantial."

b. Unmitigated Injury

To be condemned as unfair, not only must a practice cause a substantial injury, but *"the injury must not be outweighed by any offsetting consumer or competitive benefits that the sales practice also produces."* An example of this situation might be a merchant's refusal to accept defective merchandise returned for a refund. While that policy might substantially injure some consumers, it might also have benefits to others, by keeping prices down. The Commission would balance these tendencies in determining its unfairness.

c. Unavoidable Injury

If consumers could exercise a reasonable degree of care to avoid the injury under discussion, the practice is not unfair. It is only where the practice prevents consumers from protecting themselves that the Commission will intervene.

d. The Role of Public Policy

The Commission indicated in its 1980 Statement that *proof that a respondent's conduct was in violation of a public policy would constitute circumstantial evidence of consumer injury.* Public policy violations will no longer be used as an independent basis for finding behavior unfair, but solely as a factual basis upon which to infer the requisite consumer injury. Moreover, the Commission indicated that for public policy to have even this effect, it should be "declared or embodied in formal sources such as statutes, judicial decisions or the Constitution . . . rather than being ascertained from a general sense of the national values."

3. ILLUSTRATIVE UNFAIR PRACTICES

Even the narrowed and clarified unfairness doctrine articulated by the Commission in its 1980 statement is extremely open-ended. There are a number of situations, however that illustrate how and when the doctrine might be applicable. *One group of business practices likely to be "unfair" under the Commission's approach are those involving outright coercion of consumers.* Similarly, situations entailing more subtle forms of coercion are also within the unfairness concept. A finding of unfairness is also possible when a seller withholds material information in its possession that would be useful to consumers in trying to make an informed choice. Finally, cases where a seller secures the consumer's consent to draconian post-sales remedies in the event of default may also be challengeable as "unfair." (Many of these practices are now expressly forbidden by the F.T.C.'s Credit Practices Rule, 16 C.F.R. § 444 (1985)). This is *not* an exhaustive list of the business behavior forbidden by the unfairness concept, but it reveals the broad and potentially useful scope of that doctrine. Note that most of these practices do not involve advertising. It is usually easier and more straightforward for the Commission to attack false advertising practices through its deception authority.

Examples: Door-to-door salesmen working for a firm that sold furnaces made a practice of dismantling consumers' furnaces and refusing to put them back together until the consumer made a purchase. The Commission found this behavior coercive and thus "unfair" within the meaning of the Act in *Holland Furnace Co. v. F.T.C.,* 295 F.2d 302 (7th Cir. 1961). Similarly, the Commission has suggested that the use of subliminal messages in television programs or advertising would be subtly coercive and unfair. When the Commission issued regulations requiring clothing manufacturers to attach labels explaining the proper care and cleaning to each garment offered for sale, they did so on the ground that the withholding of this material information was unfair. Finally, when a mail order firm used a state long arm statute to sue defaulting consumers in a jurisdiction far from where the consumers resided, the Commission labeled that practice unfair as well. *Spiegel, Inc. v. F.T.C.,* 540 F.2d 287 (7th Cir.1976).

C. THE MEANING OF DECEPTION

1. TRADITIONAL DEFINITION

The Federal Trade Commission Act contemplates that the Commission will intervene to halt a practice before it actually has caused significant harm. In light of this, the concept of "deceptiveness" was given a broad scope almost immediately after the 1938 amendments added it to the statute.

a. Protection for the Gullible

Under the traditional formula, an advertisement or other practice is deceptive if it has any tendency or capacity to deceive a signficant number of consumers. Moreover, the consumers in question are assumed to be not hypothetical "reasonable" consumers, but instead, consumers of especial gullibility. The result is a sweeping definition of deceptiveness.

Example: Respondent marketed a skin cream which it called Rejuvenescence. Its advertisements claimed that the product "restores natural moisture necessary for a live, healthy skin" and that if a consumer used it "[Her] face need know no drought years." The Commission viewed this advertisement as representing that the product could reverse the aging process, and held it deceptive on that theory. The court of appeals affirmed, declaring that "There is no merit to [the] argument that since no straight-thinking person could believe that its cream would actually rejuvenate, there could be no deception. . . . [The] law was not 'made for the protection of experts, but for the public—that vast multitude which includes the ignorant, the unthinking and the credulous." *Charles of the Ritz Dist. Corp. v. Federal Trade Commission,* 143 F.2d 676 (2d Cir.1944).

b.   Limits on The Definition

Because the foregoing definition is so broad it is easy to pose absurd hypotheticals in which basically innocuous advertisements are condemned as deceptive. Indeed, *Charles of the Ritz, supra,* may be such a case. Subsequent cases, therefore, retreated from the most extreme applications of this formula. Under these cases, *bizzare or idiosyncratic interpretations of advertisements are not relied on to determine deceptiveness.*

Example: Respondent manufactured a swimming aid to be worn underneath a bathing suit, and advertised it as "invisible." The Commission staff challenged this as deceptive since the device was not actually invisible, but could be seen when placed on a table, etc.! In dismissing the case, the Commission itself commented that "an advertiser cannot be charged with liability in respect of every conceivable misconception, however outlandish, to which his representations might be subject among the foolish or feeble-minded." *Heinz W. Kirchner,* 63 F.T.C. 1282 (1963).

c.   No Consumer Injury or Intent Required

The Commission need not prove that the respondent acted intentionally in order to condemn a practice as deceptive. In addition, it was established early in the administration of the Federal Trade Commission Act that a practice could be deceptive even if it did not cause any economic or physical injury to consumers. This, of course, differentiates the deceptiveness doctrine from the concept of unfairness, where consumer injury is the heart of the matter. In the deception area the very status of being deceived means that one has been injured.

Example: Respondent sold lumber made from a species of tree called *pinus ponderosa* under the name California White Pine. Under the typology used by botanists, this tree was not a genuine "white pine," but rather a yellow pine. Nonetheless, respondent contended that the two types of wood were equal in quality. Consumers who requested "white pine" were often given the respondent's lumber instead of true white pine. The Commission therefore challenged the use of the name as a deceptive practice. The case ultimately reached the U.S. Supreme Court, which affirmed the finding of deception as proper, even on the assumption that the two types of lumber were identical. In reaching this result, the Court remarked that "the consumer is prejudiced if upon giving an order for one thing, he is supplied with something else. . . . In such matters, the public is entitled to get what it chooses . . ." *Federal Trade Commission v. Algoma,* 291 U.S 67, 54 S.Ct. 315 (1934).

2.   A NEW STANDARD OF DECEPTIVENESS?

Even with the limitation of the deceptiveness concept referred to above, numerous political and academic critics of the Commission claimed that it was still invoked in many questionable contexts during the 1970's.   The advent of a Commission consisting of a majority of Reagan appointees placed some of those critics in a position to reformulate the law of deception.   That was accomplished in a 1984 Commission decision, *In re Cliffdale Associates*, 103 F.T.C. 110 (Dkt. 9156).

According to that opinion, *"the Commission will find an act or practice deceptive if, first, there is a representation, omission, or practice that, second, is likely to mislead consumers acting reasonably under the cirumstance, and third, the representation, omission or practice is material."*

a.   Differences From Traditional Standard

The verbal formula in *Cliffdale* departs from the traditional definition of deception in a number of key respects.   First, the required *probability* of consumer deception is apparently different.   The traditional test is satisfied if there is "any tendency" for the ad to deceive, while the *Cliffdale* standard is only triggered if deception is "likely."   Secondly, the focus of the *Cliffdale* test is not a gullible consumer, but a consumer who is acting reasonably in the circumstances.   Representatives of the present Federal Trade Commission have argued in speeches, Congressional testimony and articles, that despite these semantic distinctions, *Cliffdale* did not change the law of deception.   They claim that while the traditional *verbal* formula had remained unchanged, the actual law being applied by the Commission and the courts had evolved away from the broad interpretation of the earliest cases, and that the language of *Cliffdale* merely reflects the present state of the law more clearly.   Others, including the two Commissioners who dissented in *Cliffdale,* have challenged this view, claiming that *Cliffdale* is a blatant and unwise attempt to narrow the deception standard and limit the protection available to consumers.

b.   Legal Status of New Standard

If *Cliffdale* does announce a new, different view of the law of deception, the legal status of the new rule is uncertain.   It has not yet been subject to judicial scrutiny and thus it is unclear if it will be endorsed by the courts. Moreover, language very similar to that used in *Cliffdale* was previously proposed to Congress as an amendment to Section 5 of the Federal Trade Commission Act, and was rejected.   That could mean merely that Congress thought it was an unnecessary amendment or it could mean that Congress disapproved of the new standard.   It will be necessary to await further developments to determine the precise status of the *Cliffdale* language.

3.   FACTORS INFLUENCING COMMISSION CASE SELECTION

Whatever deception definition the Commission uses, it does not have the resources to challenge every deceptive practice in the economy.   Thus, the principles it uses to decide which cases to actually pursue are as important as the formal legal definition of deception.   The Commission identified many of the factors it considers before filing a complaint in a 1975 "Policy Planning Protocol," as well as in subsequent speeches and publications. Some of these are reviewed below.

a. Price and Frequency of Purchase

Perhaps most important, in the eyes of the present Commission, is whether the product involved is an expensive item purchased only infrequently, or an inexpensive one purchased repeatedly. In the case of the latter types of products, the Commission is unlikely to challenge anything but the most blatantly deceptive advertisements, because it believes that if consumers buy the product and are dissatisfied due to its failure to perform as advertised, they will simply stop buying it in the future. Moreover, since sellers can predict that this is the likely outcome with small inexpensive items, they are unlikely to lie in significant respects in the first place.

b. Deterrence

The Commission is more likely to pursue a case if the practice involved is widespread and the case provides an opportunity to clarify the law with respect to that behavior. It is also more likely to file a case in situations where the failure to do so may damage the agency's credibility in the business community.

c. Risk of Lessening Information

The Commission is less likely to commence a proceeding if the proposed remedy would make it burdensome for the advertiser to provide specific information to consumers. The Commission fears that in such a case, the advertiser is likely to recast its advertisements into generalities rather than incur the cost of developing or documenting more specific claims. In the Commission's view, such a result would be counter-productive, since it reduces the amount of information available to consumers.

d. Physical Injury or Foregone Treatment

The Commission is very likely to act against deception where the result may be physical injury to the consumers involved, especially where that risk is not apparent at the time of purchase. The same is true if the advertisement falsely represents that a harmless but useless preparation or product has medicinal benefit, because in these cases, consumers may be deceived into foregoing treatment for serious conditions to their detriment.

4. APPLICATIONS OF THE DECEPTION STANDARD

The concept of deception has been invoked in an enormous variety of cases to put an end to false advertising. Some of the more interesting applications of the concept are reviewed here.

a.   Omissions

An advertisement can be deceptive not only due to explicit falsehoods, but also because of its failure to state a fact necessary to make the material which does appear truthful.

Example: A firm operating several weight reduction clinics advertised that consumers could lose weight quickly and safely by enrolling in their program. They did not reveal that their program included administration of a drug that had not been approved by the FDA for use in treating obesity. The Commission successfully challenged their advertisements as deceptive for omitting to disclose the use of the drug. *Simeon Management Corp. v. Federal Trade Commission,* 579 F.2d 1137 (9th Cir.1978).

b.   Claims of Uniqueness

If an advertising claim suggests that a firm's product is the only one with particular properties, and this implication is incorrect, the advertisement is deceptive within the meaning of the Federal Trade Commission Act. This is true both when the claim of alleged uniqueness is made explicitly and when it is merely implied.

Example: The Commission secured a consent decree preventing the manufacturers of Domino sugar from implying that its brand was superior to others on the market. *Amstar Corp.,* 83 F.T.C. 659 (1973).

c.   Type of Business

The deceptiveness doctrine has been used to challenge firms that misrepresented the type or nature of the business they were engaged in. The courts are cautious, however, to avoid depriving the respondent of the economic value of an established trade name, and thus often require disclaimers rather than a complete abandonment of the deceptive name.

Example: When a firm that did not actually grind wheat into flour sold its flour under a trade name using the words "milling company," the Commission successfully established that this was deceptive. *Federal Trade Commission v. Royal Milling Co.,* 288 U.S. 212, 53 S.Ct. 335 (1933).

d.   Testimonials

Many advertisers use either experts or celebrities to endorse their products in advertising. The F.T.C. has used its deception authority to attack a variety of misleading practices concerning testimonial endorsements, such as a false statement by the endorser that he or she actually uses the product in question. In 1975 the Commission issued guidelines governing endorsement practices, codified at 16 C.F.R. § 255 (1984).

Example: In attacking various advertisements for an acne remedy as
deceptive, the Commission specifically challenged claims by singer
Pat Boone that his daughters "got lasting help with Acne-Statin."
Apparently, they did not. *Cooga Mooga, Inc.,* 92 F.T.C. 310 (1978).

e.   Television Advertising

Determining the deceptiveness of a television advertisement can raise a variety
of problems because often an accurate demonstration of a product in the studio
will present an inaccurate image to the viewer at home, or vice versa. *If an
advertiser* tries to correct this problem by using a simulation or mock up, and
*invites the viewers to actually look at the object or demonstration in question to
see the superiority of the product, the fact that a mock up is being used must be
explicitly disclosed.   If it is not, the advertisement is deceptive.*

Example: The maker of Rapid Shave shaving cream wanted to demonstrate
the product's ability to shave sandpaper. When shown through a
TV camera, however, actual sandpaper appears to be merely a
sheet of colored paper. To obviate that problem, the firm
prepared a mock-up of plexiglass, to which sand had been applied.
It was this mock-up that was "shaved" in the TV commercial.
The Commission challenged the undisclosed use of this prop as
deceptive, and was successful in the Supreme Court. *Federal Trade
Commission v. Colgate-Palmolive Co.,*   380 U.S. 374, 85 S.Ct. 1035
(1965).

5.   DECEPTIVE PRICING AND SALES PRACTICES

The deception concept is not limited to advertising practices, nor is it confined to
misrepresentation concerning the attributes of products and services.   Hence *the
Commission has successfully challenged numerous representations about the price of
products and many other types of sales practices as deceptive.*

a.   Misrepresentation of Price or "Free" Products

For many years, the F.T.C. attacked various usages of the term "free" and
various representations that merchandise was "on sale" for being deceptive.   In
the typical case of this sort, the merchandise claimed to be "on sale" has
never been available at a higher "regular" price, or the "free" merchandise is
only obtainable after certain conditions are satisfied. The F.T.C. also issued
two sets of Guides in this area—Guide To Use of Word "Free" and Similar
Representations, 16 C.F.R. § 251.1 (1984), and the Guides Against Deceptive
Pricing, 16 C.F.R. § 233 (1984).   In recent years, the Commission has brought
very few such cases out of a concern that they may actually cause firms to
hesitate to lower prices or engage in promotions.

Example: A paint company advertised that for every can of paint purchased
by a consumer for the regular price of $6.98, the buyer would
receive a "free" can of the same quality. The Commission found

this deceptive because the firm had never sold single cans at the price of $6.98 and that, consequently, the second can was not truly free. This conclusion was sustained on review by the U.S. Supreme Court. *Federal Trade Commission v. Mary Carter Paint Co.,* 382 U.S. 46, 86 S.Ct. 219 (1965).

b. Misrepresentation of Warranty Terms

The Commission has occasionally used its deception authority against firms that have misstated the scope of product guarantees or warranties in their advertising.

Example: Where a retail store indicated in newspaper ads that its products were unconditionally guaranteed, but where the literature accompanying the products had limitations and conditions, the discrepancy was found to be deceptive under § 5 of the F.T.C. Act even though the firm normally honored the unlimited version of the guarantee that had appeared in the newspaper. *Montgomery Ward & Co. v. Federal Trade Commission,* 379 F.2d 666 (7th Cir. 1967).

c. Bait and Switch

Bait and switch is a sales practice in which customers are attracted to a store by advertisements for a product that the merchant does not really desire to sell—usually an advertisement promising a very attractive price. Once the customer is in the store, he or she is switched to a different product with a much higher profit margin for the seller. Such tactics have been successfully challenged by the F.T.C. as deceptive.

Example: A jewelry store advertised eyeglasses available "from $7.50 complete" including "lenses, frames and case." Evidence revealed that this firm sold only 10 pairs of eyeglasses each year at the advertised price out of a total of 1400 pairs sold. A Commission finding that this was deceptive bait and switch was affirmed on judicial review. *Tashof v. Federal Trade Commission,* 437 F.2d 707 (D.C.Cir.1970).

d. Door-to-Door Sales

Over the years, the Commission has used its deception authority successfully to attack a variety of misrepresentations made by firms doing business door-to-door. For instance, salespeople often falsely claim that they are taking surveys or giving away free samples in order to gain access to the consumer's home. These salespeople also sometimes use high pressure sales tactics that are within the definition of unfairness. Under a formal Commission Regulation, 16 C.F.R. § 429 (1984), *consumers must be given a three day "cooling off period" during which time they may rescind any transaction entered into with a door-to-door salesman.*

e. Mail Order Sales

Mail order firms occasionally misrepresent how soon merchandise will be shipped, or the types of items that they have on hand. In addition, they occasionally send unsolicited merchandise to customers and then follow up with sternly worded bills. The Commission has successfully stopped such practices both through case-by-case adjudication and through its Mail Order Regulations, 16 C.F.R. § 435 (1985).

6. DISPARAGEMENT

False statements by one firm about the products of a commercial rival are also within the concept of deceptiveness. Perma-Maid Co. v. Federal Trade Commission, 121 F.2d 282 (6th Cir. 1941). However, when a non-competitor with no financial interest in the matter expresses its honest opinions about a particular product, the statements are not legally "deceptive" even if they are both false and disparaging. Any other result would pose too great a risk of F.T.C. interference with First Amendment rights.

Example: Respondent published and distributed pamphlets cataloging the hazards of eating food prepared in aluminum pots and pans. The respondent was not engaged in the manufacture or sale of cooking utensils of any sort. Although the Commission found the statements in the pamphlets false and disparaging, the reviewing court held that no violation of the statute had occurred, so long as the material represented the respondent's honest opinion or belief. *Scientific Mfg. Co. v. Federal Trade Commission,* 124 F.2d 640 (3d Cir.1941).

D. ADVERTISING SUBSTANTIATION

One of the surest ways to improve the accuracy of advertising is to prevent firms from making claims unless they have advance documentation for them. While there is no explicit requirement of this sort in the Federal Trade Commission Act, administrative and judicial interpretations have now made it plain that *it is a violation of the statute to make an advertising claim in the absence of an advance reasonable basis. This is known as the advertising substantiation doctrine.*

1. DEVELOPMENT OF THE DOCTRINE

The advertising substantiation doctrine was first set out in the Commission's opinion in *Pfizer, Inc.,* 81 F.T.C. 23 (1972). In that case, Pfizer had advertised that its product Unburn "stops sunburn pain fast." The Commission staff argued that the promulgation of this advertisement, without advance substantiation of the medical claim, was both "unfair" and "deceptive."

a. The Deception Argument

The deception argument was based on a contention that the Pfizer ad contained an *implied* representation that Pfizer had a reasonable basis for the claims that it made. In the staff's view, the absence of the reasonable basis made the implied claim false and the ad deceptive. That theory was not relied on by the Commission in the *Pfizer* opinion, although it was subsequently used to attack an unsubstantiated advertising claim in *National Dynamics Corp.*, 82 F.T.C. 488 (1973).

b. The Unfairness Argument

The unfairness contention was based on the notion that advertisers may not force consumers to enter into an "economic gamble" as to whether or not unsupported claims will turn out to be true. This contention was accepted by the Commission, which declared that *"it is an unfair practice in violation of the Federal Trade Commission Act to make an affirmative product claim without a reasonable basis for making that claim."*

2. WHAT CONSTITUTES SUBSTANTIATION

a. General Rule

An advertiser is ordinarily required to have a "reasonable basis" for the objective claims it makes. Whether an advertiser had a reasonable basis for a particular claim is treated as a factual question, turning on factors such as industry standards, the cost to the advertiser to develop better data, and the value of the information consumers obtain from the ad. Thus, while controlled scientific or clinical tests may be required in certain contexts, there is no general requirement for substantiation in that form, and other types of substantiation have been accepted. Subjective product claims (such as "tastes great") or mere puffing ("best food in town") need not be supported by a reasonable basis.

b. Specific Reference to Substantiation in Ad

If the advertiser has made explicit reference to substantiation, ("controlled clinical tests prove . . ."), *the advertiser must have the type and amount of substantiation alluded to in order to avoid violation of the F.T.C. Act. Litton Industries,* 97 F.T.C. 1 (1981).

c. Basis Must Exist Prior to Disseminating Ad

The ad substantiation doctrine is only satisfied if the advertiser has an advance basis for making the claims. It is not acceptable to make claims casually, and then, after the ad has been distributed, to attempt to test those claims and prove their accuracy. Data developed after the ad was circulated may be considered, however, in interpreting the pre-dissemination material or in formulating an appropriate remedial order. As a practical matter, the Commission would be highly unlikely to challenge an unsubstantiated claim that had turned out to be true.

3. EFFECT OF SUBSTANTIATION DOCTRINE ON BURDEN OF PROOF

After the substantiation doctrine was announced some observers questioned whether it impermissibly shifted the burden of proof to the respondent in an F.T.C.

proceeding, because under the doctrine the Commission no longer needs to prove that an advertising claim is false to make out a statutory violation. Instead the Commission merely has to show that the advertiser lacked prior documentation to make out a violation of the statute. Nonetheless, the courts have indicated that any alteration in the respective burdens is not impermissible and that a requirement of ad substantiation is within the power of the Commission. *Jay Norris, Inc. v. Federal Trade Commission,* 598 F.2d 1244 (2d Cir.1979).

E. REMEDIES FOR VIOLATIONS OF SECTION 5

1. CEASE AND DESIST ORDERS
The most common Commission remedy is the entry of a "cease and desist" order against a firm that has been found in violation of F.T.C. Act § 5. Such an order operates prospectively only and forbids the respondent from engaging in specified conduct in the future. The forbidden conduct will, of course, include the behavior that gave rise to the initial charge of unfairness or deception, but may also encompass other behaviors if the Commission believes that this is necessary to "fence in" the respondent and prevent future violations.

2. ORDERS REQUIRING AFFIRMATIVE STATEMENTS
Occasionally, an order merely requiring the cessation of specified conduct would not fully remedy the unfair or deceptive behavior that led the Commission to file a complaint. For instance the respondent may have been guilty of deception arising from an omission rather than from a misstatement. In such a situation, the sensible remedy is to require the respondent to supply the missing material in the future. Yet an order of this type—affirmatively requiring the advertiser to make a specified disclosure in the future—might be challenged as beyond the Commission's remedial power to enter prohibitory "cease and desist" orders. Although numerous respondents have asserted this argument, *the Courts have sustained Commission orders that have required affirmative disclosures.*

Example: The makers of the tonic, Geritol, advertised it as effective for "tiredness due to iron poor blood." The Commission felt that these ads implied that most tiredness was due to iron poor blood, when in truth, that is not so. Consequently, it ordered the respondent to affirmatively disclose in future ads that the great majority of people who suffer from tiredness do not have an iron deficiency. The propriety of this order was affirmed on judicial review. *J.B. Williams Co., Inc. v. Federal Trade Commission,* 381 F.2d 884 (6th Cir.1967).

3. CORRECTIVE ADVERTISING

a. Conditions Where Appropriate
Sometimes a firm has repeated a deceptive claim so often, over so long a time, that even if it stopped making that claim, the erroneous impression it created

would "linger" in the minds of consumers. Where this is true, an order that merely forbids further repetitions of the falsehood does not suffice to prevent consumers from being misled in the future. Consequently, in cases such as this, the Commission argued that the only effective remedy is a requirement that the advertiser make statements in future ads to correct the lingering deception. Such orders, known as *"corrective advertising" orders, have been held to be within the Commission's cease and desist power, and have been used in a number of cases, both litigated and consent.*

Example: Listerine mouthwash was advertised for decades as effective in preventing or reducing the severity of the common cold. The Commission successfully challenged this ad as deceptive, and then entered an order requiring the respondent to state in future Listerine advertisements that "Contrary to prior advertising, Listerine will not help prevent colds or sore throats or lessen their severity." On review, the introductory phrase "contrary to prior advertising" was deleted, but the rest of the mandatory corrective language was affirmed. *Warner Lambert Co. v. Federal Trade Commission,* 562 F.2d 749 (D.C.Cir.1977).

b. Duration of Corrective Advertising Requirement

Corrective advertising orders do not usually require the respondent to run the corrective language indefinitely. Instead, the order typically specifies how long the respondent must include the "correction" in its future ads. Sometimes duration of the obligation to use corrective language is measured in terms of a specified period of months or years. Alternatively, the order may require that the correction be run until the respondent has spent a stated amount on future advertising. The latter approach was used in the Listerine case, and approved by the reviewing Court, which explained its justification: "The Commission concluded that correction was required and that a duration of a fixed period of time might not accomplish that task, since [respondent] could evade the order by choosing not to advertise at all. The formula settled upon by the Commission is reasonably related to the violation it found."

c. Differences Between Affirmative Disclosure and Corrective Advertising Orders

While orders requiring information disclosure and corrective advertising orders resemble each other, there are some differences between them. An order requiring informational disclosure presumes that certain advertising representations are misleading unless additional information is simultaneously disclosed. The advertiser can, however, avoid the duty to make the extra disclosure by discontinuing the underlying representation. For instance, in the Geritol situation, if the advertiser stopped advertising the product as a remedy for tiredness, it would no longer be obligated to disclose the fact that most tiredness is not due to iron poor blood. On the other hand, because the premise of a corrective advertising order is "lingering" deception, those types of orders require the corrective disclosure to be run for a specified time period *regardless of the ad content.* Thus, the Listerine order required the statement that the product did not prevent colds, even if the advertiser had changed the ad campaign to stress different attributes of its product, such as its effectiveness for bad breath.

d. First Amendment Limits on Commission Orders

Commercial speech is within the protection of the First Amendment. However, the courts have consistently held that First Amendment protection does not extend to false or deceptive commercial speech, and consequently, *Commission orders forbidding misleading advertising claims or requiring specific disclosures have usually been sustained when challenged on First Amendment grounds. On the other hand, some courts have suggested that the First Amendment requires the Commission to use the least restrictive order possible to remedy the deception. Beneficial Corp. v. Federal Trade Commission,* 542 F.2d 611 (3d Cir. 1976) ("any prior restraint is suspect, and . . . a remedy, even for deceptive advertising, can go no further than is necessary for the elimination of the deception.")

4. RESTITUTION

a. Restitution Provisions in Cease and Desist Orders

Firms engaged in deceptive activities often bilk consumers out of considerable sums of money. This raises the question of whether the Commission may order the respondent to return its ill gotten gains to the victimized consumers. Because the Federal Trade Commission Act only empowers the Commission to issue "cease and desist" orders, it would seem difficult to enter an order imposing an affirmative duty to make restitution of funds. Nonetheless, in the early 70's, the Commission developed a novel theory for including restitution requirements in cease and desist orders. It claimed that the respondent's continued retention of the funds was itself an unfair act, that could only "cease" if the respondent were forced to make restitution. In other words, the order required the firm to cease and desist from retaining the funds!! This theory was explicitly rejected in *Heater v. Federal Trade Commission,* 503 F.2d 321 (9th Cir.1974), which held that *restitutionary provisions are not within the Commission's cease and desist power.*

b. Restitution Sought in Civil Suits

In 1975 Congress added a provision to the F.T.C. Act permitting the Commission to file a civil suit in U.S. District Court to seek restitution from a firm that has been found guilty of an unfair or deceptive practice and against which a cease and desist order has been entered. 15 U.S.C.A. § 57b(a)(1) (1984).

5. REMEDIES FOR VIOLATIONS OF CEASE AND DESIST ORDERS
a. Parties
If a firm violates the terms of a cease and desist order entered against it, the Commission may file a suit in U.S. District Court seeking civil penalties in the amount of $10,000 for each violation. 15 U.S.C.A. § 45(*l*) (1984). If the violation is a continuing one, each day is considered a separate violation, and thus the potential maximum fine can be staggering.

> *Example:*   In the 1960's Reader's Digest ran sweepstakes promotions by sending material resembling negotiable instruments through the mail. The Commission attacked this practice as deceptive and entered a cease and desist order forbidding the firm from using "simulated items of value" in the future. Thereafter, the firm ran further promotions using simulated "travelers checks" and "cash-convertible bonds." The Commission filed suit for penalties and alleged that each of 18 million pieces of mail sent out by the firm constituted a separate violation of the earlier order. Both the district and appellate courts agreed, and the firm was required to pay $1,750,000 in civil penalties. The maximum penalty that could have been imposed was in excess of $179 billion. *United States v. Reader's Digest Ass'n.,* 662 F.2d 955 (3d Cir.1981).

b. Non-Parties
The Federal Trade Commission Act also permits the F.T.C. to seek civil penalties from firms that engage in conduct violative of cease and desist orders entered against *other* parties, provided the defendant in such a suit is shown to have acted with actual knowledge of the fact that the disputed behavior was unfair or deceptive. 15 U.S.C.A. § 45(m) (1984). In effect, this provision makes every cease and desist order a potential precedent for challenging the behavior of all firms doing business in this country. To more easily satisfy the "actual knowledge" requirement in this statute, the F.T.C. will sometimes mail copies of final cease and desist orders to all other firms in the same industry as the respondent.

F. F.T.C. RULEMAKING

1. THE COMMISSION'S AUTHORITY TO PROMULGATE RULES
Prior to 1975 there was some ambiguity as to whether the Federal Trade Commission could issue substantive rules specifying in advance particular behaviors that would be considered unfair or deceptive. The judicial authority on that question indicated that such authority did exist. *National Petroleum Refiners Ass'n v. Federal Trade Commission,* 482 F.2d 672 (D.C.Cir.1974). *The uncertainty was eliminated with the addition, in 1975, of explicit statutory authority to promulgate rules.* 15 U.S.C.A. § 57a (1984). The rulemaking procedure is spelled out in great detail in the statute and

the Commission, like all federal agencies, is also subject to the Administrative Procedure Act.

2. SCOPE AND EFFECT OF COMMISSION RULES

The Commission has issued formal rules on over two dozen different subjects. These rules are collected in title 16 of the Code of Federal Regulations and deal with such diverse topics as door-to-door and mail order sales, the proper disclosure of the leather content of belts, and impermissible credit practices in consumer loan transactions. *When a firm violates the provisions of one of these rules, the Commission may file a suit in district court seeking civil penalties.*

3. JUDICIAL LIMITS ON RULEMAKING

Before a Commission rule becomes effective it is subjected to judicial review. This requirement is not a mere formality, and a number of courts have set aside all or part of proposed rules for a variety of defects. For instance, the courts require that the Commission *first* identify unfair or deceptive practices actually being used by businesses, and then draft a rule designed to eliminate these identified problems. The Commission is not permitted to use its rulemaking authority to promulgate a code of desirable behavior and then to declare that the failure to live up to these standards is "unfair." If it were permitted to do this, it would have virtually unlimited authority to legislate about any matter affecting the economy. *See e.g. Katherine Gibbs School, Inc. v. Federal Trade Commission,* 612 F.2d 658 (2d Cir.1979).

4. LEGISLATIVE LIMITS ON RULEMAKING

Over the years, the Federal Trade Commission has embarked on a number of rulemaking proceedings that proved politically controversial. Among these were attempted rules regulating advertising directed at children, the rules concerning required disclosure of defects in used cars and the rules governing certain funeral industry practices. In these and other cases, Congress has intervened and enacted legislation either limiting how the rule may be worded, limiting the theories the Commission may rely on, or denying the Commission permission to spend any funds on a particular rulemaking in the future, thus effectively killing the rule. In addition, Congress sought to assert a general supervisory role over the Federal Trade Commission by enacting a "legislative veto" statute giving it the power to set aside Commission rules by a vote of both houses. That provision was held unconstitutional as a result of the decision in *I.N.S. v. Chadha,* 462 U.S. 919, 103 S.Ct. 2764 (1983), but pending legislation would restore a modified form of legislative veto responsive to the Supreme Court's objections. That legislation would also require the Commission to find that a practice was "prevalent" in an industry before it could institute a rulemaking proceeding.

5. THE FUTURE OF RULEMAKING

In the short term, the Commission is not likely to use its rulemaking powers to any great extent. The present political climate is not conducive to aggressive assertion of rulemaking power, and the current Commissioners have a clear preference for proceeding via case-by-case adjudication except in the clearest of cases.

REVIEW QUESTIONS

1. **T or F** An F.T.C. complaint based on a deception theory requires a showing of consumer injury, while a complaint based on an unfairness theory does not.

2. **T or F** The prohibition against unfair and deceptive acts and practices was added to the Federal Trade Commission Act by the Wheeler-Lea Amendment.

3. **T or F** Under the traditional formula for deception, an advertisement is deceptive if it has any tendency to deceive a significant number of consumers.

4. **T or F** The Commission must prove that the respondent acted intentionally if its complaint is based on a deception theory.

5. **T or F** The Federal Trade Commission may not include a provision requiring restitution in an administrative cease and desist order.

6. **T or F** Violation of the terms of an F.T.C. cease and desist order is a criminal offense.

7. **T or F** In recent years, Congress has frequently intervened in F.T.C. rulemaking initiatives.

8. **T or F** It is a deceptive practice under the Federal Trade Commission Act to use a mock-up in a television commercial.

9. **T or F** Both affirmative statements and omissions can be the basis for a charge of deceptiveness by the F.T.C.

10. **T or F** The present Federal Trade Commission is most likely to file an administrative complaint against a deceptive advertisement where the product involved is an inexpensive, frequently purchased item.

11. **T or F** Federal Trade Commission regulations require firms engaged in door-to-door sales to give consumers a three day "cooling off" period in which to cancel their purchases.

12. **T or F** If the full Commission finds in favor of the respondent, the Commission staff attorney prosecuting the complaint may not seek judicial review in the Court of Appeals.

13. In April, 1984, chemists at the Alpha pharmaceutical corporation inadvertently stumbled on a new chemical compound. They speculated that this chemical, if applied in a diluted form, could greatly slow the growth rate of regular lawn grass. Alpha began mass producing the compound and marketing it under the name LO–MOW later that same month. Their advertising claimed that "This preparation will vastly reduce the time you spend on mowing your lawn—and it is safe and easy to use." To use the product, which is sold as a powder, the consumers must mix it with specified amounts of water and use the mixture to water their lawn. The product has proven quite effective at retarding grass growth, requiring homeowners to mow their lawns only once every 6 to 8 weeks. Which of the following statements is most accurate?

    a.   Alpha violated the Federal Trade Commission Act by using the name LO–MOW for its product.

    b.   Alpha violated the Federal Trade Commission Act by promulgating its advertisements in violation of the ad substantiation doctrine.

    c.   Alpha violated the Federal Trade Commission Act by claiming in its ads that its product is easy to use, because the product must be pre-mixed with water and usual sprinkler systems cannot be used.

    d.   Alpha has not violated the Federal Trade Commission Act.

14. In 1982 Alpha was found guilty of deception in claiming in its advertisements for sneakers that they would make you "run faster." The resulting cease and desist order, which attained wide publicity in the footware trade press, forbids any advertising claim "to the effect that the product can improve athletic performance." In addition, in 1983 the Commission adopted final regulations requiring the disclosure of the materials used to make a sneaker on a label attached to each shoe. Which of the following firms is not subject to a civil penalty under the Federal Trade Commission Act?

    a.   Alpha, for running ads in 1984 stating, "Baseball season is here—if you wanna be an all star, you better wear the Alpha athletic shoe."

    b.   Beta, for selling shoes with a label attached reading "For a list of the materials used to make this product, send a stamped self-addressed envelope to Beta Shoe Corp. 123 Insole Blvd., Sneaker, Mo."

    c.   Gamma, for running ads about its cheaply made sneakers in 1985 stating "Our shoes are constructed of the finest materials available. No other brand is more durable or better made." Gamma sneakers carry labels truthfully disclosing the materials used in their construction.

d.   Delta, for running ads in 1983 stating "The new Delta Rebounder helps basketball players jump higher so they can pull down more rebounds and play ace defense."

15.   Over the past decade coffee consumption in the United States has declined markedly, as a variety of sources have stressed the adverse health effects of excess caffeine consumption. These sources have pointed out that caffeine can make you jittery, interfere with sleep and otherwise cause a high degree of nervousness.

Concerned, several coffee roasters, through their trade association—The Coffee Board—have been seeking ways to counter the trend of declining consumption. After considering a variety of options, The Coffee Board decided that the most sensible approach was a strong advertising campaign designed to emphasize the pleasure of coffee drinking in general and specifically to associate it with the image of successful active people.

The ad campaign they designed involved the use of a large number of famous athletes, singers, actors and actresses to develop a theme they called "coffee achievers." In each commercial, the celebrity would be confronted with a high energy task—singing a song, acting an intense dramatic scene, playing football, or whatever. Before actually beginning the task, the celebrity would be shown sitting down with a colleague (e.g. a coach, a producer, a sound engineer, etc.) planning it out. The celebrity would drink coffee during this scene. The narrator would say "Coffee . . . the quiet moment for the coffee achievers. It lets them think it . . . then do it . . . !" As the narrator came to the end of this phrase the celebrity would rise from the conference and proceed to perform the designated task with a great deal of energy and enthusiasm. While this occurred the narrator would conlcude by saying "Coffee—it calms you down and it picks you up. Join the coffee achievers."

Like most commercials, filming these spots took several "takes." The celebrities involved complained that the coffee they were asked to drink kept getting cold, and the producer discovered that it was a nuisance to keep brewing and repouring coffee on the set. Consequently, during the commercials the actual beverage in the coffee mugs was usually cola— sometimes regular, sometimes caffeine free.

The Federal Trade Commission has become concerned about these advertisements. A member of the staff has prepared a draft complaint alleging that they are both "unfair" and "deceptive" and seeking a cease and desist order that would require the Coffee Board to state in all future advertisements: "Coffee contains caffeine. Contrary to prior advertisements, coffee is unlikely to calm you down." You are an advisor to a member of the commission who would like to know if this complaint should issue. What will you respond, and why?

*

IX

CONSUMER REMEDIES FOR FALSE ADVERTISING AND OTHER EXPLOITATIVE PRACTICES

Analysis

Consumers are often the principal victims of false advertising and other related exploitative practices. While their interests sometimes can be vindicated through public enforcement, many frauds and deceptions inevitably go unchallenged by public agencies with limited resources. Hence consumers may desire to bring suit themselves to vindicate their rights. Their ability to do so depends on two factors—the availability of an appropriate legal theory and the existence of sufficient incentives and procedural mechanisms to make bringing suit feasible and worthwhile. The second issue is especially important because frequently a consumer who has been duped by a deceptive ad has suffered only a modest economic loss which would be far outweighed by the cost of litigation unless numerous claims can be aggregated in a class action or attorney's fees can be recovered from the defendant.

This chapter briefly explores the most commonly invoked legal theories and also considers some of the techniques that courts and legislatures have used in recent years to make it easier for aggrieved consumers to pursue their rights.

A. TRADITIONAL REMEDIES

1. COMMON LAW REMEDIES
Consumers can invoke a number of possible common law causes of action when they are victimized by a false advertisement or sales representation. Each of these, however, has elements which make success difficult and hence, make them unattractive.

a. Deceit
A party who was deceived by another's false representations has a common law action for deceit. The plaintiff must prove, however, that the falsehood was communicated knowingly (i.e. that there was "scienter") and that he or she actually relied on the representation.

b. Strict Tort Liability
If a product that was expressly or impliedly represented as safe physically injures a consumer, the consumer may recover damages in a suit based on a products liability theory. However, most jurisdictions do not allow recovery for solely economic losses, and this theory is thus ill suited for the typical false advertising case.

c. Recission or Restitution
A consumer may be able to invoke contract law to undo a transaction if the transaction was based on a false representation. Often, however, the alleged falsehood will have been oral and thus be inadmissible evidence at trial, because of the parol evidence rule. Moreover, any delay in bringing such an action may be fatal since the seller can argue that the contract was

"affirmed" by the buyer's conduct in continuing to use the merchandise after learning of the problem.

2. UNIFORM COMMERCIAL CODE

Buyers of tangible goods may be able to obtain relief under the Uniform Commercial Code if deceptive representation induced them to make their purchases. For instance, they can argue that the representations constituted a warranty, and then file suit for breach of warranty.   Alternatively, they can argue that the consideration paid for the product renders the transaction unconscionable given that the product does not perform as represented.   While these theories are useful in certain circumstances, unless the relevant state has a class action provision, many consumers will not find it economically feasible to bring suit.

B. UNAVAILABILITY OF FEDERAL REMEDIES

While Congress has, on a number of occasions, considered enacting a general statute providing private consumer remedies, no such statute has ever been adopted.   Creative counsel have sought to invoke other federal statutes to achieve the same end, but, in the case of the two most plausible statutes, have been unsuccessful.

1. NO LANHAM ACT REMEDY FOR CONSUMERS

As noted in Chapter VII, Lanham Act § 43 provides a remedy against any person who makes a "false description or representation" of goods or services, in favor of anyone who is or is likely to be injured thereby.   The plain words of this provision would appear to afford a general false advertising remedy to consumers.
Nonetheless, *the courts have concluded that this was not the intent of Congress and have thus declared on a number of occasions that consumers may not invoke Lanham Act § 43 in a false advertising case.*

Example: A group of students at a school in New York decided to take part in a ski trip organized by a tour operator.   The tour operator represented that the group would be provided with safe and reliable transportation and adequate ski lessons, but these representations proved untrue.   The buses involved broke down, lacked necessary ICC certificates and experienced numerous other problems.   There was only one ski instructor available for a group of over 150 students.   Several students filed a class action based on § 43 of the Lanham Act. The court, however, denied them relief, holding that this provision does not afford a remedy to consumers.   In its view, "The act's purpose . . . is exclusively to protect the interests of a purely commercial class against unscrupulous commercial conduct." *Colligan v. Activities Club of New York,* 442 F.2d 686 (2d Cir.1971).

2. NO F.T.C. ACT § 5 REMEDY FOR CONSUMERS

Unlike the Lanham Act, the Federal Trade Commission Act does not explicitly provide anyone with a private cause of action. Nonetheless, individual consumers and consumer groups have tried on a number of occasions to persuade the courts to find an implied cause of action under the statute that would allow cheated consumers to attack unfair or deceptive practices. The courts have uniformly declined the invitation. *There is no private cause of action under the F.T.C. Act.*

Example: The makers of Excedrin pain reliever claimed in their advertisements that the product was more effective than aspirin. A group of consumers filed a federal class action challenging this claim. The complaint was based on § 5 of the Federal Trade Commission Act. The court dismissed the case on the grounds that the statute did not provide a private right of action. *Holloway v. Bristol-Myers Corp.,* 485 F.2d 986 (D.C.Cir.1973).

C. "BABY" F.T.C. STATUTES

Every American jurisdiction has adopted a statute modeled to some degree on the Federal Trade Commission Act. Not surprisingly, these laws are often called "baby" or "little" F.T.C. Acts. The large majority of these statutes provide private remedies along with public enforcement, as was noted in Chapter VII above. By easing common law restrictions, these statutes provide a powerful new tool for lawyers representing the victims of consumer fraud. Some of the more interesting advantages of these statutes are considered below.

1. PROOF OF SCIENTER AND RELIANCE NOT REQUIRED

The chief virtue of *Baby F.T.C. Acts,* from a plaintiff's point of view, is that they *dispense with the requirement that the alleged deceptive representation have been made intentionally.* Thus, the failure to disclose a product defect about which the seller "should have known" is a sufficient basis upon which to secure relief. *Similarly, the plaintiff need not prove that he or she actually relied on the false representation in order to recover. Slaney v. Westwood Auto, Inc.,* 366 Mass. 688, 322 N.E.2d 768 (1974) ("in the statutory action proof of actual reliance by the plaintiff on a representation is not required, . . . and it is not necessary to establish that the defendant knew that the representation was false.").

2. INCENTIVES TO FILE SUIT PROVIDED

In addition, *these statutes often provide for simplified class action procedures, attorneys fees, and multiplied damage awards* (i.e. double or treble damages) which make litigation a far more plausible alternative than it is at common law.

3. DAMAGES NEED NOT BE QUANTIFIABLE

In many cases of deception, the consumer-plaintiff may have difficulty demonstrating a quantifiable amount of damages. At least one state court has held that if a deceptive representation has been made, there is sufficient injury to state a claim under the Baby F.T.C. Act, at least for injunctive relief, even if the consumer cannot demonstrate any quantifiable economic loss. *Hinchliffe v. American Motors Corp.,* 184 Conn. 607, 440 A.2d 810 (1981) ("whenever a consumer has received something other than what he bargained for, he has suffered a loss of money or property.").

Example: A seller of video recorders represents to a consumer that a particular model can be programmed to tape up to 5 programs and has a monaural sound system. When the consumer gets it home, it turns out that this model can tape only one program, but has stereo sound— a feature that this particular consumer did not want. From a pure market point of view, the product delivered may be more valuable than the product as represented. Nonetheless, the consumer did not get what he or she desired. This consumer has suffered sufficient injury to state a cause of action under the Connecticut statute construed in *Hinchliffe*.

4. RELIEF AGAINST NON-MERCHANT SELLERS

Not all unfair or deceptive practices are committed by merchants regularly engaged in the business of selling goods and services. Anyone who has ever bought a product directly from a former owner, such as a used car, knows that non-merchant sellers can also resort to deception in order to conclude a sale. *Baby F.T.C. Acts have been held applicable in cases involving sales by non-merchant sellers, when those sellers engaged in misrepresentations about the goods.* Pennington v. Singleton, 606 S.W.2d 682 (Tex.1980).

D. MAGNUSON–MOSS WARRANTY ACT

Although there is no general federal consumer statute providing consumer remedies against deception, in 1975 Congress enacted the Magnuson-Moss Warranty Act, 15 U.S.C.A. § 2301 et seq. (1984), to protect consumers from deceptive or confusing warranty practices. The statute does not require any firm to provide a warranty if it does not wish to. Instead, *the principal effect of the statute is to regulate how warranty information must be disclosed if the merchant does decide to offer one, and to create a federal cause of action for breach of warranties.* This cause of action, however, is a less helpful tool than might be supposed initially, for the reasons considered below.

1. NOT ALL WRITTEN MATERIAL IS A "WARRANTY"

If all written material transmitted with the product constituted a "warranty" within the meaning of the statute, consumers would be able to use the statute if any of that material contained false representations. However, the statutory language contains a much narrower definition, limited to written promises of only specified types. The courts have used this definition to reject broad based consumer complaints under this statute.

Example: A group of automobile purchasers discovered that their cars had a different, and inferior, type of transmission than the one specified in the brochures, manuals and other written material disseminated with the product. The buyers filed suit, claiming that the written materials constituted a warranty and that the undisclosed substitution of inferior transmissions represented a breach of a written warranty within the meaning of Magnuson-Moss. The court rejected this contention because the manuals and other literature involved did not fall within the statutory definition of a "written warranty." *Skelton v. General Motors Corp.,* 660 F.2d 311 (7th Cir.1981).

2. NO REMEDY FOR PERSONAL INJURIES

Sometimes, when a product does not perform as warranted, the result is physical injury to a consumer or family member. Nonetheless, it has been held that *the Magnuson-Moss Act does not provide a remedy for personal injuries resulting from the breach of written warranty. Gorman v. Saf-T-Mate, Inc.,* 513 F.Supp. 1028 (N.D.Ind. 1981).

3. JURISDICTIONAL HURDLES

The Magnuson-Moss Act contains some significant obstacles to federal jurisdiction. If a consumer sues individually, the amount in controversy must be $50,000. If the consumer brings a class action on behalf of a group, there must be at least 100 persons listed as named plaintiffs, each claim must be at least $25, and the sum of all claims must be at least $50,000. 15 U.S.C.A. § 2310(3) (1984). Because federal jurisdiction is not exclusive, a consumer can avoid these obstacles by bringing a Magnuson-Moss claim in state court, but that alternative may be unattractive for a variety of reasons such as congested local court calendars and restrictive discovery rules.

REVIEW QUESTIONS

1. **T or F**   There is no private right of action under the Federal Trade Commission Act.

2. **T or F**   A plaintiff must allege that the defendant made misrepresentations intentionally in order to recover under most "baby" F.T.C. Acts.

3. **T or F**   A consumer suing individually in state court for breach of the Magnuson-Moss Act must allege at least $50,000 in damages to invoke jurisdiction.

4.   **T or F**   In some states the "baby" F.T.C. Act can be used to assert a cause of action against a non-merchant seller.

5.   **T or F**   Smith, a consumer, purchased a shirt labeled "Calvin Klein" from a local department store but discovered that the shirt was not genuine Calvin Klein merchandise. Smith has a cause of action against the store for violation of Lanham Act § 43(a).

6.   **T or F**   The "baby" F.T.C. Act in all jurisdictions provides for a private cause of action in favor of consumers.

7.   Smith purchased a power lawn mower which was advertised as "the safest on the market." The owner's manual accompanying the product indicated that "there is no need to wear protective clothing" and that "you are now the proud owner of the safest power mower available today." When using the mower one afternoon, the leg of Smith's trousers was caught in the blades, and as a result he suffered severe gashes on his leg. Which of the following statements is most likely to be true?

    a.   Smith has a cause of action under his state's Baby F.T.C. Act.

    b.   Smith has a cause of action under section 5 of the Federal Trade Commission Act.

    c.   Smith has a cause of action under the Magnuson-Moss Warranty Act.

    d.   Smith has a common law cause of action for deceit.

*

X

PRICE AND SERVICE DISCRIMINATION UNDER THE ROBINSON–PATMAN ACT

Analysis

A. Jurisdictional Elements
B. Harm to Primary Line Competition
C. Harm to Secondary Line Competition
D. Affirmative Defenses
E. Brokerage Payments
F. Advertising Allowances
G. Buyer Liability
H. Remedies

In a competitive economy, prices usually reflect the costs of production (plus a fair rate of profit). All firms have an incentive to become more efficient, thereby cutting costs, lowering prices and increasing sales. Inefficient firms often go out of business because they are unable to offer prices as low as their more efficient rivals, and consumers stop patronizing them.

Of course, prices do not always reflect a firm's level of efficiency. For instance, a monopolist may sustain prices far above its costs because there are no rival firms to apply downward pressure on its prices. The legal issues surrounding monopoly pricing, however, are in the domain of antitrust law and thus beyond the scope of this outline.

Prices may also fail to reflect efficiency when a seller discriminates in price. In this situation, the firm may charge an unusually low price in one area and subsidize it with high prices elsewhere. As a result, an equally efficient rival firm that cannot discriminate may be unable to match the lower of the discriminator's two prices, and go out of business. Price discrimination, thus, is another method of unfair competition.

Price discrimination may have an additional undesirable consequence. Firms that buy from a price discriminator may discover that competition between them has been altered in ways unrelated to their efficiency. For example, if a key supplier charges two equally efficient retailers different prices, the one who must pay the higher price—the "disfavored" buyer—may not be able to survive. Yet, if it does go out of business, it will not be because it was inefficient, but because of the price discrimination of the seller.

The federal price discrimination statute, the Robinson-Patman Act, 15 U.S.C.A. § 13 (1984), addresses these issues. It has been frequently criticized, both on the merits for reflecting unsound economic policies, and as a work of legislative draftsmanship, since it is singularly vague and contradictory in places. Notwithstanding its difficulties, however, the statute is still an important aspect of the unfair trade practices landscape. It provides for both public enforcement and creates a private right of action in favor of any injured party. While public enforcement of the Robinson-Patman Act has diminished in recent years, private suits continue to be filed and it continues to influence business behavior. The following discussion provides a workable roadmap to the intricacies of the statute.

A. JURISDICTIONAL ELEMENTS

To demonstrate a violation of the Robinson-Patman Act a plaintiff or the government must show first, that several jurisdictional requirements have been satisfied, and second, that an adverse effect on competition is threatened. This section considers the various jurisdictional elements.

1. INTERSTATE COMMERCE

The Robinson-Patman Act does not invoke the full extent of Congress's power under the Commerce Clause. Activities that merely "affect" commerce are not within the scope of the statute. *The statute only applies if at least one of the two sales which, when compared, generates the alleged discrimination, involved the movement of products across a state line.* It does not matter, however, whether it was the higher or lower priced sale that took place in interstate commerce. *Gulf Oil Corp. v. Copp Paving Co.,* 419 U.S. 186, 95 S.Ct. 392 (1974).

2. A "DISCRIMINATION IN PRICE"

The statute requires a demonstration that the seller has engaged in a "discrimination" in "price." (Note that not all such discriminations are illegal. As is developed in the next section, the statute only condemns certain discriminations). Although the meaning of this phrase is now relatively straightforward, historically both the concept of "discrimination" and the definition of "price" posed problems.

a. Price

Under the Robinson-Patman Act "price" means the actual invoice price paid by the buyer, net of any rebates or refunds. In several older cases, the Federal Trade Commission claimed that this was an incorrect interpretation of the term. It argued, instead, for what is known as a "mill net" theory of price. Under this theory, any transportation costs built into the price are subtracted to arrive at the "real" or "mill net" price. The "mill net" theory has been abandoned, although there is still some case law on the books endorsing it.

Example: A shoe manufacturing plant located in Maine sells a certain type of shoe to retailers nationwide for the price of $50 a pair, delivered. The cost to ship one pair to New York is $1. The cost to ship one pair to Los Angeles is $5. Under the mill net theory, the price of the first pair was $49 while the price of the second pair was $45. Under the current modern view, the difference in transportation cost is ignored and the "price" of both pairs is deemed to be $50.

b. Discrimination

A "discrimination" means merely a difference in price. No other factors are inquired into. At one point, it was argued that two different prices do not constitute a "discrimination" unless there is a showing either (1) that the different buyers are similarly situated so as to be entitled to equal prices, or (2) that the seller was deliberately attempting to injure competition by engaging in the discrimination. The Supreme Court rejected those arguments in *Federal Trade Commission v. Anheuser-Busch, Inc.,* 363 U.S. 536, 80 S.Ct. 1267 (1960), and opted instead for the straightforward formula that "a price discrimination within the meaning of [the Robinson-Patman Act] is merely a price difference . . . ."

3. PURCHASES

a. Requirement of Completed Purchases

The Robinson-Patman Act only applies if the discrimination in price occurs in connection with two completed purchases. Thus mere offers to sell merchandise at a discriminatory price are irrelevant under the act, as are outright refusals to do business with a particular customer. In addition, non-sale transactions such as consignments and leases are not subject to scrutiny under the act.

b. The Indirect Purchaser Doctrine

The requirement of two completed purchases at two different prices suggests a technique to avoid application of the Act. Assume a seller wishes to sell to Alpha at 20 and Beta at 25. If the seller can interpose an intermediary—Omega—between itself and Beta, it could sell to Omega for 20, and have Omega re-sell to Beta for 25. The seller could then argue that the statute is inapplicable since the only 2 "purchasers," Alpha and Omega, paid the same price—20. This argument will defeat Robinson-Patman jurisdiction only if the intermediary is a genuinely independent firm. *If the intermediate seller is a sham, however, and if the original seller actually determined the prices at which the intermediary re-sold, the intermediary will be disregarded.* In that case, the court will treat Beta as a "purchaser" and compare its price of 25 with Alpha's price of 20 to find that a discrimination has occurred. *This doctrine—of ignoring sham intermediaries in determining if there are two purchasers who paid different prices—is known as the indirect purchaser doctrine.*

c. Government Purchasers

The federal government is not considered a purchaser under the Robinson-Patman Act, so sales to it are disregarded in determining whether there has been a discrimination. However, state and local government agencies are considered "purchasers" if they purchase for resale in competition with others who pay higher prices to the same seller. *Jefferson County Pharmaceutical v. Abbott Laboratories,* 460 U.S. 150, 103 S.Ct. 1011 (1983).

d. Non-profit Purchasers

An amendment to the Robinson-Patman Act makes it inapplicable to purchases of supplies, for their own use, by "schools, colleges, universities, public libraries, churches, hospitals, and charitable institutions not operated for profit." 15 U.S.C.A. § 13c (1984).

e. Parents and Subsidiaries

While some older cases suggest the contrary, several recent opinions have concluded that sales between a parent firm and its subsidiary should be ignored in determining if a seller has sold to different parties at different prices. *See e.g. Security Tire & Rubber Co. v. Gates Rubber Co.,* 598 F.2d 962 (5th Cir.1977).

4. COMMODITIES
The Robinson-Patman Act only applies to discriminatory pricing of "commodities."
Many courts have thus concluded that only sales of tangible objects are regulated
by the provisions of the act. Sales of services at different prices are not within
the reach of the statute. Other examples of things held not to be commodities
include mutual fund shares, theatre tickets, copyright licenses and bank loans.

5. LIKE GRADE AND QUALITY
*A discrimination in price is only subject to Robinson-Patman scrutiny if the different
purchasers bought commodities of "like grade and quality."* Thus, if a firm sells
regular cigarettes to retailer Alpha for 50¢ a pack, and menthol cigarettes to
retailer Beta for 60¢ a pack, no further analysis is necessary under the Robinson-
Patman Act because the sales did not involve products of like grade and quality.

a. Determining Like Grade Issues
*Goods cease to be of the same grade and quality when they have significant
physical differences that cause them to have different degrees of consumer
acceptance or marketability.* If the items differ only trivially or superficially
from each other, they will be treated as of the same grade or quality.

> *Example:* A seller sold a regular brand of ice cream and a premium brand.
> The premium brand had a higher butterfat content and was made
> pursuant to a "special formula." The two products were held not
> to be of like grade and quality in *Central Ice Cream Co. v. Golden
> Rod Ice Cream Co,* 184 F.Supp. 312 (N.D.Ill.1960). On the other
> hand, tires with different tread designs, but otherwise having the
> same construction, were held to be of the same grade and quality
> in *Goodyear Tire and Rubber Co.,* 22 F.T.C. 232 (1936).

b. Differently Labeled Physically Identical Goods
Firms occasionally market the same product under two or more separate brand
names. For instance, they may use their own trademark, and also pack the
item in containers bearing the "house" mark of a supermarket chain.
Usually, such a firm sells the nationally known brand for a higher price than
the store brand. This raises the question of whether the two items are of like
grade and quality under the Robinson-Patman Act. In *Federal Trade
Commission v. The Borden Co.,* 383 U.S. 637, 86 S.Ct. 1092 (1966), *the Supreme
Court held that physically identical goods are of like grade and quality even if
sold under different brand names.* Of course, this does not make such price
differentials illegal—it just means that they are subject to further scrutiny to
see if they are likely to produce the forbidden effect on competition discussed
in the next two sections.

6. USE, CONSUMPTION OR RESALE IN THE UNITED STATES
*The only sales considered in determining whether Robinson-Patman's jurisdictional
elements are satisfied are those made for use, consumption or resale in the United*

States. As a result, sales to foreign buyers or sales made for the purpose of subsequent export are not to be considered in determining if a price discrimination has occurred.

B. HARM TO PRIMARY LINE COMPETITION

1. OVERVIEW OF COMPETITIVE HARM REQUIREMENT

Not all price discriminations violate the Robinson-Patman Act. *Only those that pose a reasonable possibility of lessening competition are condemned.* The competition referred to can be the competition between the seller and its competitors (referred to as the "primary line") or it can be the competition that takes place at the buyers' level (referred to as the "secondary line"). In fact, the requisite unlawful harm to competition may even occur at levels further removed from the seller (i.e. "third" or "fourth" line). The judicial tests used to determine if the harm to competition requirement has been satisfied differ in primary and secondary line cases. The former are discussed in this section, the latter in the section that immediately follows. In both types of cases, however, *the risk of harm must be substantial, and the courts will only concern themselves with a general harm to the competitive process, not with harm to specfic competitors.*

2. THEORY OF PRIMARY LINE CASES

It is important to understand *how* a firm can use price discrimination to harm other firms that compete directly with it (i.e., primary line firms). The basic theory assumes that the discriminator is a large firm doing business in a number of geographic markets and that it has targeted one market where it desires to increase its percentage of sales by damaging or destroying commercial rivals. To do this, it will dramatically drop its prices in the target market, and subsidize the low prices there by raising prices in other markets where it faces little or no competition. If it drops its prices in the target market low enough, rival firms will be unable to match the reductions and will go out of business. The discriminating firm can then raise its prices in the target market and recoup its losses. This type of pricing behavior is usually called "predatory pricing." *A likelihood of harm to primary line competition exists when a firm that is engaged in price discrimination is using predatory prices in a given market.*

3. THE UTAH PIE CASE

The Supreme Court decision in *Utah Pie Co. v. Continental Baking Co.,* 386 U.S. 685, 87 S.Ct. 1326 (1967) is a frequent starting point for the study of primary line price discrimination and the problem of predation.

a. Facts

Utah Pie was a manufacturer of frozen pies doing business in Salt Lake City, where it dominated the market. Starting in 1958 three large, national food processing companies that also made frozen pies entered the Salt Lake City market. Each of these firms charged lower prices to Salt Lake City customers than to customers elsewhere. Utah Pie was forced to meet these lower prices. Its profits declined as a result and it lost some market share as well. It filed suit under the Robinson-Patman Act, alleging primary line injury. The case was taken to the Supreme Court which held in favor of Utah Pie.

b. Analysis of the Court

The Court found that each of the three defendants acted with "predatory" intent. It cited evidence that two of them had charged prices below their costs, but did not indicate what cost standard it used to arrive at that conclusion, and noted that one of the firms had engaged in some industrial espionage. It did not, however, appear to rely on these facts as essential to its conclusion that the Act had been violated. Instead, noting that the defendants' pricing had led to a "drastically declining price structure," it declared that the Robinson-Patman Act "reaches price discrimination that erodes competition as much as it does price discrimination that is intended to have immediate destructive impact." In other words, the case implied that pricing that harms the profit position of an established firm should be considered "predatory" pricing.

c. Critique

The *Utah Pie* decision was heavily criticized by academic writers. They noted that when a firm desires to enter a new market it is usually necessary for it to use promotional pricing to encourage consumers to sample its products. That, naturally, drives price levels down in the relevant market. Since the *Utah Pie* Court seemed to suggest that declining prices and loss of market share by the plaintiff are sufficient to establish a Robinson-Patman violation, these writers concluded that there would be legal risks in using promotional pricing unless prices were dropped nation-wide (thus eliminating the element of a "discrimination" in price). Because most firms would not find that economical, they would choose not to enter the new market at all. Thus the case stifled the possibility for enhanced competition in concentrated markets.

4. IDENTIFYING PREDATORY PRICES

For many years after *Utah Pie,* one of the most difficult aspects of the case law interpreting the Robinson-Patman Act was the ambiguous and conflicting way in which courts approached primary line cases. In recent years, however, a judicial consensus has begun to emerge that *prices are predatory only if they are "below cost."* This formula has, in turn, required the courts to think about the definition of the term "cost" and to select from among the many types of costs, the one most appropriate.

a. Types of Costs

Costs of production are usually divided into two broad categories—"fixed" and "variable." Fixed costs are those the firm will incur regardless of how many units it produces. For instance, rent, managerial salaries and certain utility bills. Variable costs are those that change depending on how many units the firm produces. Examples of variable costs are sums expended for raw materials and hourly wages paid to production personnel. The sum of fixed and variable costs is, not surprisingly, called the firm's total cost. For any level of production, each cost figure can be divided by the number of units produced to yield an average cost figure. If the firm, at this point, wants to produce exactly one more unit, it will have to spend an additional amount, known as the "marginal cost."

Example: Omega Widget made 1000 widgets last month. During that month its expenses were $2000 for rent, $2000 for managerial salary, $1000 in hourly wages and $1000 in raw materials. If it had wanted to make a 1001st widget, that would have cost it an additional $1.75 in materials and labor. Its fixed costs were thus $4000, its variable costs $2000 and its total costs were $6000. The average total cost was $6/per widget, and the average variable cost was $2/per widget. The marginal cost was $1.75.

b. The Areeda-Turner Test

In a highly influential 1975 law review article, Professors Areeda and Turner argued that the appropriate cost standard for resolving primary line Robinson-Patman cases is "marginal cost." Because the marginal cost for most firms is impossible to calculate, they further suggested that the courts use "average variable cost" as a surrogate. They reasoned that this cost standard operates to condemn a price as predatory only when it is so low that an equally efficient firm cannot match the price without suffering losses on each unit of production. In light of this, they concluded that *prices below average variable cost should be conclusively presumed unlawful.*

Example: Assume that Omega Widget in the previous Example is engaged in price discrimination, selling Widgets in Seattle for $6.50 and Widgets in El Paso for $1.80. El Paso Widget, a small local firm, has filed suit for unlawful price discrimination. It will succeed if it can show that Omega's prices in El Paso are predatory. Under the Areeda-Turner test, they are. Since Omega's average variable cost was $2.00, its $1.80 price is "below cost." Note that the $1.80 price was above the marginal cost of $1.75, but that the test does not use that figure because in the real world it is too difficult to calculate.

c. Judicial Response to Areeda-Turner Test

The Areeda-Turner test has proven highly influential in the courts. While not all federal circuits have accepted it verbatim, its general approach has been widely accepted. Judicial modifications to the test tend to be in the direction of making the cost-based showings less conclusive than Areeda and Turner had advocated. For instance, the 9th Circuit has adopted this formula: "If the defendant's prices were below average total cost but above average variable cost, the plaintiff bears the burden of showing defendant's pricing was predatory.   If, however, the plaintiff proves that the defendant's prices were below average variable cost, the plaintiff has established a prima facie case of predatory pricing and the burden shifts to the defendant to prove that the prices were justified . . ." *William Inglis & Sons Baking, Inc. v. ITT Continental Baking Co.,* 668 F.2d 1014 (9th Cir.1982). Other circuits have developed different formulas but follow the same cost-based approach.

C. HARM TO SECONDARY LINE COMPETITION

1. GENERAL STANDARDS

Second line competition is competition between buyers who have bought from the same seller.   The one who pays the lower price is usually termed the "favored" buyer, the one who pays the higher price is usually termed "disfavored."   There are several tests used to determine if a given price discrimination is likely to harm second line competition.   The Supreme Court has ruled that *where the favored and disfavored buyers are in direct competition, any price differential sufficient in amount to affect resale prices establishes the requisite likelihood of harm to secondary line competition. Federal Trade Commission v. Morton Salt Co.,* 334 U.S. 37, 68 S.Ct. 822 (1948).   Another test used to determine if there is a likelihood of harm on the secondary line is proof that the price difference involved is significant and profit margins in the secondary line industry are small.   Still another method of showing second line harm is proof that the profit margins of disfavored buyers have been impaired.

2. CAUSATION

A Robinson-Patman plaintiff complaining of second line injury must show a causal connection between the harm complained of and the defendant's price discrimination.   When one retailer must pay higher prices for its inventory than another, competing retailer it is usually self-evident that the injury to the disfavored buyer was caused by the price discrimination, at least where the price difference was at all significant.   In some cases, however, the connection between the price discrimination and any injury shown by the plaintiff may not be so direct. *If the defendant can show that any injury suffered by the disfavored buyers is not due to the price discrimination, it is not liable under the Robinson-Patman Act.*

Example: Borden manufactured identical evaporated milk under its own label and a "private brand" label.   It charged a higher price for the nationally branded version than for the private label.   The F.T.C. challenged this pricing structure as violative of the Act. Borden argued that any harm suffered by the disfavored buyers (i.e., those who bought only the more expensive nationally branded milk) was not caused by the price difference involved here.   The Court of Appeals agreed, noting that consumers were willing to pay more for the national brand, and "where a price differential between a premium and nonpremium brand reflects no more than a consumer preference for the premium brand, the price difference creates no competitive advantage to the recipient of the cheaper private brand product on which injury could be predicated." *The Borden Co. v. Federal Trade Commission,* 381 F.2d 175 (5th Cir.1967).

3. SPECIFIC DISCOUNTING PRACTICES

Not all price discrimination involves isolated instances of disparate pricing by sellers. Many manufacturers and wholesalers engage in specific programs of discounts to specified categories of purchasers for a variety of reasons. Obviously, all such programs pose Robinson-Patman Act risk, at least where not all buyers in the same area get the same discount. Two such discounting practices deserve specific mention.

a. Quantity Discounts

Many firms offer increasingly significant discounts for increasingly large orders. Such discounts may be permissible under two possible circumstances. First, if the largest quantity specified (to achieve the greatest discount) is "functionally available" to all customers, the discount scheme will be lawful. *Federal Trade Commission v. Morton Salt Co.,* 334 U.S. 37, 68 S.Ct. 822 (1948). This is because any injury to firms that pay higher prices is not caused by the seller, but by their own decision to buy in small quantities. Alternatively, a seller may seek to defend a scheme of quantity discounts under the cost justification defense, which is discussed in section (D)(1) below.

b. Functional Discounts

Firms will also sometimes offer a discounted price to a buyer who absorbs some of the work involved in distributing the product. For instance, assume a manufacturer sells both to retail stores and to wholesalers. (Such a manufacturer is known as a "dual distributor"). On sales to retailers the manufacturer must deliver smaller quantities, make more frequent deliveries and perhaps honor returns. These costly services need not be offered to the wholesalers who buy directly from the manufacturer. They perform these functions for themselves. Thus, the manufacturer may desire to offer these buyers a "functional" discount. Since the manufacturer saves money when it deals with the wholesaler, this type of discount may be immunized from liability under the cost justification defense, discussed below. *Even if they are not "cost justified" such discounts are not necessarily illegal, since the wholesalers and retailers are not in direct competition with each other. Thus there can be no harm to competition from this discrimination.* However, there are two scenarios in which it can pose Robinson-Patman difficulties.

1) Favored Customer is an Integrated Buyer

The legality of functional discounts becomes more complex when the party who gets the lower price runs retail outlets but performs the wholesaling functions for these outlets itself (such a firm is usually referred to as an "integrated buyer"). In this situation some have argued that the price discrimination gives the integrated buyer an unfair advantage in retail competition because it buys inventory at a lower price than the unintegrated retailers. This argument focuses on the role the integrated firm plays in reselling the goods—it resells as a retailer so it "is" a retailer. In this view, one retailer is receiving a lower price than a competing retailer, which is sufficient to demonstrate second line harm. This reasoning was followed in *Mueller Co. v. Federal Trade Commission,* 323 F.2d 44 (7th Cir.1963), which held a scheme of functional discounts unlawful. Others, however, have noted that, although the integrated firm pays a lower price because of the functional discount, it has higher costs, because it receives the merchandise in bulk and must transfer it to retail outlets at its own expense. These observers focus on the role the integrated buyer plays in purchasing—they buy as wholesalers so they "are" wholesalers. Since wholesalers and retailers don't compete, this view would immunize these functional discounts from Robinson-Patman liability. This was the position taken by the F.T.C. in *Doubleday & Co. Inc.,* 52 F.T.C. 169 (1955), but subsequently abandoned by the Commission in the *Mueller* litigation cited above. In *Boise Cascade Corp.,* 50 Antitr. & Trade Reg.Rep. 335 (F.T.C. Dkt. 9133, 1986) the Commission recently indicated that it would continue to follow the *Mueller* rule. As a result, functional discounts granted to an integrated buyer and not available to ordinary retailers will violate the Robinson-Patman Act, unless the seller can prove that the amount of the discount is equal to its own cost savings and thereby bring the pricing practices within the scope of the cost justification defense discussed below.

> *Example:* Acme Widget Mfg. sells to The Widget Shop, a retailer, for 20¢/unit and to World Wide Widgets (WWW) at a functional discount of 10¢/unit because WWW does its own wholesaling in order to get the merchandise into its chain of retail stores. Under the view in *Mueller* and *Boise Cascade,* Acme has violated the Act (unless it can successfully invoke the cost justification defense) because the WWW chain competes directly with the Widget Shop and it paid a lower price. Under the now abandoned *Doubleday* view, the difference in price could be lawful, because WWW incurs costs in transferring the merchandise into its numerous stores which justifies viewing it as a wholesaler for Robinson-Patman purposes.

2) Buyers From Wholesalers Secure an Advantage

Depending on the magnitude of a functional discount, retailers who buy from wholesalers who receive the discount may pay a lower price than the retailers who are buying directly from the manufacturer! If it was *foreseeable* to the manufacturer, when the discount was granted, that the wholesaler's customers would wind up with lower prices than the retailers who made their purchases directly from it, and if the two groups of retailers are in competition with each other, the discount violates the Act. *Cf. Standard Oil (Indiana) v. F.T.C.,* 173 F.2d 210 (7th Cir. 1949) *rev'd on other grounds,* 340 U.S. 231, 71 S.Ct. 240 (1950). Foreseeability turns on the amount of the discount. It should be stressed, however, that cases of this type are extremely rare.

> ***Example:*** Acme Widget Mfg. sells to The Widget Shop, a retailer, for 20¢/unit and to Widget Wholesalers of the World (WWW) for 5¢/unit. WWW resells to Jerry's House of Widgets, a retailer, for 15¢/unit. Jerry's is in direct competition with The Widget Shop. Acme's liability for violation of the Robinson-Patman Act will turn on whether it could have foreseen the advantage to Jerry resulting from the discount it gave to WWW. If the 15¢ price difference was a reasonable estimate of the wholesaling costs in this industry, it will probably escape liability.

c. "Reverse Functional" Discounts

Some sellers grant lower prices to customers further down the distribution chain than are offered to firms higher up. For instance, a seller might sell to retailers directly for 10¢, but charge wholesalers 20¢. It is obvious in this case that any retailer who must buy through the wholesalers winds up paying a much higher price than those lucky retailers who deal directly with the manufacturer. It is also obvious that the wholesaler's business will suffer because any retailer who can do so will shift its buying pattern away from the wholesaler in order to do business directly with the manufacturer. At least one case has held that a pricing structure of this sort violates the Act. *Krug v. International Telephone & Telegraph Co.,* 142 F.Supp. 230 (D.N.J.1956). Other courts, however, have refused to find a violation on these facts.

4. COMPETITIVE INJURY ON REMOTE LEVELS OF DISTRIBUTION

It is possible for the competitive injury in a Robinson-Patman Act case to occur on levels several steps downstream from the discriminating seller. For instance, in the example following item (3)(b)(2) in this section, the benefited party—Jerry's House of Widgets—was two steps removed from the manufacturer, and we could thus say that the injury was "third line." The wording of the statute explicitly permits allegations of third line injury. Moreover, *the Supreme Court has held that injury on even more remote levels of distribution is also cognizable under the act. Perkins v. Standard Oil Co. of California,* 395 U.S. 642, 89 S.Ct. 1871 (1969) (fourth line injury held actionable).

D. AFFIRMATIVE DEFENSES

1. COST JUSTIFICATION

It is often cheaper for a seller to deal with some of its customers than with others. *The Robinson-Patman Act permits a seller to offer lower prices in cases where cost savings are realized, provided the seller can produce detailed documentation of the cost figures involved.* Compiling cost data on a customer by customer basis is extremely difficult, so the courts permit a Robinson-Patman defendant to cost justify its price structure with data that groups customers into classifications, provided that each group is "composed of members of such selfsameness as to make the averaging of the cost of dealing with the group a valid and reasonable indicium of the cost of dealing with any specific group member." *United States v. Borden Co.,* 370 U.S. 460, 82 S.Ct. 1309 (1962).

2. MEETING COMPETITION

A firm accused of a Robinson-Patman violation will not be found liable if it can show that its "lower price . . . was made in good faith to meet an equally low price of a competitor." 15 U.S.C.A. § 13(b) (1984).

a. Nature of the Defense

The meeting competition defense has been held to be a full substantive defense. Consequently, it is irrelevant that an injury to competition may result from the discrimination, if the seller can demonstrate that it granted the lower price in response to the low prices of a competing seller. *Standard Oil Co. v. Federal Trade Commission,* 340 U.S. 231, 71 S.Ct. 240 (1951).

b. Scope of Permissible Competitive Response

The meeting competition defense permits a seller to respond to a pricing system of a competitor, as well as to specific isolated prices. Thus, it is lawful to match prices by granting discounts to all buyers within a given territory, if the seller has a good faith belief that this is what its commercial rival is doing. *It is also permissible to drop prices to the level charged by a competitor in order to aggressively obtain new customers as well as to defensively retain old customers. Falls City Industries v. Vanco Beverage, Inc.,* 460 U.S. 428, 103 S.Ct. 1282 (1983).

c. Limits on the Defense

There are a number of important limits on the meeting competition defense, the most important of which are discussed below.

1) Meet Not Beat

The defense only permits a firm to offer an "equally" low price. Thus, a firm loses the meeting competition defense if it knowingly attempts to *undersell* a rival when it offers selected customers lower prices.

2)   Product of Comparable Quality

A seller may only rely on the meeting competition defense if its own goods and the goods of the competitor whose lower prices it is matching are of similar quality. If the rival's goods are *mediocre* and the seller drops prices on its own *premium* products, the defense is unavailable.

3)   Limited to Meeting Seller's Own Competition

One of a seller's customers may do business in an area where there is intense price competition. For instance, a national manufacturing firm may sell to a retailer in a city where rival retailers have very low prices. The seller may be tempted to cut prices to that retailer to permit it to meet its retail competition. It has been held, however, that such a price reduction is not within the meeting competition defense. *F.T.C. v. Sun Oil Co.,* 371 U.S. 505, 83 S.Ct. 358 (1963). *The defense may only be invoked by a seller to match a low price offered by another firm on its own level of distribution.*

d.   Good Faith Belief, Not Actual Knowledge, Required

It is not always easy for a firm to know the prices its competitors are charging. This can make it difficult to know if a particular price reduction is genuinely necessary to "meet" a competitor's price. However, *the defense does not require actual knowledge of the competitor's pricing, only a good faith belief as to what is happening in the marketplace.* Thus an arrangement by a group of competing firms to exchange price information, was held unlawful under the antitrust laws because of its anticompetitive effect, despite the defendants' claim that it was necessary in order to comply with the meeting competition defense. *United States v. United States Gypsum Co.,* 438 U.S. 422, 98 S.Ct. 2864 (1978).

3.   CHANGED MARKET CONDITIONS

The Robinson-Patman Act makes it a defense to a charge of price discrimination that either market conditions or the marketability of the goods have changed between the time of the higher and lower priced sales. This defense is infrequently invoked and is considerably less important than the two defenses discussed above.

E.   BROKERAGE PAYMENTS

A seller might attempt to evade the prohibition against price discrimination by purportedly charging all customers the same price, but by paying nominal fees as "commissions" or "brokerage payments" back to certain favored customers. Obviously, such payments effectively reduce the price the favored customers pay, and thus resemble the direct price discrimination dealt with elsewhere in the statute. Consequently, section 2(c) of the Robinson-Patman Act forbids the payment

of any such fees by the seller to the buyer, "except for services rendered." 15 U.S.
C.A. § 13(c) (1984).

1. WHEN ARE "SERVICES RENDERED"?

The courts and the Federal Trade Commission have interpreted the "services
rendered" exception to the ban on brokerage payments very narrowly—in effect
reading it out of the act. They have held that services cannot be genuinely
rendered unless the broker is entirely independent of the buyer involved. Thus
any payment directly to the buyer—or to a broker affiliated with the buyer—is
likely to raise a risk of liability under the provision.

2. PROOF OF INJURY TO COMPETITION NOT REQUIRED

*The brokerage provision of the act does not contain any reference to adverse
competitive effects. Consequently, it can be violated even when the challenged
payment will have no effect on competition.*

3. SELLER'S BROKER

The statutory provision under discussion concerns payments to brokers owned or
affiliated by the *buyer*. Of course, a seller may also use a broker to locate
customers and compensate that broker by paying it a commission. That does not
pose problems under the statute. However, the seller's broker may be tempted to
share some of its commission with a particularly large prospective customer, in
order to induce that customer to do business with the seller that the broker
represents. This is attractive to the broker because, while the commission is
reduced, it still receives more income than if it is unable to negotiate any sale. It
is also attractive to the prospective buyer, since the commission rebate serves to
reduce the effective price it will pay. Despite its appeal to the parties, however,
this *splitting of brokerage fees by the seller's broker was held to be violative of
§ 2(c)* in *Federal Trade Commission v. Henry Broch & Co.*, 363 U.S. 166, 80 S.Ct.
1158 (1960).

F. ADVERTISING ALLOWANCES

Sellers occasionally make payments or provide services to customers to encourage
them to undertake promotional activities or to assist them in the conduct of their
business. For instance, a seller might agree to pay half the cost of a full page
newspaper ad featuring both its own name and the name of a particular retailer.
The provision of such payments or services to some, but not all, of a group of
buyers, resembles direct price discrimination because it reduces the costs of doing
business for a select group of favored buyers. Sections 2(d) and (e) of the
Robinson-Patman Act deal with this type of activity.

1. GENERAL PROVISIONS

*A firm may not make promotional payments or provide promotional services, unless
they are made available on proportionally equal terms to all of its customers.*

Absence of competitive injury is no defense to a claim of violation of these provisions. The cost justification defense is also unavailable. It is permissible, however, to defend the provision of promotional allowances on a non-proportional basis by showing that it was done to meet competition. *Federal Trade Commission v. Simplicity Pattern Co.,* 360 U.S. 55, 79 S.Ct. 1005 (1959).

2. SERVICES AND FACILITIES COVERED

A wide range of services and facilities designed to help customers promote sales have been held to be within the terms of §§ 2(d), (e). The most typical of these are joint advertising arrangements, in-store display materials, or special "cents-off" coupons. In addition, many types of services that are not literally "promotional" have also been held covered by these sections. Examples include maintenance of selected service station rest rooms by oil companies, credit card privileges granted to some but not all customers and accepting the return of unsold merchandise from only certain customers.

3. THE CONCEPTS OF PROPORTIONALITY AND AVAILABILITY

The statute requires that payments and allowances be made "proportionally" available. Sellers may "proportionalize" by basing payments or allowances either on the dollar volume or number of units purchased by each customer. Under this approach a retailer who buys 1000 units a month from a given manufacturer is entitled to double the promotional payments and services as a customer who buys only 500 units a month. It is not necessary that the exact same type of services be provided to every customer. In order for the services to be considered "available" to all customers, the seller must take affirmative steps to inform all customers about the promotional programs.

4. DUAL DISTRIBUTING SELLERS

When a seller does business with firms at both the wholesale and retail level of distribution, there is a question of who is entitled to advertising allowances. The Supreme Court has ruled that if services are provided to the direct-buying retailers, they must be made available to the retailers who make their purchases through the wholesalers as well. *Federal Trade Commission v. Fred Meyer, Inc.,* 390 U.S. 341, 88 S.Ct. 904 (1968).

G. BUYER LIABILITY

The Robinson-Patman Act was motivated, in part, by the fear that large and powerful retail firms could extort price concessions not available to smaller merchants. Consequently, section 2(f) of the statute provides that "it shall be unlawful . . . knowingly to induce or receive a discrimination in price which is prohibited by this section." Thus *a buyer who demands that it be made the beneficiary of price discrimination can be held liable for violation of the act.*

1. THE LOWER PRICE MUST BE ILLEGAL

As has been repeatedly noted, not all price discrimination is illegal. Only when all the jurisdictional elements are met, when there is the requisite showing of potential harm to competition, and when the various defenses are unavailable, does price discrimination violate the law. Consequently, if a buyer is accused of violating section 2(f), the plaintiff or the government must show as part of its case-in-chief, that all of these requirements have been satisfied, and that the buyer knew that none of the statutory defenses was available. *Automatic Canteen Co. v. Federal Trade Commission*, 346 U.S. 61, 73 S.Ct. 1017 (1953).

2. BUYER NEED NOT DISCLOSE COMPETING OFFERS

Assume that a purchaser is simultaneously negotiating for a favorable price with two sellers, Alpha and Beta. During the course of negotiations, the buyer may tell Alpha that Beta has offered it a lower price. Alpha may respond by lowering its price, in a good faith attempt to match Beta's offer. The buyer may be aware, however, that Alpha's new bid actually undercuts Beta's offer. On these facts, Alpha, the seller, has a valid "meeting competition" defense even though it undercut Beta's offer, because it acted in good faith. Consequently, the buyer will not be liable under section 2(f) despite its knowledge that Alpha's price was lower than Beta's bid. *Great Atlantic & Pacific Tea Co. v. Federal Trade Commission*, 440 U.S. 69, 99 S.Ct. 925 (1979). The Court noted that an alternative result, requiring the seller to disclose the details of the competing offer, "would almost inevitably frustrate competitive bidding and, by reducing uncertainty, lead to price matching and anticompetitive cooperation among sellers."

H. REMEDIES

1. PRIVATE REMEDIES

Parties injured by violations of the Robinson-Patman Act may file suit for treble damages. However, in such a suit the plaintiff is not entitled to "automatic damages" in the amount of the price differentials, but rather must prove specifically the magnitude of its injury. *J. Truett Payne Co. v. Chrysler Motors Corp.*, 451 U.S. 557, 101 S.Ct. 1923 (1981).

2. PUBLIC CIVIL REMEDIES

The Robinson-Patman Act may be enforced by both the Department of Justice and the Federal Trade Commission, although historically only the Commission has engaged in enforcement activity. In a proceeding before the Commission, proof of a statutory violation will result in the entry of a cease and desist order, requiring the respondent to refrain from the discrimination in the future.

3. CRIMINAL SANCTIONS

Section 3 of the Robinson-Patman Act, codified as 15 U.S.C.A. § 13a (1984), provides for criminal penalties for certain specified types of price discrimination activities. This provision is enforced solely by the Department of Justice, which has only invoked the provision a few times in the history of the act, and not at all in the last two decades.

REVIEW QUESTIONS

1. **T or F** Attorney Smith has two clients engaged in the same business, one a corporation and the other a sole proprietorship. These two firms compete with each other. Smith charges the corporate client $100/ hour and the individual $50/hour for the identical legal work. Smith has violated the Robinson-Patman Act.

2. **T or F** Most of the federal courts of appeals would conclude that where the lower of two prices was below average variable cost, the seller had engaged in illegal price discrimination.

3. **T or F** Sales to schools and hospitals will be disregarded in determining if a seller has engaged in unlawful price discrimination.

4. **T or F** Omega Widget has two retail customers, one in Miami and the other in New York. They each buy the same number of widgets each month. Omega has given the Miami customer free widget display cases that were not provided to the New York customer. This does not violate the Robinson-Patman Act since the two customers do not compete and there can thus be no harm to competition.

5. **T or F** Quantity discounts are illegal under the Robinson-Patman Act.

6. **T or F** Quart containers of regular milk and skim milk are commodities of like grade and quality for purposes of the Robinson-Patman Act.

7. **T or F** The payment of any fees by a seller to a customer in the nature of brokerage commissions is forbidden by the Robinson-Patman Act, as judicially construed.

8. **T or F** A seller accused of making advertising allowances disproportionately available to customers may defend by showing that the differences are cost justified.

9. **T or F** The interstate commerce requirement of the Robinson-Patman Act is satisfied if either of the two sales, which when compared generate the alleged discrimination, crossed a state line.

10. **T or F** Injury to competition on the second line may be found in a case where a manufacturer charges customers who are wholesalers a higher price than customers who are retailers.

11. **T or F** Functional discounts are only legal if the seller cost justifies the amount of the discount.

12. **T or F** Gamma Gadgets sells to dozens of retailers, including Alpha Stores at 50¢/unit. It does not sell to Beta Stores. Gamma just learned that its competitor, Giant Gadgets, sells comparable gadgets to Beta for 40¢/unit. Gamma has begun to sell to Beta for 40¢ while holding its price at 50¢ for all other customers. Gamma has violated the Robinson-Patman Act.

13. During 1985 Sigma Doodads had fixed costs of $100,000 and variable costs of $400,000. It sold a total of 100,000 doodads during the year, at a uniform price of $5 each. It has only done business west of the Mississippi thus far in its history, but it would like to begin selling in Boston where there is only one small firm—Delta Doodads—doing business. Delta has been selling its doodads for $6 each. Which of the following statements about *Sigma's* pricing is true?

   a. The lowest price it may charge in Boston without violating the Robinson-Patman Act is $6.

   b. The lowest price it may charge in Boston without violating the Robinson-Patman Act is $5.

   c. The lowest price it may charge in Boston without violating the Robinson-Patman Act is $4.

   d. The lowest price it may charge in Boston without violating the Robinson-Patman Act is $1.

14. Theta Gizmos sells gizmos to a variety of customers, one of which is The Gizmo Boutique (TGB), a retailer and another one of which is Atlantic Gizmo Distributors (AGD), a large gizmo wholesaler. Theta had been charging both customers the same price until AGD recently promised to increase its volume of purchases if it was given a better price. As a result, Theta revamped its pricing and now charges TGB $1/unit and AGD 80¢/unit. Which of the following statements about the new pricing is most accurate?

   a. AGD, the favored buyer, is guilty of violating § 2(f) of the Robinson-Patman Act for inducing Theta to sell to it at a lower price than is offered to TGB.

   b. Theta is guilty of a violation of the Robinson-Patman Act regardless of whether it can prove cost justification.

c. Theta is guilty of a violation of the Robinson-Patman Act unless some other gizmo manufacturer is also selling to AGD at 80¢ a unit, thus making the "meeting competition" defense available.

d. Neither Theta nor AGD has violated the Robinson-Patman Act.

15. Moonbeam Corporation is a manufacturer of electric razors. Last year, it made a total of 1,000,000 razors at its sole razor production factory in Waterloo, Iowa. That facility incurred the following costs:

Rent & Utilities	$4,000,000
Labor (on hourly basis)	3,000,000
Raw Materials	7,000,000
TOTAL	14,000,000

Although Moonbean competes with a number of different companies in different markets, its largest nationwide competitors are Flemington and Ronelco. Moonbeam has had varying success in different markets. Moonbean has never been able to interest department stores in Seattle in carrying its razors. In fact, the only razors the 3 large Seattle department stores carry are Flemingtons (which they purchase for $11 each) and Ronelcos (which they purchase for $9 each).

Last year, Moonbeam again approached the Seattle stores and offered them a deal. Although its usual price to department store customers in other markets was $15, it told the Seattle stores that it would sell to them for $13 a unit. Two stores simply refused, but a buyer at the third, Bumbershoots, told Moonbeam, "either you guys are making a killing or your competition is selling at a loss. If you come back to us with something reasonable, we'd consider picking up your product, but you should know that $13 isn't even in the ballpark." When the Moonbeam vendor inquired as to what would be "in the ballpark" he was told "Make me an offer!"

After dwelling on that comment for a week, and still determined to break into the Seattle market, Moonbeam returned to all three stores and offered them razors for $8 each. All three accepted, and placed large orders. Two of the three also informed Flemington that they no longer wished to carry its products.

Flemington has complained to the F.T.C. The Commission must determine if either Moonbeam or Bumbershoots has violated the Robinson-Patman Act. You are a staff attorney with the Commission. Please write a memorandum indicating if either firm has violated the law, giving both your conclusions and your reasoning.

APPENDIX A

ANSWERS TO REVIEW QUESTIONS

I. THE PRIVILEGE TO COMPETE

1. **False.** The fact that an existing firm will be injured does not make competition impermissible. Unless other facts are shown, the privlege to compete applies.

2. **False.** The privilege to compete does not permit firms to induce a breach of contract. Even in the absence of deception, inducing a breach is actionable.

3. **True.** Prima facie tort makes the intentional infliction of injury actionable unless the defendant's acts are privileged. The privilege to compete is lost if the defendant's sole motive is spite. Thus, proof of malevolent motive is necessary.

4. **False.** One is guilty of inducing a breach of contract even if the means used are entirely lawful and the motive is purely self-interested. Interference with prospective advantage requires some showing of deceit, coercion, or improper motive.

5. **True.** Antitrust addresses the problem of undue passivity or collusion by firms. Unfair trade is concerned with ruthless or overly aggressive behavior.

6. **c.** Omega acted intentionally to persuade Alpha to abandon its contract. Although Omega did not use any unlawful methods and did not act out of spite directed at Beta, these elements are not required to prove inducement of breach of contract. A is incorrect because the privilege to compete does not protect a firm that induces parties to abandon contractual commitments. B is incorrect because there is no indication that Omega acted out of spite. D is incorrect, because there is no indication in the question that Omega resorted to deceit, coercion, or other improper means.

II. TRADEMARKS

1. **False.** Functional shapes must be left available for other firms to duplicate. Thus, only non-functional shapes (that are also distinctive) may be protected as trademarks.

2. **True.** So long as the labels disclose the fact of repacking, it is permissible collateral use for the repacking firm to use the trademark of the original manufacturer.

3. **False.** Trademark rights can only be obtained by affixation and use. There is no way to reserve a mark for future use even if a firm has definite plans to market goods under that name.

4. **False.** If a likelihood of confusion can be shown, the owner of a trademark may enjoin infringement by the seller of non-competing goods.

5. **True.** The "r in a circle" is a device which the holder of a federally registered trademark may use to give notice that its mark is federally registered. It may not be used by firms that have only common law rights.

6. **False.** Non-use for two, rather than five, years gives rise to a prima facie inference of abandonment.

7. **True.** Suggestive terms are considered inherently distinctive and thus will be afforded trademark protection without any showing of secondary meaning.

8. *True.* If consumers view a word as designating a category of goods rather than as a brand name, the word has become a generic term, and is no longer protectible as a trademark.

9. *False.* Deceptive terms are those which materially misrepresent the attributes of the products on which they appear, and on which a consumer would rely in making a purchase. They are absolutely barred from federal registration.

10. *False.* Yellow Pages describes the most salient characteristic of the classified phone directory, and is thus descriptive, not fanciful.

11. *False.* Intent is not an element of trademark infringement, though it may be relevant to the form of relief granted.

12. *False.* Any showing of potential harm will permit a trademark plaintiff to secure an injunction. Thus limitation of future expansion or harm to goodwill and reputation are adequate showings even if there has been no diversion of sales.

13. *True.* Common law courts require genuine commercial transactions in the form of sales to actual customers, before the mark is deemed "used."

14. *True.* Geographically descriptive terms are not considered inherently distinctive, so they will only be protected in cases where distinctiveness has evolved over time. That requires proof of secondary meaning.

15. *True.* The Lanham Act specifically permits the registration of the two types of marks cited, along with trademarks and servicemarks.

16. c. Until Alpha expands its business by either selling or advertising on the West Coast, confusion is unlikely, and an injunction is premature, even though Alpha has superior rights. A is incorrect because Beta had constructive notice of Alpha's prior use when it adopted the mark, by virtue of Alpha's federal registration. That deprives Beta of the status of good faith junior user. B is incorrect because it ignores the fact that the parties are operating so far apart that confusion is unlikely. D is incorrect because ZING is a fanciful mark, making the question of secondary meaning irrelevant to this problem.

17. d. Consumers are likely to think that Delta's shirts are manufactured under licenses granted by the soft drink companies whose symbols are being used. Thus, even in jurisdictions recognizing the doctrine of aesthetic functionality, the doctrine would be inapplicable because there is likelihood of confusion as to source. Use in this fashion is not permissible collateral use. A is incorrect because use of another

firm's marks in comparative advertisements is permissible. B is incorrect because firms providing replacement parts and repair services for another firm's products may use that other firm's marks. C is incorrect for the same reason as B.

18. **c.**   Arbirtrary marks are inherently distinctive and thus secondary meaning is unnecessary. The other three types of marks all require secondary meaning since they are not distinctive per se and will only be protected if the user can show they have acquired distinctiveness over time.

19. Martini is not guilty of infringement. The first issue is whether the name MULTISTATE BAR EXAMINATION is protectible as a trademark. If not, NCBE has no basis upon which to enjoin Martini. MULTISTATE BAR EXAMINATION is certainly not inherently distinctive. It is either descriptive, since it explains the principal feature of the test involved, or generic, as the basic name for this type of test. There is probably no adequate alternative name for an objective test like this one, meant to be used in a number of states according to their own criteria. In addition, lawyers and law students probably think of the term as describing a *type* of test (e.g. a C.P.A. exam for accountants, an IQ test, a Multistate Bar Exam, etc.) rather than as a *brand* of test. These factors make the generic characterization most plausible.

If the term is considered descriptive, NCBE must show secondary meaning. While the expression Multistate Bar Exam is widely known among lawyers, that is not, in itself, sufficient to show secondary meaning unless those consumers understand the phrase to be a brand name. As noted above, there is reason to believe that they do not do so.

Finally, even if the term is protectible as a trademark, NCBE must show that Martini's use will lead to a likelihood of confusion. There are no facts in the problem suggesting that consumers think the simulated test offered by Martini is authorized, or sponsored by the NCBE. Given the sophistication of law students and their understanding of the bar preparation and examination process any such confusion is unlikely. Consequently, Martini has not committed infringement. (*See National Conference of Bar Examiners v. Multistate Legal Studies, Inc.,* 692 F.2d 478 (7th Cir.1983)).

III. COPYRIGHT

1. *True.*   For works created after the effective date of the current copyright law, copyright protection lasts for the life of the author, plus 50 years.

2. *False.* Infringement can be made out by proving copying of the structure of the work even if none of the precise words were duplicated.

3. **True.** Although originally a subject of some controversy, it now is clear that computer programs are within the subject matter of copyright.

4. **False.** An author need not register to preserve copyright rights, but registration is a pre-requisite to an infringement suit.

5. **False.** The omission of notice from a small number of copies does not invalidate copyright protection in the work.

6. **True.** The playing of the sound recording is also a "performance" of the underlying musical composition, and thus infringes the exclusive rights of the composer, unless permission is obtained.

7. **True.** Willful infringement for commercial gain is punishable by up to one year imprisonment and a $10,000 fine.

8. **False.** The 1976 statute pre-empted common law copyright. Federal copyright is the sole source of protection for a work from the moment it is fixed in a tangible medium of expression.

9. **True.** Such a use does not impair the commercial value of the work and is consistent with first amendment values and the general preference for dissemination of information.

10. **True.** Publication sufficient to extinguish common law copyright required the general distribution of copies of the work.

11. **True.** A play based on a novel is a derivative work, and the preparation of a derivative work is part of the novelist's exclusive right of adaptation.

12. **False.** Trademarks are not eligible for copyright protection.

13. **True.** The inference of copying is so overwhelming where the two works are identical that a showing of access is not necessary.

14. **False.** There is no intent requirement in suits for copyright infringement.

15. **b.** The method of how to build bookshelves is an idea, and thus not eligible for copyright protection (although the words use to describe that idea would be protectable). A is incorrect because there is no requirement that a work of art portray reality or have any level of artistic merit in order to qualify for copyright protection. C is incorrect because data compilations are within the subject matter of copyright. D is incorrect because the selection of which birds to tape and where to place the microphones is sufficient orginality on the part of the author to make this tape a protectable sound recording.

16. c. The lengthy quote as part of a scholarly debate is consistent with First Amendment interests and does not undermine the economic value of the original work. A is incorrect because Glenn may have intended to ultimately publish the diary when the time was ripe, and the acts described lessen the value of any ultimate publication. B is incorrect even though the purpose of the use is education, because the activity obviously deprives the author of the textbook of valuable sales. D is incorrect, even though parody is sometimes fair use, because the satirist here has gone beyond conjuring up an original and instead appropriated the entire work.

17. *Yes.* The first issue is whether the Johnson novel is copyrightable subject matter. While clearly based on pre-existing material, and thus not original in the colloquial sense, it is sufficiently original to qualify for copyright since it constituted more than a mere copying of Shakespeare's work. Moreover, since the original Shakespearean play is in the public domain, Johnson was free to prepare a derivative work based upon it. Copyright protection thus attached to the novel from the moment it was "fixed" on the page.

Although the copy left on the plane did not bear a notice of copyright, that does not affect Johnson's rights since he did not publish the work. Omission of notice is signficant only for published works. The facts do not indicate if Johnson registered his work with the Copyright Office, but he need not have done so prior to the alleged infringement in order to preserve his rights. He may register now and then file suit. He will not be able to recover statutory damages, however, unless he registered before the infringment.

Ms. Smith's preparation and performance of the play are clearly infringing acts. The play was a derivative work of the Johnson novel. Preparation of a derivative work without the permission of the copyright owner violates the owner's exclusive right of adaptation.

Ms. Smith might argue that since the play was performed in an educational setting, her acts are protected by the fair use doctrine. Her use was not originally commercial in nature and it has not yet affected the market for Johnson's work, which he prepared simply to amuse himself. The sales to other teachers at $5 each are also for educational purposes and may merely cover her duplicating costs. On the other hand, she copied virtually the entire work, and her acts would certainly diminish the reward Johnson could attain if he subsequently published his novel. Although application of the fair use doctrine is subjective, there is a reasonable basis to conclude that it would not be available on these facts.

IV. MISAPPROPRIATION

1. *False.* The *INS* case was decided under federal common law and thus ceased to have binding effect with the decision in the *Erie* case.

2. *True.* The courts have split on the descendability of the right of publicity, with some holding that it terminates on death, and others holding that it passes to the heirs of the celebrity.

3. *False.* The media may not report on entertainers in such a way as to destroy the economic value of their performance. Thus, notwithstanding the First Amendment they may not depict an entire performance on the news.

4. *True.* Acts that deprive creative firms the economic rewards for their labors will likely undermine incentives for firms to be creative in the first place. Consequently courts focus on destruction of incentives in deciding misappropriation cases.

5. *False.* Such a party may also rely on theories such as implied-in-fact contract, unjust enrichment, breach of confidential relationship, or taking of property.

6. *False.* The right of publicity is not limited to people whose fame is derived from profit-making activities.

7. *False.* Jurisdictions relying on privacy theories to protect celebrities against name or likeness appropriation will probably terminate the right on death, since the right of privacy is considered a personal right that does not descend to one's heirs.

8. *False.* While some jurisdictions require a direct competitive relationship in misappropriation cases, others do not.

9. *True.* There is no right of compensation for an idea unless it is valuable, and the requirements of novelty, concreteness and usefulness thus must be satisfied by the plaintiff.

10. *False.* If the idea is routed to the research department and the firm later develops a similar idea on its own, it will be unable to prove independent development. Submitted ideas should therefore be segregated from the research department.

11. c. Here, the material being protected by state law, a videocassette, is within the subject matter of copyright, and the rights at issue—the exclusive right to perform the work by showing publicly—are also

among those listed in the copyright statute. Therefore, this cause of action would be pre-empted. A is incorrect because the physical appearance of the musicians at their live concert is not "fixed in a tangible medium of expression" and thus state law may protect it. B is incorrect, because the right to receive royalties on the re-sale of art work is not a right conferred by the copyright law, and thus state law may confer that right. D is incorrect because the copyright act does not pre-empt causes of action for breach of express or implied promises to pay compensation.

12. b.   The publication of the pamphlet is almost certainly privileged under the First Amendment. Any publicity rights of the Senator must yield to the interest in open political debate. A is incorrect because although the baseball player may not be nationally known, he is presumably well known in the town where he plays and the merchant is clearly making commercial use of his name. C is incorrect because the archbishop has a right of publicity even though his fame does not derive from profit-seeking activities. D is incorrect because the sale of cup-cakes is commercial activity and the use of the professor's name is undoubtedly the principal reason the cup-cakes are being purchased.

13. Louie is probably guilty of misappropriation. The initial question is whether any Ohio cause of action is federally pre-empted. While architectural plans are copyrightable subject matter, the appearance of buildings has been held outside of the copyright act. Thus, under section 301 of the copyright statute, states are free to provide protection in this area if they wish to do so.

Assuming Ohio follows the general common law on misappropriation the next question is whether the plaintiff, CWF, created a valuable intangible with the expectation of profit. There is every indication that it did. While it did not design the buildings at the fair, it expended the effort necessary to secure the participation of the various cities, and presumably also determined where each pavilion would be sited, and thus how the buildings would look as a group. The appearance of the fair was the creation of CWF. That it expected some financial return from this effort is revealed by the fact that it charged admission, and granted numerous limited concessions, including one for postcards.

The second element of misappropriation is the taking of the intangible by the defendant without consent and with little effort. There is no claim that Louie acted with consent. He might argue that he did not merely "take" the appearance of the buildings, but added his own artistic elements by deciding how to compose his pictures and what photographic settings to use. Postcards, however, are purchased chiefly as straightforward representations of notable sights. Nothing here suggests that these cards were purchased primarily for Louie's photographic artistry. It is more likely that they were bought because the fair was popular and people wanted pictures of the buildings. Therefore, this second element is satisfied.

Finally, there is the question of financial harm to the plaintiff. CWF had granted a postcard license to Acme so there might be injury if the payments under that license were based on the volume of cards to be sold. Also, some people might buy Louie's cards downtown and decide, as a result, that they did not have to travel to the fair since they now knew what all the buildings looked like. In addition, if Louie's behavior were held lawful, it might destroy future incentives to organize fairs of this sort because the organizers could not assure licensees of exclusive rights and it would be more difficult to raise money. Consequently, CWF has a good chance of success. *See New York World's Fair 1964–1965 Corp. v. Colourpicture Publishers, Inc.,* 21 A.D.2d 896, 251 N.Y.S.2d 885 (2d Dept. 1964).

V. PATENTS

1. *False.* A claim of novelty is defeated only if a *single* source fully anticipates the invention in question.

2. *False.* The commercial success suggests that there was a strong demand for the device and therefore that it would have been made previously if the manner of doing so had been obvious. Commercial success is considered evidence of non-obviousness.

3. *True.* The fact that the device has been on sale more than a year before the application is filed gives rise to a statutory bar to patentability.

4. *False.* The manner in which an invention was developed is irrelevant to its patentability. There is *no* requirement that patentable inventions be the product of a "flash of genius."

5. *False.* While industrial processes incorporating computer programs can be patented if the statutory tests are met, programs themselves are considered like mathematical formulas and are not patentable subject matter.

6. *True.* The prior art is to be drawn from material addressing the same technological problems as the invention, not from the same commercial field.

7. *False.* Kerosene is a "staple" commodity. It has many uses other than as a part of the patented process. Thus it is not contributory infringement to make such sales.

8. *False.*   Treble damages are awarded in the discretion of the court, not as a matter of right.

9. *True.*   File wrapper estoppel prevents a patentee from claiming that an allegedly infringing device is equivalent to his invention if the patentee gave up claims describing the other device during the patent examination process.

10. *True.*   The statute explicitly provides for a re-examination process, during which the applicant may provide additional information to the patent office in support of patentability.

11. *True.*   The statute requires a disclosure that will permit others to learn how the invention is made so that, when the patent expires, the learning it represents is available to the public.

12. *False.*   So long as the device in question has been used in its ordinary way, the use need not have been either widespread or particularly obvious to casual observers.

13. b.   Under the so-called "negative" tests of invention, the development of a new product by tinkering with the ratio of ingredients of an existing compound is something that anyone might try, and is therefore unpatentable because it is obvious. A is incorrect, because the praise and wide adoption of the device indicate that others would have tried to invent it previously if they could have. That they did not do so suggests that it was non-obvious. C is incorrect because the prior art for cushioning impacts to the human body would almost surely not include literature bearing on nuclear plant engineering. D is incorrect because the development of a new device through meticulous trial and error does not render the invention any less inventive than something developed through a flash of genius.

14. c.   Omega's patent forbids others from making the device, even if they do so entirely innocently and without knowledge of the patent. Thus, Gamma's construction of the single unit for his own use is infringing. A is incorrect because, under the first sale exhaustion doctrine, it is not infringement to use a patented object that has been purchased from one who owns it. B is incorrect because the consumers themselves are not engaged in infringement and therefore the sale of the videotape cannot be considered contributory infringement. D is incorrect because repair of patented devices short of complete reconstruction does not constitute infringement.

15. Yes, the patent should issue. The problem requires consideration of issues of novelty, obviousness, and statutory bar.

The first issue is whether the October, 1982 publication in Cardiac Medicine was anticipatory, so as to destroy Kildare's claim of novelty. A documentary source is anticipatory only if it fully discloses the entirety of an invention (i.e., it is an enabling disclosure). Here, that is not the case. The description in the article was of a combined administration of two drugs in equal doses, not the combination of different proportions of the two, along with heat, in order to produce a wholly new compound.

The September 1983 French publication also does not affect the novelty of Kildare's invention, since it did not appear until after he developed the new preparation.

The next problem is whether Kildare's patent should be denied on obviousness grounds. Although the discovery of the drug was accidental, rather than the product of a "flash of genius," that does not require a conclusion that the drug was not inventive, or was obvious, since the statute specifically indicates that "patentability shall not be negatived by the manner in which the invention was made."

The problem does not reveal the full content of the prior art. Assuming the October 1982 article is the only relevant prior art reference, the question is whether it permits one skilled in the relevant art—pharmacology—to deduce how to make the drug. The article described the combined administration of two drugs as a treatment for high blood pressure. While it is a judgment call, it is unlikely that this article makes obvious a wholly new drug, produced by a chemical reaction, which is useful for treating heart palpitations, a different condition than high blood pressure. The conclusion of non-obviousness is fortified by the fact that, prior to Kildare's activities, there were few effective drugs for heart palpitations. If the method of making Gammadol was obvious, some other researcher would have previously developed it and made it available. On the other hand, the virtually simultaneous discovery of the same preparation in Europe is some evidence that the new drug may have been obvious.

Assuming the invention was non-obvious, Kildare must finally show that the statutory bar provisions do not preclude a patent here. The September 1983 French publication is not an event on which statutory bar can be based because it did not occur more than a year before the (August 1984) date of the application. The October 1982 American publication does not give rise to statutory bar because it is not an enabling disclosure. Finally, Kildare's own use of the invention more than one year before applying for a patent (i.e. from June through August of 1983) does not trigger the bar, because the use was for genuine experimental purposes.

Since the statutory requirement of utility is obviously satisfied on these facts, there is no obstacle to patentability, and the patent should issue.

VI. TRADE SECRETS

1. ***True.***   Overbroad covenants of this sort are considered to be against public policy and may violate the antitrust laws.

2. ***True.***   Reverse engineering involves the mechanical or chemical analysis of another firm's products. It is always permissible to engage in this kind of activity in an attempt to discover trade secrets.

3. ***True.***   Review is available under the Administrative Procedure Act, but the complaining firm must be able to invoke some statutory authority in support of its contention that the material should not be disclosed.

4. ***False.***   The contractual commitment to pay royalties continues for whatever term is specified in the contract. It does not terminate when the secret becomes public information.

5. ***False.***   Any means that are successful in overcoming reasonable precautions to maintain secrecy will be condemned as improper.

6. ***True.***   While minimal novelty and utility are required before something can be the subject of trade secret protection, the material involved need not meet the standards of patentability.

7. ***False.***   Although some courts would grant perpetual injunctive relief in this situation, that view is not universal. Other courts deny relief entirely or grant limited "head start" injunctions.

8. ***False.***   Most courts would imply a confidential relationship between employer and employee forbidding use of the secret even if one was not explicitly imposed by contract.

9. ***True.***   A third party incurs no liability for use of the secret until told of its status, and may not be enjoinable thereafter if it has materially altered its position.

10. ***False.***   A head start injunction is one which lasts for a period of time equal to the period from the date of the theft of the secret to the date the secret became publicly known.

11. **d.**   A trade secret license is a valid contract and the revelation of the secret is considered sufficient consideration to sustain the obligation of the licensee to pay royalties. Such contracts are enforced according to their terms regardless of whether the secret has become public. A is wrong because the concepts of unreasonable scope and duration are applied to covenants not to compete, not to trade secret licenses. B is

wrong because the Supreme Court has indicated that there is no conflict between enforcement of a trade secret license and the patent laws that gives rise to pre-emption. C is wrong because the magazine learned the secret through reverse engineering, which is a proper means by which to learn a secret.

12. Zenith is probably not guilty of trade secret misappropriation, although it is a close question. The problem requires consideration of (1) whether the customer lists were proper subject matter for trade secret protection, (2) whether the degree of secrecy maintained was adequate and (3) whether the secret was learned through improper means.

A trade secret may consist of any information that is not generally known. In the case of customer lists the question is whether the identified customers were readily ascertainable as likely prospects or not. If not, the list is a valuable trade secret. Here, there must be thousands of companies that buy machinery. Only a small minority purchase made-to-order material. Apex had spent time and effort identifying that group. Thus, its customer lists are valid trade secret subject matter.

The adequacy of the secrecy here is the most difficult question. The production of only a limited number of diskettes and the attempt to treat them carefully represents some degree of security. Merely placing them in the New Jersey plant manager's desk, however, may be inadequate, unless that desk was locked or kept in a locked office.

A further problem arises from the retention of the material in the machine's memory which was made accessible through a password, which could be found in a book that was kept out in the open on a desk. This does not demonstrate the degree of care that is reasonably calculated to keep the information secret. Certainly, a procedure requiring either that the books be secured each night or that the operator erase the machine's memory would be relatively easy to implement and would provide considerably greater secrecy.

Third, the computer containing these files was sold to Zenith without being checked to see if any confidential material was retained in its memory. Such carelessness may constitute a waiver of secrecy even if the somewhat casual procedures reviewed above were adequate. Consequently, it would appear that secrecy was not adequately maintained here and plaintiff has no basis to recover.

If the court were to conclude otherwise, however, and reach the issue of "improper means," it would find that Zenith behaved improperly. First, Zenith knew that it did not purchase the customer lists and yet Hal Modem explicitly misrepresented this fact to Ms. Johnson. While this lie was not criminal, it was nonetheless sufficiently wrongful to constitute improper means.

Similarly, the offer of financial inducement to Ms. Johnson is in the nature of a bribe and even if not technically criminal, is easily categorized as wrongful. Thus, if Apex had taken more careful precautions with its customer list it probably would have had a valid cause of action on these facts.

For a judicial discussion on similar facts, *see Defiance Button Machine Co. v. C & C Metal Products Corp.,* 759 F.2d 1053 (2d Cir.1985).

VII. COMPETITOR REMEDIES FOR FALSE ADVERTISING AND DISPARAGEMENT

1. ***True.*** Lanham Act § 43(a) only reaches false statements about one's own goods, therefore an explicit disparaging statement about a rival's goods does not violate the statute.

2. ***True.*** The "sole source" rule limited the right to recover for false advertising to firms who had a monopoly in the genuine goods, since only they could demonstrate clear injury due to the false ads.

3. ***True.*** A likelihood of economic injury in the future will suffice to show entitlement to injunctive relief, but a more specific showing is required for damages.

4. ***False.*** A false statement must be material, and it must pertain to the defendant's own merchandise, before it is actionable under the Lanham Act.

5. ***True.*** Those cases gave great weight to the fact that the Lanham Act was a trademark statute and thus limited § 43(a) to cases like passing off, which are analogous to trademark infringement.

6. ***False.*** State statutes have tended to abrogate the sole source rule and permit any merchant who is likely to be injured by false advertising to recover.

7. ***False.*** Droit Morale is a European doctrine that provides a cause of action for artists whose work is altered or mutilated by other parties.

8. ***True.*** A common law disparagement plaintiff must correlate the defendant's false comments with specific lost sales in order to recover for disparagement.

9. ***True.*** Because of first amendment considerations, where there is a public debate about the merits of a product, a party is liable for

disparagement only if he knows that his comments are false, or disseminates them with reckless disregard for their truth or falsity.

10. *False.* There is no intent requirement to make out a valid cause of action under the Lanham Act

11. b. This statement concerns the goods of a competitor, not the goods of the party making the statement, and thus is not actionable under § 43(a). A is incorrect because at least some courts would conclude that the use of the Coca-Cola color scheme and script constituted a false representation that the pro-drug tee shirt was sponsored by Coca-Cola. C is incorrect because it is an explicit false statement by a merchant about his own services that is material to prospective purchasers. D is incorrect because the edited version, a creation of the defendant radio station, is being misdescribed as the original song as recorded by the record company.

12. d. This statement is a false description or representation of the services Jerry provides. It is violative of Lanham Act § 43(a) and ComputerHaus can recover damages if it can document its economic injury and show a causal connection between that injury and Jerry's ads. A is wrong because ComputerHaus is not the sole source of full service computer retail services. A consumer who was tricked into patronizing Jerry by these advertisements would not necessarily have patronized ComputerHaus even if he had known the truth. B is incorrect because the statements involved do not disparage ComputerHaus or make reference to it in any way. C is incorrect because only injunctive relief is available under the Uniform Deceptive Trade Practices Act.

13. Yes, CPI has valid causes of action under both the common law and Lanham Act § 43(a) for a variety of false implications contained in the P & G advertisements. It probably also has a remedy under state statutory law, depending on the particular jurisdiction where it is located.

CPI may be able to secure relief in a suit at common law by relying on the newer cases that relax, to some degree, the "sole source" requirement that made such actions historically difficult. Even though CPI does not have a monopoly on the manufacture of genuine hand lotion—because many companies make such lotions—CPI can point out that the P & G ads are directly targeted at its product, VECL, which is mentioned by name explicitly. Thus, success on this cause of action will depend on CPI's ability to prove falsity and injury. Both of those factors are considered below in connection with the discussion of the Lanham Act suit.

The Lanham Act makes any "false description or representation" actionable provided the plaintiff can show that it is likely to be injured. Here, the plaintiff and the defendant are direct competitors. Consequently, there is almost surely a chance of injury to CPI. Any objective evidence it can produce concerning a decline in sales would, naturally, further bolster this contention, but many courts would accept the mere existence of a direct competitive relationship as sufficient evidence of likely injury, at least to support injunctive relief.

The real question under section 43(a) then, is whether the P & G advertisements are false. Viewed literally, they are not. However, the statute reaches misleading, as well as literally false, claims. There are several misleading implications here.

First, the reference to independent tests implies that the tests were conducted by a firm with no interest in the results. Here, the testing firm was paid by P & G and thus, it might be argued, the failure to disclose this fact renders the ads misleading. More importantly, the advertisements suggest a much more overwhelming preference for New Supra than the actual data indicate. If consumers who had no preference are disregarded, it appears that the two products were virtually tied in two markets, and that VECL was rated clearly superior in the third. This is hardly the impression communicated by CPI. Third, the advertisements ignore the results in the Boulder test. The omission of this information paints a false picture.

Moreover, these inaccuracies in the advertisements are clearly material. Consumers are likely to rely on the reported experience of other consumers in deciding which product to pick. The representations here are thus highly likely to influence consumer product choice. Consequently, CPI has a strong cause of action under § 43(a).

Depending on the state where CPI is located it may also be able to invoke a "baby" FTC act. Some of those statutes do not provide for private causes of action and many limit remedies to injunctive relief, so further research would be necessary to determine precisely how useful such a statute might be in this precise case.

For a variant on these facts, *see Procter & Gamble Co. v. Chesebrough-Pond's, Inc.,* 747 F.2d 114 (2d Cir.1984).

VIII. FEDERAL TRADE COMMISSION REGULATION OF UNFAIR AND DECEPTIVE PRACTICES

1. *False.* The statement is backwards. The very definition of unfairness is consumer injury, while in a deception case the Commission need not prove any injury at all.

2. *True.* The original version of the statute only dealt with "unfair methods of competition." The 1938 Wheeler-Lea Amendment added the "unfair and deceptive acts and practices" language.

3. *True.* Actual deception is not required, and there is no requirement that a "reasonable" consumer be deceived if a significant number of gullible consumers would be misled.

4. *False.* There is no intent element in either the "unfairness" or the "deception" doctrine.

5. *True.* It has been judicially held that a restitution provision is beyond the Commission's power to enter "cease and desist" orders.

6. *False.* Violation of the terms of an order will subject the violator to civil penalties.

7. *True.* Because the Commission tackled a number of politically controversial issues, Congress has been repeatedly involved in the F.T.C.'s rulemaking activities.

8. *False.* The use of mock-ups, per se, is not forbidden. It is only deceptive if the viewer is invited to scrutinize the mock-up for first-hand proof of a product claim and the use of the mock-up is not disclosed.

9. *True.* The Commission may attack both explicit misrepresentations and the failure to disclose information as deceptive.

10. *False.* The present Commission is unlikely to act if the product is inexpensive and frequently purchased because consumers will quickly discover the falsehood and simply stop buying the offending product, making F.T.C. action unnecessary.

11. *True.* Because it is difficult to regulate high pressure sales tactics directly, the F.T.C. regulations impose the cooling off period so that consumers can reconsider unwise transactions.

12. *True.* Only the respondent may appeal an adverse Commission decision to the courts. The Commission staff does not have this right.

13. b. By making the product claim based solely on a speculation that the product would work, Alpha has violated the requirement that it possess an advance reasonable basis for all advertising claims. A is incorrect because the product name is not, itself, deceptive and would probably be considered "puffing" by most consumers in any event. C is incorrect because many products require the addition of water and it is unlikely that this minimal effort renders the claim "easy to use" deceptive. D is incorrect because the claim was not substantiated.

14. c. Although Gamma has probably violated the F.T.C. Act's prohibition against deception because of its false claims, this does not subject it to civil penalties, but rather to an administrative proceeding before the Commission. Based on the limited facts in the question, the false claim about the quality of the sneaker does not violate a cease and desist order previously entered against Gamma, nor one previously entered against another party, nor does it violate any F.T.C. regulation. A is wrong, because Alpha's claim here violates the order that was entered against it in 1982, in that the reference to being an "all star" clearly suggests superior athletic performance. B is wrong because Beta did not comply with the regulation requiring materials to be listed on the tag, and is thus subject to civil penalties. D is wrong because Delta's claim violates the terms of the 1982 order against Alpha, and that order received wide publicity. Therefore Delta probably knew that its conduct was "deceptive" and is liable for civil penalties under section 5(m) of the F.T.C. Act.

15. At a minimum, the complaint should be modified to eliminate the charge of unfairness and the request for a corrective advertising disclosure. Depending on which definition of "deception" is used, the advertisements may or may not violate the standard.

To constitute "unfair" conduct, an advertisement or commercial practice must pose a risk of substantial, unmitigated, unavoidable consumer injury. Those conditions do not appear to be met here. While many consumers may become jittery if they drink coffee, the magnitude of that injury is relatively slight. Moreover, consumers are likely to quickly learn that coffee has this effect on them and therefore to avoid the product in the future. Thus any injury is "avoidable." There is no element of coercion in these advertisements, nor is there the withholding of any information uniquely in the possession of the advertiser. Consequently, the unfairness doctrine seems to be inappropriate on these facts.

These advertisements may be deceptive, however, if analyzed under the historic definition of that term. Under the classic test, an advertising claim is deceptive if it has any tendency to deceive a significant number of consumers. One of several themes of these ads is that coffee is relaxing—that it promotes contemplation. The advertisements specifically state that coffee "calms you down." This is obviously contrary to the weight of scientific evidence about the effect of caffeine. While very many sophisticated consumers will dismiss this claim as contrary to their own experience, or recongnize the distinction between the pyschological effect of "relaxing with a cup of coffee" and the chemical effect of coffee on the body, there are undoubtedly numerous gullible consumers who will take these representations at face value. Perhaps they will have a hot cup of coffee just before bed to help them sleep! Thus, the traditional test of deception is satisfied here.

Under the newer *"Cliffdale"* standard, the advertisment should be condemned only if it is likely to mislead reasonable consumers. Here, the common knowledge about coffee as a stimulant is so widespread that it is difficult to conclude that there is a high probability of a reasonable consumer being led astray. Moreover, because coffee is relatively inexpensive and frequently purchased, consumers can discover for themselves what effect the product has. Therefore this is a poor case for Commission action.

The substitution of cola for coffee in the mugs does not change this result. The cola is not the focus of the commercials. The announcer does not suggest that consumers look at the thick rich color of the beverage while the camera zooms in on the mug. Thus no deception charge can be predicated on the innocuous use of a prop here.

If any of the celebrities who request caffeine-free cola in the mugs does not actually drink coffee, however, there may be deception through the use of an inappropriate endorsement. The F.T.C. guides on endorsements suggest that an endorser must actually use the product in question if the ad makes an express or implied representation to that effect. The facts in this problem are insufficiently detailed to determine if that is a problem here.

Finally, even if a complaint were to issue, this is an inappropriate case for corrective advertising. The "coffee achievers" campaign is quite new. Any deception involved would not "linger" after the advertisements were discontinued. Since lingering deception is the justification for corrective advertising, such a remedy would be unnecessary here and might even pose First Amendment problems.

IX. CONSUMER REMEDIES FOR FALSE ADVERTISING AND OTHER EXPLOITATIVE PRACTICES

1. *True.*   No cause of action is explicitly provided and the courts have refused to imply one out of a concern that such suits would interfere with the F.T.C.'s enforcement activities.

2. *False.* Most Baby F.T.C. Acts dispense with the "scienter" requirement, thus making even inadvertent misrepresentations actionable.

3. *False.* The minimum amount in controversy requirements specified in the Magnuson-Moss Act apply only to suits brought in federal court.

4. *True.* Such statutes have been applied against defendants who were making casual sales of used goods.

5. *False.* Consumers do not have standing to invoke section 43(a) of the Lanham Act. It is strictly a competitor remedy.

6. *False.* While private causes of action are widespread, not every jurisdiction provides for them.

7. a. Unless Smith lives in one of the few states that does not provide a private right of action under its Baby F.T.C. Act, the representations about the safety of the machine and the lack of need for protective clothing appear to have been deceptive in light of his injury and thus would be grounds for a suit under the statute. B is wrong because there is no private cause of action under F.T.C. Act § 5. C is wrong because the advertisements and owner's manual involved here are not within the statutory definition of a "warranty", and thus there is no indication of a breach of warranty. D is wrong because the problem does not indicate that the seller knew these representations were false, and scienter is an element of a cause of action for deceit.

X. PRICE AND SERVICE DISCRIMINATION UNDER THE ROBINSON–PATMAN ACT

1. *False.* The Act only applies to discriminatory pricing of commodities. Legal services are not within the scope of the statute.

2. *True.* While specific standards differ, most circuits have accepted the general outline of the Areeda-Turner tests for predatory pricing and condemn prices that drop below average variable cost.

3. *True.* Specific statutory provisions exempt purchases by charitable organizations for their own use from consideration under the act.

4. *False.* The prohibition against providing promotional facilities on a non-proportional basis applies even where there is no adverse competitive effect.

5. *False.* There is no blanket prohibition of quantity discounts. They are allowed if cost justified or if functionally available to all customers.

6. *False.* The two types of milk are not physically identical and they do not have the same degree of consumer acceptance, so they are not of like grade.

7. *True.* The brokerage payment provisions of the act operate as a complete ban on all such payments.

8. *False.* The cost justification defense does not apply to alleged violations of the advertising and promotional allowance provisions of the act.

9. *True.* If all sales are within a single state, the jurisdictional element of Robinson-Patman is not satisfied even if those sales have an effect on interstate commerce. Actual sales across a state line are required.

10. *True.* The wholesale customers of the discriminator will be injured because any retailers who are free to do so will shift to become direct customers of the discriminator. Thus there is injury on the second line here.

11. *False.* They may also be legal because the recipient of such a discount (e.g. a wholesaler) does not compete with firms paying the higher price (e.g. retailers).

12. *False.* Gamma is protected by the meeting competition defense. The defense applies even though Gamma dropped its prices to obtain a *new* customer rather than merely to retain an *old* customer.

13. c. The lowest price that would not be held predatory by most courts is a price equal to average variable cost. Here, the average variable cost is $4 ($400,000 in variable costs divided by 100,000 units of production). A is incorrect because it implies that Sigma may not drop its prices in the Boston market at all. B is incorrect since $5 is the average *total* cost. C is incorrect since $1 is the average *fixed* cost.

14. d. Since AGD and TGB are on different levels of the distribution chain, they do not compete. Therefore the price advantage to AGD cannot have any effect on second line competition and is not unlawful. A is incorrect because a buyer cannot be liable under § 2(f) unless the pricing behavior of the seller violates the act and, as noted, that is not true here. B is incorrect because cost justification is a defense to a charge of price discrimination. C is incorrect because, as noted, there is no violation regardless of the meeting competition defense.

15. Neither firm has violated the Robinson-Patman Act because the meeting competition defense applies to shelter what would otherwise be unlawful predatory pricing.

The first issue in any Robinson-Patman Act case is whether the jurisdictional requirements of the statute have been satisifed. Here, it is clear that they have. Since products were shipped from Iowa to buyers around the country, the interstate commerce requirement is satisfied. Since most buyers paid $15 but Seattle stores paid only $8, there has been a discrimination in price between different purchasers. The razors involved are all of like grade and quality and are plainly commodities destined for resale in the United States.

The more important inquiry here is harm to competition. For second line injury, competing buyers must be charged different prices. Since all buyers in Seattle paid the same price and since the buyers who paid higher prices are apparently located in other cities, no favored and disfavored buyers do business in the same market and there cannot be any second line problems.

Primary line competition was affected here, since Moonbeam's aggressive entrance into Seattle displaced Flemington entirely and presumably cut into Ronelco's sales volume as well. Harm to primary line competition is usually demonstrated by the defendant's use of a price below its average variable cost. Here, Moonbeam's variable costs were apparently $10,000,000/year (labor plus raw materials). Since it produced one million units, the average variable cost was $10. Thus the $8 price it charged was predatory. Consequently, unless it may invoke an affirmative defense, it has violated the act.

Fortunately for Moonbeam, however, its conduct satisfied all the requirements of the meeting competition defense. Although its $8 price actually undersold its competitors, rather than merely matched them, Moonbeam apparently did not know that at the time. Its attempt to get some indication of competitive price levels was rebuffed by the buyer from Bumbershoots and if it had attempted to verify price levels with Flemington or Ronelco it might well have been guilty of antitrust violations. All indications are that it acted in good faith. There is also no indication that the competitor's products were anything other than comparable in quality to the Moonbeam razors, so Moonbeam was free to try to match its rivals' prices.

Moreover, it is irrelevant that Moonbeam had not previously done business with the Seattle stores and therefore was not acting "defensively" to retain customers against a price raid by a competitor. The Supreme Court has ruled that the meeting competition defense also applies to "offensive" attempts to garner new customers, and may permissibly encompass an area-wide price response—which seems to be what Moonbeam did here.

The availability of a meeting competition defense for Moonbeam is also conclusive on the question of buyer liability on the part of Bumbershoots. A buyer cannot be liable unless the seller engaged in illegal price discrimination. The fact that Bumbershoots knew that Moonbeam's price offer was lower than that of the competing firms is of no consequence, since a buyer in this position is not obliged to reveal the details of the competing offer. Thus, neither firm has violated the act.

*

APPENDIX B

MODEL EXAMINATION

[**Note:** The questions which follow are extremely lengthy and challenging. I suggest you use them by actually writing up answers and then exchanging those answers with others in your class before reviewing the sample answer which follows. You should attempt to do that, initially, on a closed-book basis. Each question involves material from several different topics in the course.]

I.

In 1972 a wealthy Philadelphia philanthropist, K. Baresford Tipton, resolved to do something to help the starving children of Asia and Africa. Recognizing that even his vast resources could barely scratch the surface of the problem, he decided to solicit funds from the public. He conceived of a plan whereby donors would have their contributions routed to a particular child, and would receive photographs of the child and reports on the child's health, diet and well-being. To administer this program, Tipton formed a non-profit corporation called Save the Children, Inc. ("STC").

STC began soliciting funds for the child relief effort through direct mailings to potential donors living across the United States. A typical mailing included a photograph of a hungry child, and a leaflet. The leaflet read in part:

Don't just sit there—SAVACHILD
Just $25 a month can save a child through SAVACHILD
Make your contribution payable to
SAVE THE CHILDREN, INC.
1500 Walnut Street, Philadelphia, PA.

By 1983 Tipton's plan had proved only moderately successful. About $1.7 million annually was being received from some 23,000 contributors living in 22 states in the Northeast and Midwest. Indeed, Tipton was disappointed by a survey appearing in the June, 1983 issue of Charitable Organizations Magazine. According to that poll, 46% of those surveyed thought that Save the Children provided training in water safety to lifeguards planning to work as camp counsellors at children's summer camps. Tipton was, however, undeterred. To demonstrate his continued optimism he applied for Lanham Act registration for the marks SAVACHILD and SAVE THE CHILDREN, which was granted in 1983.

Unbeknownst to Tipton, in 1982 Sue Beth Miller, a former Miss Mississippi best known for her participation in a nationwide ad campaign for tomato juice, decided to speak out against the proliferation of statutes and ordinances guaranteeing rights to gay persons in the areas of employment (especially as public school teachers) and housing. To organize her campaign, Ms. Miller formed a corporation called Save Our Children, Inc. and began making direct mail solicitations from mailing lists obtained from fundamentalist church groups. Most of the persons on these lists lived in the Southeast. Her literature read, in part, as follows:

Homosexuals do not belong in our schools. They exert an unwholesome influence on our children. It is to protect our children that we must fight these so-called "gay rights" laws. Help us. Don't delay. Act now.

SAVE YOUR CHILDREN

Prevent the spread of the homosexual menace by sending in your check today. Mail it to:

SAVE OUR CHILDREN
100 Righteousness Road, Downright-Upright, MISS.

Ms. Miller had also left instructions with her staff to try to enlarge their mailing lists. One of her employees, on a visit to his grandmother in Philadelphia, noticed a large dumpster outside the offices of Tipton's organization, STC. Naturally curious, he decided to investigate, and began rummaging through the trash. At the bottom of the dumpster he found a 17 page document headed "SAVACHILD Participants, January 1981—CONFIDENTIAL". The first page of the document had been stamped in red with the word "Superceded." The employee pocketed the list and on his return to Mississippi, he turned it over to

Ms. Miller, who added the names appearing on it to her Save Our Children mailing lists.

By 1984, Tipton and STC noticed that their contributions had fallen off by about 10%. In that year, they also received about half a dozen letters from contributors protesting their involvement with, what one writer called, "this stupid anti-gay crusade." All six of these letters indicated that the authors would withhold future contributions from STC. Tipton had read about Ms. Miller's activities in Newsweek over the preceding few months and now realized that her conduct was posing a threat to the continued health of STC. Tipton has also learned that Ms. Miller plans to seek Lanham Act registration for the mark "Save Our Children."

Tipton has come to see you. He wants to know what remedies he may have against Ms. Miller and her organization. Please write a memo reviewing his options.

II.

Of the many manufacturers of men's knit shirts, one of the most successful is Bif Laurenn. Three years ago Bif introduced a new line of shirts—"Bowlo by Bif"—with a cute breast pocket embroidered emblem of an overweight bowler getting ready to roll a strike. These shirts have become extraordinarily popular and are in heavy demand everywhere.

Bif manufactures the shirts in a wide variety of colors at his plant in South Carolina. Although his average total cost per unit is only $6, the strong demand permits him to mark them up heavily. Bif sells the shirts to both wholesalers and directly to a number of large department stores throughout the country. Both wholesalers and department stores pay the same price for the shirts—$15.

Starting last year wholesalers became eligible for a new "Baker's Dozen" program instituted by Bif. Under the program, the wholesaler receives one shirt free of charge with each box of 12 shirts it buys. Bif exercises no control over these wholesalers, who make independent decisions about how much to charge their customers for the shirts. Most of the retail buyers from these wholesalers are medium and small sized men's stores.

Recently, Bif noticed that orders from the department stores were down significantly. When he contacted the buyers at several stores they all gave him the same story. They were afraid that the popularity of the item had crested and they did not want to get stuck with excess inventory. As one of them put it "Better to run out than to overbuy and have to mark them down." Although Bif tried to allay their fears, they were not persuaded to increase their orders.

After consulting with his marketing staff, Bif returned to the department stores. He told them that he had designed a new "Discount Protection Plan."

Under the plan, the department stores would be permitted to return any shirts which remained unsold after 10 days at a 20% off sale. The store would get a full credit on all returned shirts. In other words, if the store normally sold the shirts for $30 at retail, it would have the right to return the shirt for a refund if it remained unsold after 10 days on sale for $24. The department stores were delighted with this program and most of them significantly increased their orders. When wholesale customers of Bif inquired about their eligibility for this program, he told them "Don't be ridiculous—who ever heard of a wholesaler having a sale!" Some of the wholesalers were sufficiently annoyed that they threatened litigation.

Not one to take threats lightly, Bif has consulted you. He has asked you to review his entire pricing structure and alert him to any problems you see. Please indicate if any of his activities violated the Robinson-Patman Act, and explain your conclusion.

III.

One of the most popular programs on TV for the past several years has been a filmed adventure series on the National Broadcasting System (NBS) called "Delano, M.E." It concerns the exploits of a county coroner who not only performs autopsies, but also solves crimes. In virtually every episode Delano, the main character, is seen talking over the crime in question with his best friend, Marcus. The Marcus character operates a restaurant. As portrayed in the show the restaurant is unique, having what might be called a medical motif. For instance, the patrons of this hypothetical restaurant are served their drinks in miniature intravenous bottles; the actors who portray the waiters and waitresses are dressed in surgeon's green operating suits; and on different episodes the actors playing the customers were heard in the background ordering such items as an "Emergency Room Burger" or a "Transfusion Salad." The name of the restaurant on the show is "The Emergency Room."

Last year, a young man in Stamford, Connecticut, named Craig Phillips, decided to go into the restaurant business. Having watched Delano, M.E. a number of times he decided to model his real establishment after the one depicted on the show. Although he called the restaurant "The Operating Room," the menu items, mode of service, and decor all replicated those depicted on the show.

While planning his menu, Craig recalled his favorite drink—a concoction he had frequently when he was stationed in Whahoowa, Thailand, as an Air Force Sergeant during 1981. This consisted of one ounce each of vodka, gin, bourbon, scotch, tequilla and amaretto along with a dash of tomato juice and four ounces of hot pepper sauce. In Thailand this drink was called the "Thai Surprise." Craig decided to offer the same drink, but concluded that because of Americans' more sensitive palates, he should modify the recipe. He substituted Worcestershire sauce for the hot pepper sauce, doubled the amount of amaretto, and used pineapple juice instead of the tomato juice. He decided to call this drink the Major Surgery (price $4.50).

Shortly after opening Craig filed two patent applications—one for "a method of performing restaurant services consisting of a medical motif . . . etc." and the other for "a composition of matter consisting of a mixture of alcoholic beverages, juices and condiments, as follows . . . etc." The second of these, of course, referred to his new drink, the Major Surgery. Around the same time Craig also began distributing handbills on street corners in Stamford which read: "Delano says, 'When I'm in Stamford I eat at the Operating Room. That's because they serve only Grade A prime beef and you can't get a stronger drink anywhere.' "

It happens that NBS, the network which exhibits Delano, also publishes a restaurant rating book. Restaurants listed can receive from one to four smiling faces, reflecting increasingly positive opinions of the establishment. A restaurant can also be given a rating illustrated by a picture of a skillet, and called "a pan." This rating indicates severe disapproval. The edition of this guide published six months after Craig opened listed the Operating Room in the section for Stamford and gave it "a pan." The rating said in part: "The shocking bad taste of this restaurant's theme is matched only by the bad taste of its food. The meat dishes are all made with inferior cuts of beef, and the vegetables were rotten. The drinks, we might add, contain virtually no liquor." This book carries a notice of copyright and has been registered with the Library of Congress pursuant to the Copyright Act.

When the review described above was called to Craig's attention he thought it was very funny. He put a big blow up of it on a large poster in his window under the heading "NBS can't take a joke!!" He also handed out handbills with the same heading that also reproduced this review, along with a large number of favorable comments about the restaurant by leading Stamford citizens.

All of the meat served at The Operating Room is Department of Agriculture graded "U.S. Choice," the second highest rating given beef (the highest rating is "Prime"). Vegetables are bought fresh every morning. A feature story in the Stamford newspaper two months after Craig's opening indicated that his Bloody Mary contained 11% vodka, making it tenth in potency out of a total of 17 Stamford restaurants surveyed.

Craig Phillips has come to see you. He has heard through the rumor mill that NBS is thinking of bringing legal action against him. He would like your opinion as to (1) whether NBS has any valid causes of action against him; (2) whether he has any valid causes of action against NBS that he might assert as counterclaims if NBS were to sue and (3) whether he will be issued the patents he has applied for. Please prepare a memo for him responding to those inquiries.

MODEL EXAMINATION ANSWER

I.

Tipton has possible remedies for both common law and federal trademark infringement, along with a potential claim for trade secret theft.

The first thing Tipton must do to succeed in trademark litigation is to defend the validity of his marks. Because his federal registrations were granted in 1983 his marks have not yet become incontestable. (This answer was prepared in 1986. The marks will become incontestable in 1988.) Thus they are subject to challenge on any grounds which would have prevented their registration initially.

[It can be noted at the outset that the validity of the marks (SAVACHILD and SAVE THE CHILDREN) is not affected by the fact that they are used in connection with charitable services rather than goods. The Lanhan Act permits registration of servicemarks as well as trademarks (provided all other statutory requirements are satisfied) and the common law protects them as well, viewing them as "trade names."]

The initial difficulty is whether the words SAVE THE CHILDREN are actually being used in a trademark sense to identify a particular variety of services or alternatively merely as the name of the business or organization providing those services. If the words are not being used as a device by which to identify Tipton's services and distinguish them from those provided by others, they are not properly registrable and his 1983 registration may be cancelled. That, of course, would prevent him from bringing a Lanham Act § 32 suit for infringement of a registered mark. Nonetheless, he would still be able to prevent the use of confusingly similar trade names or marks by Ms. Miller by invoking § 43(a)'s prohibition against false designations of origin.

Factually, the use of SAVE THE CHILDREN in Tipton's leaflets does seem to be more in the nature of a business name than as a servicemark. The name appears only once, and seems to be merely the first line of the address to which contributions are to be sent. That conclusion is reinforced by the use of the alternative designation SAVACHILD to describe the actual program at issue elsewhere in the leaflet. The facts do not indicate any other usage of SAVE THE CHILDREN that would qualify as true servicemark use.

Another potential problem with both SAVE THE CHILDREN and SAVACHILD is that a court might consider them to be merely descriptive. If that were so, they could only be protected on a showing of secondary meaning. Descriptiveness turns on how closely the words of the mark actually describe the products or services involved and the need other merchants in the same field have to use the same or similar words.

Here, while both terms provide some information about the charitable activities of Tipton's organization, they do not plainly disclose his activities. Although the words suggest a service organization designed to help children the words do not indicate which children will be helped and how the help will be provided—that is, they do not specifically describe an organization devoted to providing food and medical relief to Asian and African children. Moreover other organizations seeking to provide services of this type probably do not need these precise words to describe their activities, as there are any number of alternative names imaginable (e.g. Third World Children's Relief Fund, Food for Kids, etc.). Thus there is a good chance the marks would be considered suggestive.

If a court were to disagree and considered them descriptive, Tipton would have to demonstrate that they have acquired secondary meaning. That might be difficult. In mid-1983 close to half of those responding to a survey thought the organization was involved with lifeguard training rather than the provision of food and medicine to poor children. On the other hand, Tipton has apparently been using these marks since 1972, thus triggering the Lanham Act presumption of secondary meaning that arises after five years of continuous use. This long use of the marks would also be probative of secondary meaning at common law. That 23,000 persons have contributed and that the organization's leaflets have presumably been mailed to many thousands more people is also indicative of secondary meaning. Further survey evidence might be useful here, but Tipton has a good chance of proving secondary meaning if required to do so.

If Tipton can persuade a court that his marks are valid he can allege that Ms. Miller's use of the phrase SAVE OUR CHILDREN is infringing, by asserting claims under Lanham Act §§ 32, 43(a) and under the common law. To succeed under any of these theories he will have to show that her use gives rise to a likelihood of confusion.

The first factor relevant to confusion is the similarity of the marks themselves. SAVE THE CHILDREN and SAVE OUR CHILDREN are virtually identical. There are greater differences with respect to SAVACHILD, since it consists only of a single coined word, unlike the three conventional words that make up Ms. Miller's mark. Nonetheless, the two marks sound a great deal alike, and convey the same meaning, so this factor cuts in Tipton's favor.

A second relevant inquiry is the geographic scope of use of the marks by the various parties. If a junior user of a mark operates in an area "remote" from that of the senior user, and if the junior user was "innocent" when he or she first adopted the mark, there will be no infringement. Here, Ms. Miller made her first use of the mark in 1982, and Tipton did not receive his Lanham Act registration until 1983. Thus, he cannot rely on the constructive notice provision of the statute to defeat her claim that she adopted the mark innocently. Moreover, nothing in the facts indicates that she had actual knowledge of Tipton's prior use when she first adopted her mark. Consequently it is likely that she would be found to be an "innocent" junior user.

Tipton received the bulk of his contributions in the Northeast and Midwest while Miller solicited persons living in the Southeast. While this might suggest that the rival operations were conducted in areas that are legally "remote" from each other, the facts also indicate that Tipton's solicitation letters went out via "direct mailings to potential donors living across the United States." This destroys any possibility that a court would find the areas of competing use to be "remote." As a result, even though Ms. Miller's adoption of the mark may have been "innocent" the overlapping areas of use also militate in favor of a finding of infringement.

Another important factor is whether the parties here are in direct competition. Infringement is much more likely to be found where that is the case. While the charitable activities of these two organizations are quite divergent, they are both fund raising entities. In other words, they are arguably direct competition for the limited dollars that most people have available for charitable contributions. On the other hand, the individual "customers" of the rival groups are likely to be distinct, since Mr. Tipton's activities are more likely to appeal to those on the left of the political spectrum, while Ms. Miller's appeal to those on the right, and the former is more traditionally charitable while the latter is political. However, even if not held to be directly competitive in every respect, the activities of the two are sufficiently similar—the politically and socially motivated solicitation of funds by mail—so that they would be held to be related in any trademark infringement case.

Beyond the factors of similarity of marks, markets and services, there is, in this case, evidence of actual confusion. Six individuals wrote to Tipton in a way suggesting that they thought his group was sponsoring the anti-gay-rights activities that were actually being conducted by Ms. Miller. The evidence of a 10% decline in contributions is further evidence of actual confusion. Consequently, there is an excellent chance that Tipton will succeed in a suit for trademark or tradename infringement.

Tipton might also claim that Miller wrongfully appropriated a trade secret when she used the names on the January 1981 contributor list. He would first have to show that the names on the list constituted confidential information giving him a commercial advantage—the definition of a trade secret. Such a list normally consists of the names of those persons who have a predilection to making charitable contributions in general, and who are inclined to contribute to a particular charity specifically. It cannot be compiled through random sampling or any other method except through the monitoring of previous contributions. Moreover it is in the interest of a charity to keep its contributor lists confidential lest the individuals involved become so deluged with solicitations that they decide to cease donations to all charities. This analysis suggests that the material is suitable for protection as a trade secret.

The second requirement for trade secret protection, however, is that the owner of the information take reasonable precautions to keep it secret. Here, after the information had been updated, the superceded list was merely discarded in a dumpster. Certainly, Tipton could have taken other inexpensive, elementary precautions to better safeguard the information. For instance, he could have shredded the papers containing the old list or he could have even burned them. His failure to do so may destroy the trade secret status of the information.

Even if it did not, it is not at all clear that the information was obtained by improper means. While it is both irregular and distasteful to go rummaging through another person's trash, it does not involve any illegal, tortious or unethical behavior (assuming no trespassing was involved in gaining access to the dumpster, which the problem suggests was on a public street in Philadelphia).

If, despite these problems, a court were to find trade secret theft here, relief might be difficult to fashion. Miller could be enjoined from soliciting the individuals in question in the future, but since they have already been contacted a number of times, it might be a rather ineffectual remedy. A damages award would be very difficult to design given the fact that both entities are not-for-profit organizations.

II.

Bif's Baker's Dozen plan probably does not pose a serious risk of liability under the Robinson-Patman Act, but the Discount Protection Plan probably should be revised to avoid future difficulties.

1. *The Baker's Dozen Plan*

Bif is a "dual distributor" of sorts, selling both to wholesalers and directly to certain retailers (i.e. the department stores). Under the Baker's Dozen plan, wholesalers receive thirteen shirts for the price of twelve. This results in an effective price reduction to them, since their per shirt cost drops to approximately $13.85 per shirt. Since the department stores continue to pay $15, there is at least a potential price discrimination problem.

All of the jurisdictional pre-requisites of the Robinson-Patman Act appear satisfied here. Because Bif's plant is in South Carolina and his customers are located nationally, clearly there are sales in interstate commerce. The requirement of a "difference in price" is satisfied by the numbers set out in the preceding paragraph. Clearly the shirts are "goods or commodities" and since the identical shirts are being sold to the various customers there is no difficulty involving the "like grade and quality" requirement, or the "two purchasers" requirement. Finally, all of the shirts are destined for use, consumption or resale in the United States since they are being sold to conventional domestic retail and wholesale outlets.

That means that liability will turn on harm to competition and the availability of affirmative defenses. The problem here does not refer to any competing shirt manufacturers and the affected parties all seem to be further down the distribution chain, hence we are dealing with a potential second line case. Normally, second line harm can be made out by showing any price differential in an amount sufficient to affect the resale price of the buyers.

Here, however, it is important to note that the favored buyers—the wholesalers—do not compete directly with the retailers, because the firms are on different levels of distribution. As a result, secondary line harm would be unlikely. It is possible, however, that problems could emerge if the customers of the wholesalers (i.e. the medium and small sized men's stores referred to in the problem) wind up paying either vastly more than, or vastly less than, the $15 paid by the department stores who buy directly from Bif. (It should be noted at this point that many instructors do not cover the Robinson-Patman implications of pricing situations like this one. Obviously, you should not be concerned about your inability to set out this analysis if you are not responsible for the underlying substantive material.)

If the wholesale mark-up is very modest, the small men's stores may wind up paying less than the department stores. For instance, if the wholesalers typically mark up each shirt only 15¢, the small stores would pay $14 for an item that costs the larger stores $15. That would affect the ability of the department stores to compete in the resale of these shirts to the ultimate consumer. If this situation was foreseeable by Bif, there is a risk that he might be held to have violated the statute under the reasoning in both the *Standard Oil (Indiana)* and *Perkins* decisions of the Supreme Court. (*See* discussion on p. 199–200 of text of outline).

On the other hand, if the wholesale mark-up is normally considerable, such as $6.00 a shirt, the small stores would pay close to $20 per item, while the department stores cost would only be $15. If some of those small stores are permitted to do so, they may stop buying from wholesalers and start making purchases from Bif directly. That would naturally harm the business of the wholesalers. There is some tenuous authority suggesting that where this is the case, the competitive injury requirement of the Robinson-Patman Act can be deemed satisfied. It should also be noted that there are cases on the same facts going the other way. Since Bif does not seem willing to do business with these small stores this is, at most, a purely theoretical observation.

Because the precedents and theories discussed in the preceding two paragraphs are dated and infrequently invoked, the risks described are probably quite minimal unless the small men's stores are paying prices grossly out of line with the $15 price paid by the department stores. Consequently, there is probably little risk in advising Bif that he may continue this program if he wishes, so long as he is made aware of the outside possibility of liability on the theories alluded to.

2. *Discount Protection Plan*

This plan does not result in a price reduction to the favored customers—the department stores. They wind up paying the same $15 as they always did for those shirts that they can sell either at full retail price, or on sale. In addition, however, they may also return all unsold merchandise. This is probably best conceived of as the provision of a sales or promotional service, thus requiring analysis under § 2(e) of the act.

Under that section of the statute, services such as these must be provided to all customers on a proportionally equal basis. Here, Bif has explicitly declined to make the return policy applicable to wholesalers. Under the decision in the *Fred Meyer* case, however, a dual distributing seller like Bif need not make services provided to direct buying retailers (i.e. the department stores) available to direct buying wholesalers. Rather, such a seller is obliged to make the services available to the competing retailers who buy indirectly, through the wholesaler (i.e., the small men's stores in this case).

Thus Bif must allow retail stores who buy through the wholesalers to return merchandise on a basis comparable to that available to the department stores. Since the current plan is devoid of any such features it violates the statute. As a result, Bif must either extend the program to the small men's stores or discontinue it entirely.

III.

1. *The Patent Applications*

Craig's patent applications will be denied. Under the case law interpreting the patent statute, a method of performing business is not patentable subject matter. Consequently, the first application for "a method of performing restaurant services" will necessarily fail. Even if this were not the case, the business method in question here was fully anticipated by its portrayal on the Delano, M.E. television show. Thus it lacks novelty and cannot be patented.

The application pertaining to the drink recipe does encompass patentable subject matter, as the combination of liquors and mixers involved is within the statutory concept of a composition of matter. Nonetheless, this patent will be denied because the "invention" it describes is obvious. If an innovation described in a patent application would have been apparent to one skilled in the relevant art, a patent will be denied. Here, Craig arrived at the new drink recipe through a very ordinary substitution of ingredients in a previously known drink. Courts often cite substitution of ingredients and alteration of proportions as indicative of obviousness. Indeed, it is arguable that almost any mixture of alcoholic beverages and mixers would be found by a court to be obvious, since there are only a limited number of alcoholic beverages and mixers, and the fact that they can be combined in a variety of proportions is a well known fact.

Craig can still attempt to protect his drink receipe as a trade secret, however, since his rejected patent application will not be published and since novelty requirements for trade secrets are considerably less than those imposed for patents.

2. *Suits by NBS Against Craig*

a. *Unauthorized Use of Restaurant Format*

The concept of a restaurant based on a medical motif was first created by NBS or its agents. Craig's restaurant adopts the same unusual and striking format, without permission. Consequently, NBS may allege that this constitutes either copyright infringement or common law misappropriation. The network may also claim that it will give rise to public confusion over the sponsorship of the restaurant, thus raising questions under § 43(a) of the Lanham Act.

The format of the restaurant is expressed in both the written scripts and in the videotapes of the Delano, M.E. episodes. Since both of these media are tangible, they constitute legitimate subjects for copyright protection. NBS may therefore file suit for copyright infringement.

There are two important questions raised by such a suit. First, the court must determine whether Craig has copied merely the idea embodied in the NBS works, or whether he has taken the actual expression developed by NBS. If he has done only the former, there is no copyright infringement. Second, the court must determine if Craig has actually performed an act that is within the grant of exclusive rights contained in § 106 of the Copyright Act. He is only liable for infringement if he (1) made copies of a protected work; (2) adapted a protected work; or (3) performed or displayed a protected work.

The idea of a restaurant based on a medical motif cannot, itself, be protected by NBS under the copyright laws. Only the manner in which that idea is expressed—the particular details and features of such a restaurant—are covered by the statute. The facts here indicate that "the menu items, mode of service, and decor" of Craig's restaurant "replicated those depicted on the show." Thus, Craig may have done more than duplicate just the notion of a restaurant with a medical format. Rather he may have taken the precise expression of this idea first formulated by NBS.

It must therefore be determined if the use of a copyrighted expression as the basis for a restaurant design is an activity constituting infringement. The most typical infringement cases involve the making of unauthorized "copies" of a protected work. The statute defines a copy as "material object in which a work is fixed . . . and from which the work can be perceived, reproduced or otherwise communicated." Whether the reproduction of elements of a protected work in the decor and menu of a restaurant satisfies this definition is probably a question of first impression. Since statues and paintings are material objects, the combination of two and three dimensional attributes that make up a restaurant's decor are probably also within that definition. On the other hand, the courts have held that buildings are not "works of authorship" within the scope of the copyright laws and that no infringement occurs when an individual duplicates another's building without permission. (See outline at page 78). That makes it somewhat likely that Craig's activities would be held non-infringing, although the result is far from clear. Similar issues would be raised if NBS contended that Craig's activities constituted an unauthorized adaptation of their work (i.e. "transformation of a work into another form, such as dramatization, translation, condensed version, or musical arrangement") or unauthorized display (i.e. the showing of a "copy of it, either directly or by means of . . . any device").

If NBS seeks to proceed alternatively on a misappropriation theory they would first have to surmount the contention that this cause of action is pre-empted. The copyright statute pre-empts any claim involving material with the scope of copyright as defined in § 102, and involving any of the exclusive rights itemized in § 106. If the copyright analysis in the foregoing paragraphs results in a conclusion of infringement, that necessarily means that any common law action is pre-empted. On the other hand, if there is no finding of infringement there will be no pre-emption.

Assuming that pre-emption is not a problem, NBS will have to prove that the medical motif concept was created by them at considerable effort, that its protection is within the policy of the misappropriation concept, and that Craig took it without payment for commercial purposes to the detriment of NBS. The first element should not be too difficult. The originality of the concept is some indication of the effort involved in its creation. It is also worth noting that the network probably pays the writers and program developers very considerable sums of money to come up with ideas like this. Similarly, there can be no dispute that Craig is using the idea for commercial purposes since he derives revenue from his restaurant.

The difficult issues for NBS here will be showing that protection of a concept such as this is within the scope of the misappropriation tort and that Craig is harming them economically by using the concept with payment or permission. Misappropriation is usually said to be grounded in the desire to protect incentives for firms to engage in creative activity. Therefore, many courts would ask if allowing Craig to make uncompensated use of the medical restaurant theme, will deter NBS from either continuing to produce the Delano, M.E. show, or from investing effort in developing other new shows? That seems unlikely. Incentives are most affected when the intangible in question is the "stock in trade" of the creator—that is, the very thing that the creator sells for a profit. That is not the case with the restaurant motif at issue here. It is true that NBS might have hoped—at some indeterminate time in the future—to license a chain of restaurants based on this theme. That might have been a profitable activity, the value of which has diminished because of Craig's action in opening such a restaurant. Nonetheless, the loss of the prospective licensing revenues may not be the kind of loss that would drive them from the field of network television.

The foregoing observations also bear on the nature and extent of harm to NBS. While there is a loss of potential future licensing fees, the parties here are not in direct competition. At the moment, NBS operates no restaurants. Some courts explicitly require competition between plaintiff and defendant to provide a remedy for misappropriation. Even with respect to those courts that do not, the absence of competition suggests an absence of harm. It is not as if each person who patronizes Craig's restaurant would have made a purchase from NBS but for the duplication of the format. Thus, while it is not free from doubt, NBS would probably not succeed on a misappropriation theory.

Finally, there is a question of whether the use of the format by Craig will engender public confusion as to the sponsorship of his restaurant. Lanham Act § 43(a) precludes any false designation of origin. If the medical motif is associated in the public's mind with NBS, they might erroneously conclude that Craig is operating under the supervision of the network.

NBS would first have to show the distinctiveness of the medical motif concept in order to proceed on this theory. In other words, they would have to offer proof of secondary meaning. Their ability to do so will turn on how unique the concept is, and the degree to which the public has come to associate it exclusively with them. Survey evidence of public perception would be important on this issue. Also relevant would be the prominence and frequency with which the hypothetical restaurant appears on the show. If it is only for a minute or two and if the camera stays largely focused on the characters, secondary meaning is less likely than if the scenes set in the restaurant last for ten minutes and there are numerous "long shots" of the entire set showing the decor and other attributes of the hypothetical establishment. The fact that the restaurant is used as a setting in "virtually every episode" strengthens NBS's showing of secondary meaning. It would also be important to ascertain if anyone else is using a medical motif for a restaurant. If there are numerous similar restaurants scattered throughout the country, the NBS case is seriously weakened.

Once distinctiveness is shown, NBS must then show a likelihood of confusion. Numerous factors bear on this issue and the problem provides little factual information. For instance, any incidents of actual confusion would be revealing. These could be made out by showing that NBS has received letters from patrons of Craig's restaurant either complaining about or complimenting the food, or requesting recipes. The overlap of customers would be another issue. If the Delano, M.E. program appeals largely to a younger audience and Craig's restaurant is patronized largely by older customers, that would detract from the requisite showing. The fact that Craig intentionally and consciously mimicked the format of the program is supportive of a likelihood of confusion. Survey evidence would again be crucial here.

A similar analysis could be made with respect to Craig's choice of the name "The Operating Room." While not literally identical to the name used on the show ("The Emergency Room") the two are quite similar in meaning and might generate further confusion as to sponsorship.

b. *Unauthorized Use of Rating Book Excerpts*

NBS's Restaurant Rating Guide is clearly copyrightable material. Since copies of the book bear a copyright notice, and the work has been registered, Craig's use of the language from the book involving his restaurant is an arguable case of copyright infringement. In response to such a suit, he could invoke the fair use defense.

Four factors are relevant in analyzing the fair use defense: (1) the nature of copyrighted work; (2) the amount of the work taken; (3) the purpose of the use; and (4) the effect on the market for the copyrighted work. Here, the nature of the work—a guidebook—suggests that a variety of persons may wish to quote excerpts, and that the creator of the volume should have anticipated that. It is quite customary for restaurants to post favorable reviews in their windows. Thus, this factor favors Craig.

The amount of the work used also favors Craig. He only has duplicated that portion of the book that described his own restaurant. If the book describes as few as 100 restaurants, this is only 1% of the material at issue.

Craig's purpose in using the work is somewhat ambiguous. It is not the conventional commercial use that restaurants often make of favorable reviews. Instead, it seems to be an attempt to tease or poke fun at NBS, evidenced by the reference in the window poster "NBS can't take a joke!!" and by the juxtaposition of the unfavorable review with the laudatory comments by Stanford citizens in the handbills. To the extent that this use would be considered part of a "right of rebuttal" there are First Amendment interests in tolerating this use. Consequently, this factor also seems to favor Craig.

Finally, the use in question here is unlikely to significantly affect the market for the book. People buy a restaurant rating book to have simultaneous and comparative access to a large number of restaurant reviews. The public display or distribution of an isolated review to the public is unlikely to displace any sales or otherwise affect the economic reward that NBS can earn from the book. As a result, Craig's assertion of the fair use defense is well taken and an NBS copyright infringement suit based on unauthorized use of the book language would probably fail.

c. *False Advertising in the Handbills*

The handbills initially distributed by Craig contain three possibly false statements. First, the language "Delano says . . ." implies that either NBS or the
actor that plays Delano endorses Craig's restaurant. This is apparently not true.
Second, the statement that the meat at The Operating Room is "prime" is false,
since the meat served there is graded "choice"—a lower grade. Finally the contention that you "can't get a stronger drink anywhere" seems inconsistent with the
newspaper survey on the strength of Bloody Mary's.

NBS does not have standing to challenge the latter two representations. Under all legal theories for challenging false advertising (common law, state baby FTC
Acts, or Lanham Act § 43(a)) the plaintiff must show at least a possibility that it
will suffer injury due to the falsehoods being promulgated by the defendant. The
common law implemented this requirement through its sole source rule, which
would require here that NBS be the sole source of "prime" meat and strong drinks
in Stanford. The Lanham Act relaxed this stringent standard, but a plaintiff still
must identify some plausible theory as how the falsehood will injure it by conceivable diverting sales. Here, because NBS and Craig do not compete either directly or
indirectly in the restaurant business, it is impossible for NBS to make such a
showing.

The lack of any sort of competitive relationship also makes it unlikely NBS
could use a conventional false advertising theory to challenge the reference to Delano in the handbills. It might, however, invoke § 43(a) to allege that the inaccurate reference to Delano constitutes a false designation of origin. Much like the
unauthorized use of the restaurant format discussed above, the reference to Delano
may give rise to a public perception that Craig's restaurant is sponsored by NBS.
The harm to the network here is a reduction in their ability to capitalize on the
popularity of the Delano character by licensing. Whether the network will succeed
on the facts depends on (1) whether Delano is a distinctive name associated with
the network (i.e. secondary meaning) and (2) they can prove a likelihood of confusion—the same two issues discussed in the later portion of part 2(a) of this answer,
above. (The actor who portrays Delano may be able to claim that the use of the
character name in the handbills violates his "right to publicity." Since the question asks you to consider only suits between Craig and NBS, discussion of that possibility is beyond the scope of the question. Similarly, the FTC might want to
challenge the handbills as a "deceptive act or practice" under § 5 of the FTC Act,
but that too is beyond the scope of the question.)

3. *Suits by Craig Against NBS*

Craig might allege disparagement because of the highly critical and somewhat
inaccurate review of his restaurant that appeared in the NBS rating book. To succeed at common law he would have to show that the review contained false statements, show that those statements tend to harm his business reputation and
demonstrate special damages—that is, itemize specifically the revenues he has lost

as a result of the review. Under certain circumstances he might also have to prove "actual malice." He might also be able to bring his disparagement claim under the Connecticut Baby FTC Act. There is no federal cause of action, however, because Lanham Act § 43(a) only reaches false statements made by a merchant about his own goods, not those discussing the goods or services of another party.

It should be fairly easy to demonstrate that the review was partially false. It states that Craig serves "inferior cuts of beef." While USDA "choice" is not the highest grade on the market, it is far superior to the bulk of commercially available meat, which is ungraded. In this regard the review communicates a false impression. The allegation that the "vegetable were rotten" seems grossly at odds with the fact that vegetables are purchased fresh every morning. The claim that "the drinks . . . contain virtually no liquor" is also false. The Major Surgery drink is stated to contain a considerable 6 ounce portion of alcoholic beverages and while Craig did not top the bloody mary poll in the local newspaper, that poll suggests that his bloody mary contains more vodka than 7 other local restaurants. It should be equally straightforward to demonstrate that such falsehood would tend to disparage a restaurant. Clearly people will be disinclined to patronize a place with bad food and overpriced drinks.

If Craig's restaurant is deemed a "public figure" or if its quality has become a matter of public debate, Craig will also have to show that the falsehoods here were made with "actual malice" under *N.Y. Times* and *Bose* cases. There is no indication that this restaurant is anything other than a local establishment so its status as a public figure is at best questionable—it is not a national corporation like General Motors or Kodak. On the other hand it probably does seek the public eye through advertising and implicitly invites public comment on its food and drink by the very nature of the restaurant business. A court might, therefore, very well conclude that the actual malice standard must be satisfied here. To do that, Craig would have to show that the falsehoods were printed either with knowledge that they were false or with a reckless disregard for their truth or falsity (i.e. he would have to negate the possibility of an innocent or merely negligent mistake). There is not enough information given to resolve this issue, but it seems highly unlikely that the person who wrote the review did not know that the drinks had considerable alcoholic content. Certainly just a few sips of the Major Surgery would have put that thought out of a reasonable person's mind. The claims here seem so much at odds with the facts that Craig might succeed in demonstrating actual malice if he is obliged to do so.

The real difficulty Craig will encounter will be demonstrating special damages. To do this he must show a specific loss of sales directly attributable to the disparaging statement. He might attempt to show—based on daily revenue figures—that his business declined after the review was published. His showing in this regard is complicated, however, by his decision to give the review such great prominence in his own window and on his handbills. A court might justifiably conclude that any damages suffered were largely self-inflicted. Thus a disparagement counterclaim would be a long shot.

Finally, it should be noted that while the NBS book refers to Craig's restaurant by its trade name—The Operating Room—Craig has no plausible trademark or trade name infringement claims because use in this fashion is a legitimate "collateral" use.

GLOSSARY

A

Abandonment   In trademark law, the loss of trademark rights due either to (a) non-use with an intent to abandon or (b) failure to supervise licensees. There is a statutory presumption of abandonment under the Lanham Act if the mark is not used for two consecutive years.

Adaptation Right   In copyright law, the exclusive right of the holder of a copyright to prepare "derivative works" based on the copyrighted item. For instance, the right to prepare a screenplay based on a novel or the right to publish an English translation of a work originally written in French.

Advertising Substantiation   A doctrine propounded by the Federal Trade Commission making it an unfair and deceptive act to promulgate an advertisement unless the advertiser has an advance reasonable basis for believing that each claim in the advertisement is true.

Aesthetic Functionality   In trademark law, a doctrine of ambiguous scope and vitality, under which a non-owner of a trademark may use the mark to decorate goods of different types than are sold by the owner of the mark because of the mark's aesthetic appeal, without incurring liability for infringement.

Affixation   The requirement that a trademark must actually appear on goods or their containers before any trademark rights can attach. Under the Lanham Act, if the mark appears on "displays" associated with the sale of the goods the affixation requirement will be deemed satisfied.

Anticipation   A patent will be denied to a party if the invention in question has been previously patented by another, or has been described in print by another, or has been

251

known or used in the United States. These events constitute an "anticipation" of the invention. For a documentary source to be anticipatory it must fully disclose how to make the invention. *See* Enabling Source.

Arbitrary Mark A trademark consisting of a coined or made-up word, which will be protected from the date of first use at common law, and which is eligible for registration under the Lanham Act without any further showing of distinctiveness.

Areeda-Turner Test A presumption that prices below average variable cost are predatory and illegal. Variations of this test have been widely adopted as the controlling standard in Robinson-Patman primary line cases.

Article of Manufacture Any man-made object other than a "machine" or a "composition of matter." Articles of manufacture constitute one of the categories of inventions within the subject matter of the patent statute.

Average Total Cost The total of all costs incurred by a firm over a given period of time divided by the number of units produced during that same period of time. This is one of several cost figures courts may calculate in resolving primary line Robinson-Patman claims.

Average Variable Cost Costs which fluctuate with the number of units produced, such as raw material costs, are considered variable. If all costs of this type during a given period are divided by the number of units produced during that period, the result is average variable cost. Prices below this level are considered predatory under the Areedo-Turner Test and may give rise to Robinson-Patman liability.

B

Baby F.T.C. Act A state statute outlawing unfair and deceptive acts and practices either generally or through an itemized list, modeled on the Federal Trade Commission Act. Many, but not all, of these statutes provide private causes of action to both competitors and consumers.

Bait and Switch A sales practice in which an attractive item is advertised at a very favorable price, but not actually available for sale. When consumers seek the item they are pressured into purchasing something else carrying a higher profit margin for the seller. This practice has been successfully challenged by the F.T.C.

Blanket License Various performing rights societies obtain authorization from copyright owners to license others to use their musical works. Those societies then grant blanket licenses, allowing the licensee to perform any copyrighted works within the repertoire of the society during a specified time.

C

Cancellation The Lanham Act permits any party who will be damaged by the continued registration of a trademark to file a petition to cancel that mark. During the first five years after registration, the petition may be based on any grounds that would have barred registration initially. Thereafter, only specified grounds may be asserted. Cancellation petitions are heard by the Trademark Trials and Appeals Board with review by the U.S. Court of Appeals for the Federal Circuit.

Cease and Desist Order After a firm or person has been found guilty of an unfair or deceptive act or practice in a proceeding before the Federal Trade Commission, the Commission will enter an order restraining the party from engaging in the impermissible conduct in the future. These cease and desist orders operate prospectively only, but they may include requirements that the firm make affirmative disclosures or corrective advertising.

Certification Mark Under the Lanham Act, a mark used on goods other than those of the mark owner in order to certify regional or other origin, material, mode of manufacture, quality, accuracy, or other characteristics of the goods, is called a certification mark. Certification marks are registrable on the same basis as trademarks.

Claims The portion of a patent which sets forth the specific elements of the invention which are alleged to be novel. The claims define the scope of protection of the patent. Only devices that contain all the elements and limitations recited in a particular claim will be deemed to infringe the patent.

Collateral Use The right of a non-party to make use of another firm's trademarks to truthfully describe the origin of goods that have been repaired or repackaged, or to communicate truthful information about the scope of services, or to make truthful comparisons in advertising.

Collective Mark A mark used by the members of a comparative, an association or other collective group or organization is defined as a collective mark in the Lanham Act. Such marks are registrable on the same bases as trademarks.

Common Descriptive Name In Lanham Act terminology, the common descriptive name of a product is the term by which all products of that type are known—such as "shoes" or "razors." Since such a term cannot ever designate the origin of goods, it cannot be registered as a trademark. A registered mark may be cancelled at any time if it has become the common descriptive name of the goods in question. The term is equivalent to the common law term "generic" (*see below*).

Common Errors In a suit for copyright infringement the plaintiff must prove that the defendant copied the protected work. The fact that the defendant's work and the copyrighted work both contain identical inaccuracies—common errors—is circumstantial evidence of copying that the courts consider highly probative.

Common Law Copyright Prior to the adoption of the 1976 Copyright Act, a work of authorship was protected against misappropriation prior to its first general publication by remedies under state law. This "common law copyright" in unpublished works was eliminated in the new statute by virtue of the pre-emption provision.

Composition of Matter A combination of chemicals or other ingredients that yields a wholly new substance is considered a composition of matter. Such compositions are one of the listed subject matters eligible for patent protection.

Comprehensive Nonliteral Similarity Copyright infringement plaintiffs often prove that the defendant copied their protected work by pointing to resemblances between the two works at issue. If the defendant's work does not use any precise words or phrases of the plaintiff's work, but duplicates its overall plot structure in some detail, the works are said to bear a "comprehensive nonliteral similarity" to each other and infringement will usually be found.

Compulsory License Several provisions of the Copyright Act provide that certain parties may make certain types of uses of copyrighted material without the explicit permission of the copyright owner, on payment of a specified royalty. These compulsory licenses are regulated, in certain respects, by an agency called the Copyright Royalty Tribunal.

Consent Order Prior to commencing formal administrative proceedings against a party accused of unfair or deceptive practices, the Federal Trade Commission will give that party an opportunity to resolve the matter informally. If the party agrees, it will enter into a consent cease and desist order (*see* cease and desist order, above), forbidding certain conduct in the future.

Copy Under the copyright statute, a copy is defined as a material object (other than a phonorecord) in which a work is fixed by any method now known or later developed, and from which the work can be perceived, reproduced, or otherwise communicated, either directly or with the aid of a machine or device. Only the owner of the copyright may make copies of the work.

Copyright Royalty Tribunal A government agency which performs a number of functions in connection with the administration of compulsory licenses provided for in the copyright statute—including the setting of royalty rates and the distribution of royalties.

Corrective Advertising If an advertiser has persisted in using a deceptive claim for an extended period of time so that the claim lingers in the minds of consumers even after it is deleted from advertising, the Federal Trade Commission may order that firm to undertake corrective advertising to inform consumers about the earlier representation and to provide them with corrected information.

Cost Justification Under the Robinson-Patman Act a seller has an affirmative defense against a charge of price discrimination if it can prove that it incurs lower costs in servicing those customers who pay lower prices. This cost justification defense requires precise documentation of the magnitude of cost savings.

Covenant Not to Compete A contractual obligation imposed on an employee or seller of a business forbidding competition after the employment is terminated or the sale is finalized for a specified period of time in a specified locale. Such covenants are only enforceable if they are reasonable in scope and duration.

D

Deceptive Act or Practice The Federal Trade Commission makes deceptive acts unlawful. Historically an act was deceptive if it had any tendency to deceive a non-trivial number of customers. A more recent reformulation of the test defines a deceptive act as one which is likely to deceive a consumer acting reasonably in the circumstances. The nature of the difference between these two tests and which of them will be accepted as proper is currently still a matter of debate.

Deceptive Mark A mark which falsely describes a material attribute of the product to which it is attached, and on which consumers would rely in selecting the goods, is deceptive. A deceptive mark will not be protected at common law and may not be registered under the Lanham Act.

Deceptively Misdescriptive Mark An objectively inaccurate mark is considered deceptively misdescriptive if consumers would be likely to take the representation implicit in the mark seriously, but do not consider the misdescribed trait important in selecting the product. A mark of this sort may be protected or registered only upon a showing of secondary meaning. An absurdly inaccurate mark that consumers would not believe is considered arbitrary, not deceptively misdescriptive.

Deposit Once a work is published, the copyright owner or publisher must deposit two copies with the Library of Congress. The requirement for such a deposit is independent of copyright registration and must be satisfied within three months after publication. There is no deposit requirement for unpublished works.

Derivative Work Under the copyright law, a work based on a pre-existing work, such as a translation, musical arrangement, fictionalization, motion picture version, abridgment or any other form in which a work may be recast, transformed or adapted, is a derivative work. Only the holder of copyright in the underlying work (or one acting with his permission) may prepare a derivative work. The preparation of such a work by any other party constitutes infringement.

Descriptive Mark   A trademark which merely describes the goods to which it is affixed is considered "descriptive" and will only be protected or registrable if the user can demonstrate secondary meaning.

Design Patent   The unique appearance or design of an article of manufacture may be protected against duplication by a design patent if it is original, non-obvious and ornamental. Design patents may be issued for both surface ornamentation or the overall configuration of an object. Such patents last for a term of 14 years. Material that is eligible for design patent protection may also be copyrightable.

Dilution   A trademark doctrine protecting strong marks against use by other parties even where there is no competition or likelihood of confusion. The doctrine exists by virtue of state statutes in a number of jurisdictions but there is no federal dilution cause of action.

Disparagement   A falsehood that tends to denigrate the goods or services of another party is actionable in a common law suit for disparagement. The same conduct is also actionable under certain state statutes and can form the basis for an F.T.C. complaint. There is no private federal cause of action for disparagement under the Lanham Act.

Display Right   To display a work is to show a copy of it publicly, either directly, or in conjunction with any device. The holder of the copyright in the work has the exclusive right to display it; however, the owner of a particular copy of the work may display that copy at the place where that copy is located.

Distinctiveness   An essential element of a device claimed to be a trademark is that it identify the goods of a particular merchant and distinguish them from the goods of others. A word, symbol, shape, or color serving this purpose is said to be distinctive. Certain marks are inherently distinctive while others only acquire distinctiveness over time (*see* secondary meaning). A distinctive mark may lose its distinctiveness over time and become generic.

Distribution Right   The copyright owner of a work is granted the exclusive right to distribute copies of that work. The distribution of copies by others without consent constitutes infringement.

Doctrine of Equivalents   A doctrine which declares a device infringing of a patented invention if it does the same work as the invention in substantially the same way, even if it is outside the literal terms of the claims of the patent. The doctrine prevents parties from infringing patents with impunity by making merely trivial changes in an invention. The more significant the patented invention the greater the scope of this doctrine.

Droit Morale   A European doctrine of "artistic integrity" that gives artists the right to prevent others from altering their work without permission.

Dual Distributor   A firm that sells goods simultaneously to buyers on two different levels of the distribution chain—such as a manufacturer who sells directly to both wholesalers and retailers—is called a dual distributor. Such sellers often offer discounts to some, but not all, of their customers, which can raise complex problems under the Robinson-Patman Act.

Duty of Candor   A patent applicant is under a duty to provide the patent office with all information that bears on the patent. This duty of candor can be violated either by affirmative misstatements or by the failure to disclose material information relating to such issues as the prior art, the priority of invention or other parties' public use of similar devices. Violation of the duty makes the patent unenforceable and may also lead to charges of antitrust violations.

E

Enabling Source   When a patent is denied on the grounds that the invention has been anticipated, and the anticipation is predicated on the contents of a documentary source, that source will defeat patentability only if it makes an enabling disclosure—in other words, contains sufficient information to permit a party skilled in the art to make the invention. The disclosures in a patent must themselves also be enabling, to insure that the new technology will be dedicated to the public upon the expiration of the patent.

F

Fair Use   Certain limited uses of copyrighted works will not be deemed infringing even if carried out without the consent of the copyright owner. Whether a use is "fair use" is determined by application of criteria set out in the copyright statute, including (1) the purpose and character of the use, (2) the amount of the work used, (3) the nature of the copyrighted work and (4) the effect the use will have on the market for the work. A typical example of fair use would be the quotation of a passage of a novel in a book review critiquing that novel.

Fanciful Mark   A trademark consisting of a made-up or coined word, such as KODAK, is said to be "fanciful." Such marks are considered inherently distinctive, and thus are protected at common law, and are eligible for Lanham Act registration, from the time of first use.

File Wrapper Estoppel   If a patent applicant, during the patent examination process, surrendered certain claims or interpretations of the invention, file wrapper estoppel prevents that party from subsequently invoking the doctrine of equivalents (*see above*) in an infringement suit to claim that such constructions are within the scope of his patent.

Fixed in a Tangible Medium of Expression   A work of authorship is copyrightable only if it is recorded in some way permitting it to be perceived, reproduced or otherwise communicated, either directly or with the aid of a machine. Works that are not fixed in a tangible medium may be protected under state law, such as the misappropriation doctrine.

Flash of Genius Requirement   For a period of time after a 1941 decision of the Supreme Court, some parties believed that a device was not patentable if it was invented as the result of trial and error or accident. Language in that case seemed to suggest that only the products of a "flash of genius" could be protected by patent. Section 103 of the patent statute, added in 1952, eliminated any such requirement by stating that "patentability shall not be negatived by the manner in which the invention was made."

Fragmented Literal Similarity   A copyright infringement plaintiff can prove copying by the defendant by showing that scattered throughout the defendant's work are words (or musical phrases, or artistic symbols or images) that constitute part of the protected work. This type of resemblance between the two works is known as Fragmented Literal Similarity.

Function of an Apparatus   The invention of a novel machine permits the inventor to secure a patent on the machine. It does not entitle the inventor to a patent on all other theoretical ways of accomplishing the same result. Thus the patent is on the apparatus itself, not the function of the apparatus.

Functional Discount   A discount granted to a buyer who performs certain distributional or warehousing functions for itself where other parties require the seller to perform those functions. *See* Integrated Buyer. Such discounts raise a number of difficulties under the Robinson-Patman Act when those who receive the discount compete with those who do not.

Functionality   A shape, configuration or color scheme will only be protected as a trademark if it is non-functional. Functionality exists if the design or color is so superior to available alternatives that competition would be hindered by giving the first user exclusive rights. *See also,* Aesthetic Functionality.

G

Generic   A word that describes a type of merchandise and does not serve any source designating function—such as "car" or "hat"—is considered a generic term. Generic terms will not be protected as trademarks. *See also* Common Descriptive Name.

Geographically Descriptive Mark   A geographic word used as a trademark that indicates where the goods are grown or manufactured is considered geographically descriptive. Such marks will only be protected at common law and registered under the Lanham Act upon proof of secondary meaning.

Geographically Deceptively Misdescriptive Mark   A geographic word used as a trademark that plausibly suggests where the good might have been grown or manufactured but is, in fact, inaccurate, is considered geographically deceptively misdescriptive. Such marks are only protected at common law and registered under the Lanham Act upon proof of secondary meaning.

Grey Market Goods   Foreign firms often license one U.S. company to use their trademarks in the United States and sell their goods as exclusive importer. Others may buy the products of that foreign firm abroad and import them into the United States without authorization. Such goods are called grey market goods because they often do not carry the same warranties as merchandise sold by the official importer. The sale of grey market goods can constitute trademark infringement under certain circumstances but the case law in this area is in disarray.

H

Head Start Injunction   In trade secret litigation, if the secret has become public by the time of trial some courts will deny relief entirely and other courts will perpetually enjoin the defendant from using the secret. A compromise position is to enjoin the defendant for a period equal to the time between the date of the theft of the secret and the date the secret became public, since that period equals the "head start" that the defendant unfairly obtained over the rest of the industry.

I

Improper Means   A trade secret owner may recover against any party who learns the secret through improper means. Improper means are defined as any means that are independently illegal or tortious, or any means that are effective in overcoming reasonable precautions for secrecy.

Incontestability   After a trademark has been federally registered for 5 years, the registrant may have the mark declared incontestable, preventing the assertion of certain claims against the mark. The most important claims that are cut off are (1) that the mark is merely descriptive and lacks secondary meaning and (2) that the mark in question was previously used by a party other than the registrant prior to the registrant's first use.

Indirect Purchaser Doctrine   In Robinson-Patman litigation the government or plaintiff must be able to identify two purchasers who paid different prices. If all parties who dealt directly with the seller paid the same price but one buyer is a sham intermediary whose pricing decisions are controlled by the seller, the sham party will be ignored and the courts will focus instead on the price paid by those indirect purchasers who bought through or from this sham party.

Innocent Junior User   A party who, without actual knowledge, adopts a trademark that has been previously used by another in a distant geographic market is an innocent junior user. Innocent junior users may continue use of the mark within their own area of trade. Because the Lanham Act provides constructive notice of a registrant's claim of ownership of a trademark, however, no party making first use of a mark after another party's registration can attain the status of "innocent" junior user.

Integrated Buyer A firm that performs more than one distributional function for itself. For instance a chain of retail stores that does its own wholesaling, by buying in bulk and maintaining its own warehouses, is integrated. Sellers often offer functional discounts to integrated firms that are not offered to competing firms that do not do their own wholesaling. This can raise difficulties under the Robinson-Patman Act.

J

Junior User The second party, chronologically, to make use of a trademark is usually referred to as the "junior user."

L

Lanham Act The federal trademark statute, which provides for a registration scheme conferring valuable procedural and substantive rights. It also contains, in § 43(a), an important cause of action for any person injured by another's use of a false description or representation in connection with the sale of goods.

Legislative Veto As a device for exercising political control over the rulemaking activities of the Federal Trade Commission, Congress enacted legislation permitting it to set aside such rules upon the vote of both houses. That procedure was subsequently declared unconstitutional, but pending legislation would revive the legislative veto in a format designed to respond to the Supreme Court's objections.

Like Grade and Quality For sales at different prices to be subject to Robinson-Patman Act scrutiny, the higher and lower priced sales must involve goods of like grade and quality. Physically identical goods are considered of like grade regardless of differences in labeling. Goods are not of the same grade and quality if they have significant physical differences that cause them to have different degrees of consumer acceptance or marketability.

Likelihood of Confusion This is the legal test for trademark infringement both at common law and under The Lanham Act. Whether the defendant's acts give rise to likelihood of confusion requires consideration of a number of factors, including similarity of the marks, similarity of the products, evidence of actual confusion, cost of the product, sophistication of consumers and the geographic scope of each party's use of the mark. This standard is also used in suits under section 43(a) of the Lanham Act and in administering the Lanham Act § 2(d) bar against registration of marks that have been previously used by another party.

M

Machine Any mechanical apparatus is considered a "machine" under the patent laws and machines are one of the listed categories of patentable subject matter.

Magnuson-Moss Warranty Act A 1975 Federal statute prescribing how warranty terms must be disclosed and providing certain federal remedies for breach of warranty. The statute contains numerous procedural hurdles for suits in federal court, and has been given a somewhat limited construction by the courts.

Marginal Cost The cost to increase production by exactly one more unit at any given time is called the "marginal" cost. Although suggested as the theoretically most appropriate cost figure to use in determining if predatory pricing is taking place, marginal cost is almost always incapable of measurement in the real world. Most courts use "average variable cost" (*see above*) as a workable substitute in analyzing predatory pricing cases.

Meeting Competition Defense A seller has a complete defense to a charge of Robinson-Patman Act violations if it can prove that the lower price was offered in good faith to match what it believed to be an equally low price of a competitor. This defense is also available to a charge of unequal provision of promotional payments or services.

Mill Net Theory of Price In a number of older cases, the F.T.C. argued that, for Robinson-Patman purposes, freight charges should be subtracted from prices of delivered goods before comparing prices to determine if discrimination had taken place. This is known as a mill net theory of price. Under this theory, a firm that sold from a single plant to customers nationwide for a single price would be deemed to have charged customers in different regions different prices because of the difference in transportation costs. This theory has now been abandoned.

Misappropriation A state law doctrine permitting a party who creates a valuable intangible asset to recover when another party takes that asset without permission for commercial purposes and thereby deprives the creator of a profit. The doctrine was created by the Supreme Court's *INS* decision and apparently is not pre-empted by the copyright statute.

N

Non-Obvious To be patentable, an invention must be non-obvious. To determine if that requirement is satisfied the courts will first identify the scope and content of the prior art bearing on the subject matter of the invention, then identify the differences between that prior art and the invention under scrutiny, and then determine the level of skill that prevails in the relevant art. If, based on these determinations, the invention would

have been obvious to a party having ordinary skill in the art, it is not patentable.

Novelty An invention will only be patentable if it is novel. Evidence that the invention was anticipated (*see above*) by any single prior art reference will destroy the claim of novelty as will evidence that the device was known or used by others prior to the applicant's date of invention.

O

Opposition In trademark practice under the Lanham Act, any party who believes that he may be injured by the registration of a particular mark may file an opposition with the trademark office specifying the grounds why the mark should not be registered. Such petitions are adjudicated in the first instance by the Trademarks Trials and Appeals Board with review in the U.S. Court of Appeals for the Federal Circuit.

Originality A work is eligible for copyright protection only if it is "original." Originality means merely that the work was created through the independent effort of the author, rather than having been copied from another source, and does not imply any requirement of artistic or intellectual merit.

P

Palming Off *See* Passing Off.

Passing Off A general term used to refer to any act in which a seller misrepresents its goods as being the merchandise of another party. Trademark infringement is one type of passing off, although many courts reserve use of the phrase "passing off" for those cases where the infringement is intentional.

Performance Right To perform a work is to recite, render, play, dance, act or show images of the work directly or by means of a device. Transmission of the work by broadcasting it or otherwise also constitutes a performance. The owner of the copyright in the work has the exclusive right to perform it publicly, except in the case of sound recordings, as to which there is no performance right.

Phonorecord   A material object in which sounds are fixed, by any method now known or later developed, and from which those sounds can be perceived, reproduced, or otherwise communicated, either directly or with the aid of a machine or device. The most common types of phonorecords are long playing stereo records, cassette tapes and compact discs. The owner of copyright in a work has the exclusive right to reproduce the work in phonorecords and to distribute those phonorecords to the public.

Plant Patent   A type of patent which may be issued to the discoverer of a new variety of asexually reproducing plants, provided the other conditions for patentability are satisfied.

Pre-emption   A state doctrine, whether based on common law or statute, must give way to inconsistent federal law under the supremacy clause. When that occurs, courts frequently say that the state law is "preempted." Although there are many seeming conflicts between federal copyright law and state misappropriation law as well as between federal patent law and state trade secret law, the bulk of the cases directly addressing preemption issues have concluded that the state doctrines survive intact.

Predatory Pricing   Pricing that is below cost and designed to deliberately destroy a commercial rival is considered "predatory." Under contemporary cases, courts will focus on a firm's "average variable cost" (*see above*) in determining if particular prices are predatory. A firm that uses predatory pricing in one market, and subsidizes those prices with higher prices elsewhere, is guilty of a violation of the Robinson-Patman Act, because the behavior is likely to cause harm to competition on the primary line.

Prima Facie Tort   A general tort concept that makes any unjustified intentional infliction of injury actionable. The doctrine has been used by competitors who alleged that others had entered into competition solely out of spiteful desire to injure them. The doctrine is not available in ordinary competitive situations despite the potential of harm to competitors because there is a privilege to compete.

Primary Line   In Robinson-Patman Act cases the plaintiff or the government must prove that the price discrimination at issue is likely to cause harm to competition. If the theory of the case is that this harm will occur to competition on the same level of competition as the one on which the seller operates, the case is usually characterized as a primary line case.

Prior Art   In determining the patentability of an invention, the patent office and the courts will compare the invention to the documentary material that already exists in the same field of technology and also consider the range of devices currently known and in use. This body of comparative material is known as the prior art. If a single prior art reference completely discloses how to make the invention, the invention is not novel. If the prior art references considered in the aggregate would permit someone skilled in the relevant art to deduce how to make the invention, the invention is obvious. In either case, the patent will be denied.

Privilege to Compete   Although entry into a new market and competition with established firms is likely to harm those firms, this behavior is not actionable because of the social and economic benefits of competition. This result is often summarized by the statement that there is a privilege to compete.

Promotional Payments or Facilities   Sellers often provide customers who are in the retail trade with cash payments or facilities to help them promote sales of the product. For instance, they may provide display racks or share the cost of newspaper advertising. The Robinson-Patman Act requires that such promotional payments or allowances be made proportionally available to all customers.

Publication   The distribution of copies of a work to the public is defined as publication under the copyright statute.   The copyright owner must make sure that all copies bear a notice of copyright if the work is to be published, and the obligation to deposit copies with the Library of Congress is triggered by publication.   Under the prior law, publication marked the dividing line between state common law protection for the work and federal statutory protection, but common law copyright was abolished in the 1976 copyright statute, thus greatly lessening the significance of publication.

R

Reasonable Basis   Under the Federal Trade Commission's advertising substantiation doctrine, it is an unfair and deceptive practice to promulgate an advertisement unless the advertiser possesses a reasonable basis for the claims made therein.   What constitutes a reasonable basis is determined on a case-by-case basis.   Data in the form of clinical tests, a review of relevant literature or information about the performance of the product in the hands of consumers all might constitute reasonable bases under certain circumstances.   The data relied upon as providing the reasonable basis must be in the possession of the advertiser in advance of circulation of the advertisement.

Reissue   If a patent contains errors or inaccuracies that were the result of inadvertent mistakes by the patent applicant, that party may return to the patent office to have the errors corrected and the patent reissued.   A reissue patent runs only for the unexpired term of the original.

Related Goods   Courts will find trademark infringement in cases where the goods sold by the defendant and the mark owner do not directly compete, if the goods are related. Goods are considered related if consumers would assume that, when marked with the same trademark, they come from a common source or are sponsored by the same party.

Reproduction Right   The owner of the copyright in a work has the exclusive right to reproduce that work in copies or phonorecords.   The unauthorized production of copies by others constitutes infringement unless protected by the fair use doctrine (*see above*).

Reverse Engineering   The process of determining how a product is manufactured by disassembling it and analyzing its parts or otherwise conducting experiments on it is called reverse engineering.   Reverse engineering is not an improper way to deduce another firm's trade secrets and thus may be engaged in without risk of liability.

Reverse FOIA Suits   If an agency plans to disclose trade secret material in its possession to the general public against the wishes of the owner of the secret, that party may bring suit for review of the agency action under the Administrative Procedure Act to enjoin the disclosure.   Such suits are known as reverse FOIA (Freedom of Information Act) suits.

Right of Publicity   The right of a celebrity to preclude others from using his or her name, likeness, voice or other attributes for commercial gain without consent.   There is theoretical uncertainty over whether the right of publicity is an independent doctrine or merely the successful assertion of trademark, misappropriation or privacy theories. There is also a dispute over whether the right survives the death of the celebrity.

Robinson-Patman Act   The Federal price discrimination act, which makes price discrimination unlawful when a variety of jurisdictional tests are satisfied and when there is also a likelihood of harm to competition.   The statute also reaches certain impermissible brokerage payments, the disproportionate provision of promotional payments and services and the inducement of unlawful price discrimination by buyers.

S

Second Line In Robinson-Patman Act cases the plaintiff or the government must prove that the price discrimination at issue is likely to cause harm to competition. If the theory of the case is that this harm will occur to competition on the level at which the buyers from the discriminator operate, the case is usually characterized as a second line case.

Secondary Meaning Some words or other devices used as trademarks may not be distinctive when first adopted, but may acquire distinctiveness over time. When such a mark has come to signify that an item is produced or sponsored by a particular merchant it is said that the mark has secondary meaning. The existence of secondary meaning can be proven by resort to consumer surveys, evidence of high sales volume and intensity of advertising, among other factors. Types of marks requiring secondary meaning before they will be protected include (1) descriptive and misdescriptive terms; (2) geographically descriptive and misdescriptive terms and (3) surnames. Under the Lanham Act, five years of exclusive use of a mark is deemed prima facie evidence of secondary meaning.

Section 301 This provision of the copyright statute deals with the scope of federal preemption of state causes of action. It provides that states may protect intellectual property that is outside the scope of copyright and may also confer any rights that are different from those conferred by the copyright statute. Any state doctrine or statute that purports to provide rights equivalent to those in the statute for subject matter within the scope of copyright is pre-empted.

Senior User The first party, chronologically, to make use of a trademark is usually referred to as the "senior user."

Service Mark Under the Lanham Act, a mark used in the sale or advertising of services to identify the services of one person and distinguish them from the services of others, is considered a service mark. Service marks are registrable under the same conditions as trademarks. The term "service mark" was unknown at common law, but the names used to identify services were protected as common law trade names.

Sole Source Rule In suits for false advertising at common law, the plaintiff may not recover unless it can demonstrate that it has a monopoly in the sale of goods possessing the advertised trait, because only in that situation were the common law courts confident that the plaintiff would be harmed by the defendant's false advertising. This restrictive doctrine is known as the sole source rule.

Sound Recordings The copyright statute defines a sound recording as a work that results from the fixation of a series of musical, spoken or other sounds, but not including the sounds accompanying a motion picture or other audiovisual work, regardless of the nature of the material objects in which they are embodied. The rights of the owner of copyright in a sound recording are narrower, in a number of respects, than those of owners of copyright in other types of works.

Specification The portion of a patent application which describes the invention, including a description of how to make and use it, in sufficient detail to permit any person skilled in the relevant art to do so.

Statutory Bar If an inventor delays more than one year after the occurrence of certain events, that inventor will be barred from securing a patent on the invention. The events that will give rise to this bar include a description of the invention, a printed publication, the issuance of a patent here or abroad on the invention, or the placing of the invention by anyone on sale or into public use in the United States. Experimental use of the invention by the patent applicant more than one year before the application will not give rise to a statutory bar.

Suggestive Mark   A trademark which requires the consumer to use imagination to determine the precise nature of the goods, is considered suggestive. Such marks are deemed inherently distinctive. They may be protected at common law and registered under the Lanham Act without any showing of secondary meaning.

T

Technical Trademark   In some of the older common law cases, a mark that was inherently distinctive was denominated a "technical" trademark. Such marks were protected in a cause of action known as "trademark infringement." The term is now largely obsolete.

Trade Dress   The overall appearance of a product or its packaging. Duplication of the trade dress of another's goods is actionable as passing off at common law and under Lanham Act § 43(a). Commercial prints and labels constituting key elements of trade dress may be protectible under the copyright laws as well.

Trade Name   Under Lanham Act definitions, a trade name is the name of a business. Trade names are not registrable but a party who makes unauthorized use of another's trade name can be enjoined under Lanham Act § 43(a). In some older common law cases, marks that required secondary meaning before they would be protected were sometimes referred to as "trade names." These common law trade names were protected in a cause of action known as "unfair competition." This use of the term trade name is becoming increasingly obsolete.

Trade Secret   Any information that derives independent economic value, actual or potential, from not being generally known to, and not being readily ascertainable by proper means by, other persons who can obtain eco-

nomic value from its disclosure or use and is the subject of reasonable efforts to maintain its secrecy.

Trademark   Any word, name, symbol or device or any combination of those which is adopted and used by a manufacturer or merchant to identify its goods and distinguish them from those manufactured or sold by others.

U

Unfair Acts or Practices   The Federal Trade Commission Act forbids unfair acts or practices. The Commission has declared that behavior is unfair if it will lead to a substantial, unmitigated and unavoidable consumer injury. Coercive behavior and the withholding of useful information are examples of unfair practices. The Commission's test is likely to be codified by statutory amendments pending as this book goes to press.

Uniform Deceptive Trade Practices Act   One version of a "baby" F.T.C. Act that provides private remedies for a variety of unfair and deceptive acts, including false advertising and disparagement. The remedies under this particular statute are limited to injunctive relief.

Use in Commerce   Because the Lanham Act is predicated on the federal power to regulate interstate commerce, the statute requires proof that a mark has been used in commerce before the mark is registrable. This requirement is satisfied by evidence that goods with mark affixed have been sold or transported in any commerce which may be lawfully regulated by Congress.

Utility   A patent applicant must demonstrate that his invention performs some function that is of benefit to society. This utility requirement is in addition to the requirements of non-obviousness and novelty. Examples of items that have been held to lack utility include devices the sole purposes of which were immoral, and compositions of matter that, although new, have no purpose other than further research.

Utility Patent The customary type of patent issued to any novel, non-obvious, and useful machine, article of manufacture, composition of matter or process. This is one of three types of patents provided for by the statute, the others being design and plant patents.

W

Wheeler-Lea Amendment This 1938 amendment to the Federal Trade Commission Act added a prohibition against "unfair or deceptive acts or practices" to the pre-existing bar on "unfair methods of competition." It thereby made it plain that the Commission could take steps against unscrupulous conduct that harmed consumers even if there was no adverse effect on competing firms.

APPENDIX D

TEXT CORRELATION CHART

	Oppenheim, Weston, Maggs & Schechter, Unfair Trade Practices and Consumer Protection (4th ed., 1983)	Goldstein, Copyright, Patent, Trademark and Related State Doctrines (2d ed., 1981)	Kitch & Perlman, Legal Regulation of the Competitive Process (1979)	Chisum Intellectual Property: Copyright, Patent and Trademark (1980)
I. THE PRIVILEGE TO COMPETE				
A. The Dilemma of Competition	1–7	———	1–9	———
B. The Significance of Motivation	7–11	———	1–4	———
C. The Stability of Contract	16–31	———	5–7, 463–474	———
II. TRADEMARKS				
A. The Rationale for Protecting Trademarks	32–38	19–23	———	———
B. The Dual System of Trademark Protection	38–71	———	281–286	11–1—11–2
C. Obtaining Trademark Rights: Affixation, Use and Registration	38–48	84–88, 279–293, 325–339, 355–359, 384–386	286–291, 340–347, 350–354	11–1—11–38, 13–1—13–26, 14–1—14–3

	Oppenheim, Weston, Maggs & Schechter, Unfair Trade Practices and Consumer Protection (4th ed., 1983)	Goldstein, Copyright, Patent, Trademark and Related State Doctrines (2d ed., 1981)	Kitch & Perlman, Legal Regulation of the Competitive Process (1979)	Chisum Intellectual Property: Copyright, Patent and Trademark (1980)
D. Distinctiveness	72–121	80–84, 96–100, 113–114, 118–128, 293–325	268–276, 291–331	12–1—12–48
E. Unusual Trademark Types	12–138	128–140, 339–355	331–340	11–2—11–12, 13–24—13–26
F. Impermissible Marks	138–143	323–325, 353–354	302–303	12–1—12–2
G. Using Another's Mark	144–209	92–94, 101–107, 113–115, 359–384, 395–418	347–350, 354–414	14–11—15–18
H. Trademark Abandonment	221–222	323, 381–382	423–428	12–6—12–8
I. Remedies	209–220	94–95, 387–395	414–419	15–18—15–22
III. COPYRIGHT				
A. Copyrightable Subject Matter	367–385, 393–425	684–713	627–658	1–1—2–29
B. Publication	———	197–212	486–488, 624–625	3–1—3–17
C. Copyright Formalities	385–393	654–669	625–626	3–17—3–40
D. The Rights of a Copyright Owner	425–446	713–811	658–665, 772–795	3–41—4–74
E. Infringement	425–446	830–855	665–708	5–1—5–36
F. Fair Use	425–446	763–786	708–761	5–36—5–89
G. Remedies	———	811–830	———	5–89—5–97
IV. MISAPPROPRIATION				
A. Protection for Business Schemes	226–236	36–70	474–486	———
B. Protection for Intangible Stock-In-Trade	236–254	107–113, 115–116	18–38, 489–490	16–27—16–42
C. Protection for Celebrities' Fame	281–298	242–268	604–619	———
D. Pre-emption Problems	254–281	213–232	39–48, 486–507	16–1—16–27
V. PATENTS				
A. Types of Patents	———	497–556	———	6–1—6–91
B. Patentable Subject Matter	———	497–556	798–847	6–1—6–91

		Oppenheim, Weston, Maggs & Schechter, Unfair Trade Practices and Consumer Protection (4th ed., 1983)	Goldstein, Copyright, Patent, Trademark and Related State Doctrines (2d ed., 1981)	Kitch & Perlman, Legal Regulation of the Competitive Process (1979)	Chisum Intellectual Property: Copyright, Patent and Trademark (1980)
	C. The Requirement of Novelty	———	454–463, 472, 478–485	915–923, 927–931, 947–950	7–13—7–34
	D. Statutory Bar	———	454	924–927, 931–947	7–108—7–127
	E. The Requirement of Non-Obviousness	———	432–454, 478–485, 569–573	860–901, 950–970	7–34—7–108
	F. The Requirement of Utility	———	485–494	847–860	7–1—7–13
	G. Patent Application Procedure	———	557–562	1020–1032	8–1—8–42
	H. Patent Infringement	———	633–651	1042–1090	9–1—10–18
VI.	TRADE SECRETS				
	A. Material Constituting Trade Secrets	298–305	141–145, 156–157, 178–191	532–537	17–10—17–23
	B. Appropriation by Parties with Legitimate Access	305–310, 354–366	141–149, 162–175	508–528	———
	C. Trade Secret Theft by Strangers	310–314	150–155	528–532	———
	D. Trade Secret Disclosure by Government	324–330	161–162	542–551	———
	E. Remedies for Trade Secret Theft	315–332	158–160	552–557	———
	F. Pre-emption Problems	332–354	6, 64–70, 178–194, 224	563–595	17–10—17–29
	G. Trade Secrets and Other Unfair Trade Concepts	———	———	551–563	———
VII.	COMPETITOR REMEDIES FOR FALSE ADVERTISING AND DISPARAGEMENT				
	A. Common Law Remedies for False Advertising	448–457	71–80, 89	75–85	16–39—16–40
	B. State Statutory Remedies for False Advertising	457–467	———	113–114	———
	C. Federal Lanham Act Remedies for False Advertising	467–480	418–429	116–123, 136–142	———
	D. Common Law Remedies for Disparagement	480–498	———	85–110	———

APPENDIX E

TABLE OF CASES

†